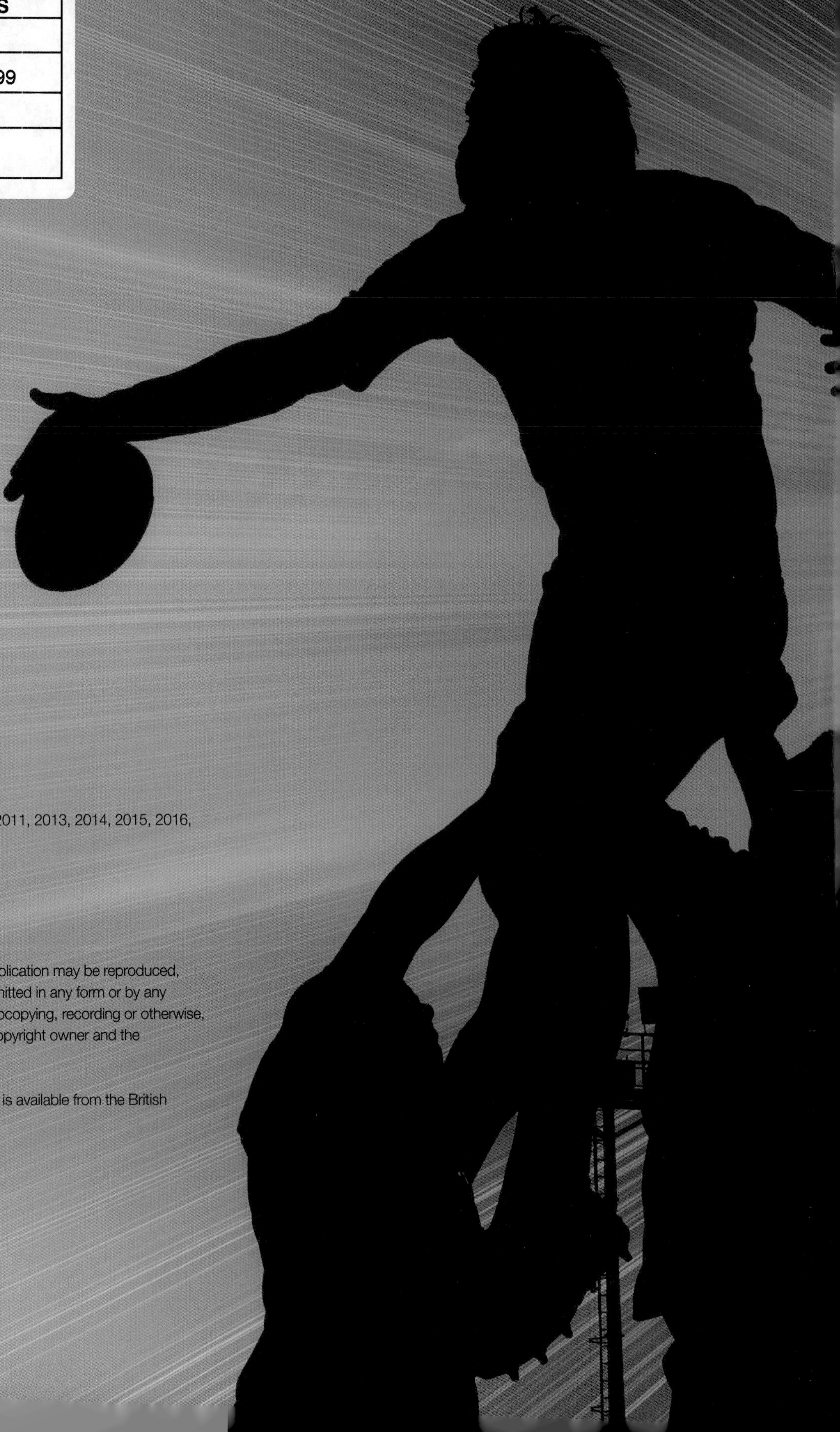

First edition published in 2011
Reprinted with updates in 2012
Second edition 2013
Third edition 2014
Fourth edition 2015
Fifth edition 2016
Sixth edition 2017
Seventh edition 2018

Copyright © Carlton Books Limited 2011, 2013, 2014, 2015, 2016, 2017, 2018

Carlton Books Limited
20 Mortimer Street
London W1T 3JW

A CIP catalogue record for this book is available from the British Library

10 9 8 7 6 5 4 3 2 1

ISBN: 978-1-78739-172-7

Project Editor: Martin Corteel
Project Art Editor: Luke Griffin
Picture Research: Paul Langan
Production: Ena Matagic

Printed in Dubai

WORLD RUGBY RECORDS

SEVENTH EDITION

CHRIS HAWKES

CARLTON
BOOKS

CONTENTS

**FROM LEFT TO RIGHT: Sergio Parisse (Italy),
Stuart Hogg (Scotland), Conor Murray
(Ireland), Beauden Barrett (New Zealand),
Willie le Roux (South Africa), Elliot Daly
(England), Dan Biggar (Wales), Mathieu
Bastareaud (France), Michael Hooper
(Australia).**

INTRODUCTION

Welcome to the sixth edition of *World Rugby Union Records*, a book that covers the full breadth of this much loved game, from the traditional 15-a-side international format to sevens, women's and youth international rugby, from an entirely new perspective – from the long list specific moments and achievements that have added extra glitter to the game's long established appeal over the years. The challenge, of course, came in trawling through rugby's numerous and comprehensive archives to find the hidden gems – one's that have made legends out of some individuals and villains out of others. As a passionate fan of the game it was a privileged task, and a process that allowed me to rediscover almost-forgotten rugby-related memories from my earliest days as a fan. The hope is that this book will evoke a similar response in every one of its readers.

The considerable task of compiling such an extensive list of records was made easier by the availability of numerous and comprehensive archives on the game, with match reports and statistics available for every international match that has been played since the very first, when England travelled to Raeburn Place in Edinburgh on 27 March 1871 to play Scotland.

As is the case with all sports in this television money driven era, rugby today is a 12-month-a-year affair, so there had to be a cut-off point. In this instance, all statistics and records in this book are correct as of 17 March 2018, the day Ireland beat England 24–15 at Twickenham to win their third Grand Slam and 11th Triple Crown.

Particular thanks for the production of this book are due to Martin Corteel, whose encouragement and assurance while putting a book of this type together remain invaluable, to Lorraine Jerram, for her assiduous eye to detail while editing the book, to Luke Griffin, whose design flair has helped to bring the words to life, to Paul Langan for his meticulous search through rugby's photo archives in an attempt to illustrate even the most obscure of records, and to Maria Petalidou for her considerable skill in ensuring the book's production was achieved in a seamless manner. The various aspects of producing a book of this type would not have come together without their considerable input. Final thanks are due to you, the reader. I hope that the time you spend within the pages of this book will be as enjoyable an experience as it was to put them all together.

Chris Hawkes
Salisbury, May 2018

OPPOSITE: The defining moment of the 2018 Six Nations Championship came when Jonny Sexton nailed an 83rd-minute drop-goal to hand Ireland a 15–13 victory over France in Paris.

OVERLEAF: Peri Weepu leads the All Blacks in their traditional call to battle, the Haka, one of the most stirring and anticipated sights in world rugby

PART I
THE COUNTRIES

Although a lack of firm evidence suggests that the legendary moment in 1823 when Rugby School pupil William Webb Ellis picked up a ball and ran with it during a game of football to create an altogether different sport may well be apocryphal, no one can dispute the rapid nature of rugby's spread throughout the world.

    The first set of rudimentary rules were written in 1845, the first international match took place in March 1871, in which Scotland beat England by one goal to nil at Raeburn Place in Edinburgh, and by 1881 both Ireland and Wales had established international teams. Two years later, in 1883, the world's

first international competition – the Home Nations Championship – was staged and within a few years the rugby gospel had spread beyond the confines of Britain and Ireland.

In 1888, a touring team from the British Isles travelled to Australia and New Zealand, the same year saw a New Zealand side tour Britain for the first time, and by the end of the first decade of the twentieth century, teams from Australia and South Africa had played in the northern hemisphere. And the game's expansion to the furthest reaches of the globe did not stop there: France played its first rugby international in 1906, Argentina in 1910, the USA in 1912, Fiji, Samoa and Tonga in 1924, Japan and Canada in 1932. Many other countries followed and by 2018 the 102 member nations and 17 associate member nations of World Rugby – ranging from Andorra to Zimbabwe – had played over 8,500 internationals between them. This section looks not only at the major rugby-playing nations' records in the international arena, but also at the performances of the game's lesser nations, as well as highlighting the players whose performances have made them legendary figures in the game's history.

BELOW: Twickenham, in south-west London, played host to the 2015 Rugby World Cup final.

EUROPE

Europe is the cradle of world rugby. It is the continent in which the game has its origins, in which the laws of the game were first drawn up, in which the world's first international match took place, in which the world's oldest international tournament – the Home Nations Championship – was first contested and from which the game of rugby spread to the furthest reaches of the globe. Europe is also home to some of the world's most powerful rugby-playing nations and features more top-20 ranked countries (ten) than any other continent on the planet.

BELOW: Ireland's Jacob Stockdale ran in seven tries during the 2018 Six Nations and was voted Player of the Tournament.

ENGLAND

The birthplace of the game, England has more registered players than any other country. They have also achieved considerable success in the international area winning the now Six Nations Championship on 37 occasions: (with 13 grand slams), but their finest moment came in Sydney in 2003, when they beat Australia 20–17 in the final to become the first, and to date only, country from the northern hemisphere to win the Rugby World Cup. England are also two-time finalists in the Rugby World Cup, in 1991 and 2007.

ENGLAND DEMOLISH HAPLESS ROMANIA

When England played Romania at Twickenham on 17 November 2001 it was a day of records. First, Jason Leonard, making his 93rd appearance, became the most capped forward in international rugby history and then his team-mates, as if to celebrate the popular prop's achievement, ran riot. They scored their first try after nine minutes and then overwhelmed their awestruck opponents, scoring 20 tries en route to a staggering 134–0 victory – the biggest win in their history. It was a day to remember for debutant Charlie Hodgson, too: the 21-year-old Sale fly-half bagged 44 points – including two tries – to break Paul Grayson's individual points-scoring record for England, with only the width of a post preventing him from breaking Simon Culhane's world-record haul of 45 points (set while playing for New Zealand against Japan in the 1995 Rugby World Cup).

OVERALL TEAM RECORD

Span	Mat	Won	Lost	Draw	%	For	Aga	Diff	Tries	Conv	Pens	Drop	GfM
1871–2018	724	396	274	50	58.47	12275	9133	+3142	1606	951	1211	142	4

BACK TO THE DRAWING BOARD

England may well have pointed to the absence of many of their star players as an excuse for their abject capitulation, but there is no escaping the fact that their side – featuring seven debutants – suffered nothing short of total humiliation against Australia at Brisbane on 6 June 1998. Trailing 33–0 at half-time, they collapsed to a sorry 76–0 loss: it was their largest ever international defeat.

BELOW: Debutant Charlie Hodgson had a day to remember against Romania on 17 September 2001, bagging an England record 44 points.

LOSING START FOR ENGLAND

In December 1870, a group of Scottish players issued a letter of challenge to England in the *Scotsman* and *Bell's Life* newspapers to contest a match in the 'carrying game'. It could hardly be ignored and three months later, on 27 March 1871 at Raeburn Place in Edinburgh, the world's first rugby international took place. Scotland won the 20-a-side affair by scoring one try and a goal to England's solitary try – a points system had still to be devised.

ENGLAND RISE AGAIN

After suffering the ignominy of being dumped out of their own World Cup in 2015, English rugby was at its lowest ebb. But in came new coach Eddie Jones, and the transformation was immediate. England claimed a Grand Slam in the 2016 Six Nations, beat Australia away (3–0 in the series), swept all before them in the 2016 autumn internationals, and extended their winning run to a joint world record 18 matches. The dream died in Dublin (Ireland won 13–9), but England had, once again, become a force to be reckoned with.

HONOURS

Rugby World Cup:
(best finish) – champions (2003)

Six Nations:
winners – 1883#, 1884#, 1886*, 1890*, 1892#, 1910, 1912*, 1913 (GS), 1914 (GS), 1920*, 1921 (GS), 1923 (GS), 1924 (GS), 1928 (GS), 1930, 1932*, 1934#, 1937#, 1939*, 1947*, 1953, 1954#*, 1957 (GS), 1958, 1960#*, 1963, 1973*, 1980 (GS), 1991 (GS), 1992 (GS), 1995 (GS), 1996#, 2000, 2001, 2003 (GS), 2011, 2016 (GS), 2017

* = shared; (GS) = Grand Slam; # = triple crown

ABOVE: Martin Johnson lifted the Rugby World Cup for England in 2003.

COACHES

Name	Tenure
Don White	1969–71
John Elders	1972–74
John Burgess	1975
Peter Colston	1976–79
Mike Davis	1979–82
Dick Greenwood	1983–85
Martin Green	1985–87
Geoff Cooke	1988–94
Jack Rowell	1994–97
Sir Clive Woodward	1997–2004
Andy Robinson	2004–06
Brian Ashton	2006–08
Rob Andrew	2008
Martin Johnson	2008–11
Stuart Lancaster	2011–2015
Eddie Jones	2015–present

BELOW: A Rugby World Cup winner in 2003, Josh Lewsey stands seventh on England's all-time try-scoring lists with 22 tries.

MOST TRIES: TOP TEN

Pos	Tries	Player (Span)
1	49	Rory Underwood (1984–96)
2	31	Ben Cohen (2000–06)
=	31	Will Greenwood (1997–2004)
4	30	Jeremy Guscott (1989–99)
5	28	Jason Robinson (2001–07)
6	24	Dan Luger (1998–2003)
7	22	Josh Lewsey (1998–2007)
8	20	Mark Cueto (2004–11)
9	19	Chris Ashton (2010–14)
10	18	Cyril Lowe (1913–23)

ON TOP OF THE WORLD

Their detractors may have dubbed them 'Dad's Army' (half of their squad was over the age of 30) and pointed to a one-dimensional style of play based on a muscular pack and the unerring accuracy of Jonny Wilkinson's boot, but England entered the 2003 Rugby World Cup as the world's no.1 ranked team and were supremely confident of victory, having beaten all-comers both home and away in the build-up to the tournament. And they did not disappoint, easing through the group stages before beating Wales in the quarter-finals, France in the semi-finals and edging out Australia 20–17 in a closely contested final (thanks to a last-gasp, extra-time Wilkinson drop goal) to become the first team from the northern hemisphere to win rugby's greatest prize.

ABOVE: Rob Andrew, a stalwart for England between 1985 and 1997, during which time he won 71 caps for his country, was inducted into the World Rugby Hall of Fame in 2017. The fly-half appeared in the 1991 Rugby World Cup final, but will be best remembered for his stunning, last-gasp drop-goal against Australia in the 1995 Rugby World Cup quarter-final.

HALL OF FAME INDUCTEES

Name (Span, Caps)

Maggie Alphonsi (2003–14, 74 caps)
Rob Andrew (1985–97, 71 caps)
Gillian Burns (1988–2002, 73 caps)
Bill Beaumont (1975–82, 34 caps)
William Percy Carpmael (1948–54, 23 caps)
Lawrence Dallaglio (1995–2007, 85 caps)
Jeremy Guscott (1989–99, 65 caps)
Alfred Hammersley (1871–74, 4 caps)
Carol Isherwood (1987–92, 7 caps)
Martin Johnson (1993–2003, 84 caps)
John Kendall-Carpenter (1949–54, 23 caps)
Jason Leonard (1990–2004, 114 caps)
Edgar Mobbs (1909–10, 7 caps)
Ronald Poulton-Palmer (1909–14, 17 caps)
Alan Rotherham (1882–87, 12 caps)
Robert Sneddon (1888, 3 caps)
Henry Vassell (1881–82, 5 caps)
Wavell Wakefield (1920–27, 31 caps)
William Webb Ellis (inventor of game)
Clive Woodward (1979–88, 23 caps)
Jonny Wilkinson (1998–2011, 91 caps)

EVER-PRESENT LEONARD SETS CAPS LANDMARK

When Jason Leonard won his first cap for England on 28 July 1990, against Argentina, he became his country's youngest ever prop forward: it was the start of a record-breaking career. Capable of scrummaging with equal effect at both loosehead and tighthead, he was a cornerstone of a pack that helped England to the Rugby World Cup final in 1991 and to back-to-back grand slams in 1991 and 1992, and he made the first of five British Lions appearances in 1993. Coaches and players may have come and gone, but Leonard remained an ever-present in the England set-up throughout the 1990s, and in November 2000 passed Rory Underwood's haul of caps to become England's most capped player. By the time he bowed out of international rugby, following England's 2003 Rugby World Cup triumph, he was the most capped player in rugby history with 114 caps – a record since broken by several players.

RIGHT: A regular source of points for England for more than a decade, Rory Underwood scored a record 49 tries for his country.

ENGLAND'S YOUNGEST PLAYER

Colin Laird holds the distinction of being the youngest player ever to pull on an England shirt. The fly-half was a mere 18 years and 134 days old when he made his debut during England's 11–9 victory over Wales at Twickenham on 15 January 1927. He went on to make ten appearances for his country (scoring five tries) and was an ever-present in the side when England won their sixth grand slam in 1928.

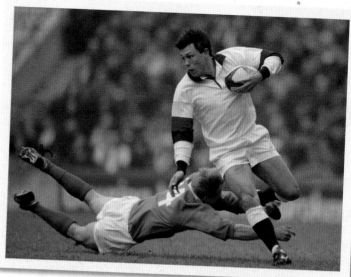

ENGLAND'S FLIER ON THE WING

An RAF flight lieutenant, Rory Underwood burst on to the international scene in 1984, scoring his first try in only his second Test (against France in Paris); it was an opportunistic

LEFT: Jason Leonard is the only player in history to have won more than 100 caps for England.

effort that highlighted the searing turn of pace that would become the hallmark of his career. Equally comfortable on either wing, he was a constant presence in the England side until his retirement in 1996, during which time he won three grand slams, collected six British Lions caps (scoring one try), and appeared in the 1991 Rugby World Cup final. The first England player to appear in 50 internationals, the quicksilver winger ended his 12-year career with 85 caps – a record for an England back – having scored an all-time national record 49 tries.

ALL-TIME LEADING TRY-SCORERS: BY POSITION

Position	Player (Span)	Tries
Full-back	Jason Robinson (2001–07)	13*
Winger	Rory Underwood (1984–96)	49
Centre	Will Greenwood (1997–2004)	31
Fly-half	Charlie Hodgson (2001–12)	8
Scrum-half	Matt Dawson (1995–2006)	16
No.8	Lawrence Dallaglio (1995 –2007)	10†
Flanker	Neil Back (1994–2003)	16
Lock	Joe Launchbury (2012–17)	4
Prop	Bruno Brown (1911–22)	4
	Dan Cole (2010–17)	4
Hooker	Phil Greening (1996–2001)	6

* also scored 15 tries as a winger. † also scored 7 tries as a flanker.

MOST POINTS: TOP TEN

Pos	Points	Player (Span)
1	1179	Jonny Wilkinson (1998–2011)
2	652	Owen Farrell (2012–18)
3	400	Paul Grayson (1995–2004)
4	396	Rob Andrew (1985–97)
5	301	Toby Flood (2006–13)
6	296	Jonathan Webb (1987–93)
7	269	Charlie Hodgson (2001–12)
8	240	Dusty Hare (1974–84)
9	220	George Ford (2014–18)
10	210	Rory Underwood (1984–96)

RIGHT: Jonny Wilkinson is England's leading points-scorer with 1,179.

BELOW: Clive Woodward celebrates his ultimate achievement, coaching England to Rugby World Cup glory in 2003.

BOTTOM: Will Carling led England 59 times between 1988 and 1996.

CAPTAIN CARLING REVIVES ENGLAND

Appointed England's youngest-ever captain in November 1988 at the tender age of 22, Will Carling played a major role in reviving his country's floundering rugby fortunes, leading them to the Rugby World Cup final in 1991 (which they lost to Australia) and to grand slam success in 1991, 1992 and 1995. He led his country on 59 occasions – a national record – and by the time he relinquished the reins in 1996 he had recorded 44 wins, making him England's most successful captain of all time.

MODERN APPROACH PAYS DIVIDENDS FOR COACH WOODWARD

A talented player in his own right, making 21 appearances for England at centre between 1980 and 1984, Clive Woodward succeeded Jack Rowell as England coach in 1997. Success initially eluded him – and a quarter-final defeat to South Africa at the 1999 Rugby World Cup left many questioning his credentials for the job – but his man-management skills and an innovative approach to pre-match preparation soon brought the best out of the talented group of players he had at his disposal. It culminated, of course, in English rugby's proudest moment: victory at the 2003 Rugby World Cup. When he left the post the following year, England had won 59 of the 83 Tests under his charge – no England coach in history has notched up more wins. He was knighted in 2004.

WILKINSON PROSPERS FOR ENGLAND

Jonny Wilkinson won his first cap for England against Ireland on 4 April 1998 aged 18 and established himself as a regular within a year. Showing an unerring accuracy with the boot, he helped England to the Six Nations crown in both 2000 and 2001 and by 2003 was considered the best player in world rugby: helping England to back-to-back wins over New Zealand for the first time; playing a leading role in England's first-ever victory on Australian soil; landing the crucial drop goal that secured England the Rugby World Cup; and ending the year as the IRB's Player of the Year. Then injury struck: he missed four years of international rugby, but returned in 2007 to lead England to a second successive Rugby World Cup final. In 2008, he overhauled Neil Jenkins as all-time leading points-scorer in international rugby and is one of only two players in Six Nations Championship history (alongside Ronan O'Gara) to have passed 500 points.

MOST CAPS: TOP TEN

Pos	Caps	Player (Span)
1	114	Jason Leonard (1990–2004)
2	93	Dylan Hartley (2008–18)
3	91	Jonny Wilkinson (1998–2011)
4	85	Lawrence Dallaglio (1995–2007)
=	85	Rory Underwood (1984–96)
6	84	Martin Johnson (1993–2003)
7	82	Dan Cole (2010–18)
8	81	Danny Care (2008–18)
9	78	Joe Worsley (1999–2011)
10	77	Matt Dawson (1995–2006)

FRANCE

A gold medal in the 1900 Olympic Games apart, France made a stuttering start to international rugby – winning only one of their first 31 matches. It wasn't until the late 1950s that French rugby truly came of age: they won the Five Nations Championship for the first time outright in 1959, claimed a first grand slam in 1968 and have since gone from strength to strength. Three-time finalists in the Rugby World Cup (in 1987, 1999 and 2011), France currently stand eighth in the World Rugby rankings.

SO NEAR AND YET SO FAR

Rugby World Cup semi-final upsets have been a French speciality over the years: in the inaugural edition of the event in 1987, they stunned hosts and pre-tournament favourites Australia when Serge Blanco dived over the line in the dying moments of the game to secure a 30–24 victory. And they were at it again against much-fancied New Zealand at Twickenham in 1999 – a match described by many as the greatest of all time. Trailing 17–10 at half-time, they rallied in spectacular fashion to secure a memorable 43–31 victory. But that was where the fun ended: France went on to lose the final on both occasions and a third final defeat in 2011 – 8–7 to New Zealand – meant the French had become the first team in history to lose in three Rugby World Cup finals.

MOST TRIES IN A MATCH

The French record for the most tries by one player in a match is four, a feat achieved by two men: Adolphe Jaureguy (against Romania at Colombes on 4 May 1924); and Maurice Celhay (against Italy at Parc des Princes on 17 October 1937).

LEADING LES BLEUS

Fabien Pelous is France's most-capped player of all time with 118 appearances), and he also holds the distinction of having led his country on more occasions than any other player in history. The giant lock captained his country for the first time in March 1997 and went on to lead the side a record 42 times (notching up 27 wins in the process) until his retirement in November 2006.

RIGHT: Vincent Clerc scored his 31st try for France in their 26–12 Rugby World Cup 2011 quarter-final victory over England at Auckland, taking him one clear of Philippe Sella and alone in third place in France's all-time try-scorers' list.

EVERY CLOUD HAS A SILVER LINING

In 1931, just when it seemed French rugby was on an upward curve, France made the headlines for all the wrong reasons. Their ferocious style of play had been upsetting their Five Nations rivals for some time, but when rumours of professionalism in French rugby that contradicted the games's strict amateur principals started to emerge, they were summarily thrown out of the tournament and condemned to play matches against the game's lesser nations. They took full advantage: between 6 April 1931 and 17 October 1937, they put together a run of ten consecutive victories – still an all-time record winning streak for France.

HONOURS

Rugby World Cup:
(best finish) – runners-up (1987, 1999, 2011)
Six Nations:
winners – 1955*, 1959, 1960*, 1961, 1962, 1967, 1968 (GS), 1970*, 1973*, 1977 (GS), 1981 (GS), 1983*, 1986*, 1987 (GS), 1988*, 1989, 1993, 1997 (GS), 1998 (GS), 2002 (GS), 2004 (GS), 2006, 2007, 2010 (GS)

* = shared; (GS) = Grand Slam

MOST TRIES: TOP TEN

Pos	Tries	Player (Span)
1	38	Serge Blanco (1980–91)
2	34	Vincent Clerc (2002–13)
3	32	Philippe Saint-Andre (1990–97)
4	30	Philippe Sella (1982–95)
5	26	Philippe Bernat-Salles (1992–2001)
=	26	Emile Ntamack (1994–2000)
7	25	Christophe Dominici (1998–2007)
8	23	Christian Darrouy (1957–67)
=	23	Aurélien Rougerie (2001–12)
10	20	Yannik Jauzion (2001–11)
=	20	Patrique Lagisquet (1983–91)

OVERALL TEAM RECORD

Span	Mat	Won	Lost	Draw	%	For	Aga	Diff	Tries	Conv	Pens	Drop	GfM
1906–2018	755	404	311	33	56.21	13653	11334	+2319	1722	1031	1256	223	1

MOST CAPS: TOP TEN

Pos	Caps	Player (Span)
1	118	Fabien Pelous (1995–2007)
2	111	Philippe Sella (1982–1995)
3	98	Raphael Ibanez (1996–2007)
4	93	Serge Blanco (1980–1991)
5	89	Olivier Magne (1997–2007)
6	86	Damien Traille (2001–11)
7	85	Nicolas Mas (2003–15)
8	84	Sylvain Marconnet (1998–2011)
9	83	Dmitri Szarzewski (2004–15)
10	82	Imanol Harinordoquy (2002–12)

RECORD-BREAKING TRIUMPH FOR FRANCE IN TOULOUSE

Namibia may not have provided the strongest opposition in their pool but, following a morale-sapping opening-game defeat against Argentina (17–12), France needed to win and win comfortably when they faced off against the African minnows in Toulouse if they wanted to get their 2007 Rugby World Cup campaign back on track. They did not disappoint and thrilled the 35,339 crowd by running in 13 tries en route to a crushing 87–10 victory – the biggest win in their history.

NEW YEAR'S DAY BLUES FOR FRANCE

A crowd of 3,000 people made its way to the Parc des Princes in Paris on New Year's Day 1906 to watch France contest an international rugby match for the first time, against New Zealand, who were playing in the last match of their first-ever tour to the northern hemisphere. It did not turn out to be the happiest of occasions for the home side or the partisan crowd: trailing 18–3 at half-time, they ended up losing the match 38–8, with New Zealand outscoring Les Bleus by ten tries to two.

FAILING TO FIND THE WINNING FORMULA

France made a troubled start to international rugby, managing to win just one of their first 31 matches over a period of 14 years. During that time, between 28 January 1911 (a 37–0 defeat to England) and 17 February 1920 (a slender 6–5 reverse against Wales), they lost 18 matches in a row – the longest streak in international rugby history. It came to an end when France beat Ireland 15–7 in Dublin on 3 April 1920.

ABOVE: Philippe Sella shone at centre for France for 13 years and was the first Frenchman to achieve the 100-cap milestone.

CLASSY CAMBERABERO SHINES FOR FRANCE

After a stuttering performance in their opening match of the inaugural Rugby World Cup in 1987 (a 20–20 draw against Scotland), France bounced back with a dominant victory over Romania (55–12). However, it was still all to play for in the final round of group matches, and only a convincing win against minnows Zimbabwe (who Scotland had beaten 60–21) could guarantee Les Bleus top spot in the pool – and thus avoid a potentially awkward quarter-final tie against hosts New Zealand. They played staggeringly well, crushing the Africans 70–12 to top the group with Didier Camberabero the star of the show. The flamboyant fly-half scored three tries and slotted nine conversions to amass 30 points in the match – an all-time record for France.

BELOW: Didier Camberabero helped France to reach the 1987 Rugby World Cup quarter-final with 30 points against Zimbabwe (three tries and nine conversions in a 70–12 rout). No France player has scored more points in a match.

HALL OF FAME INDUCTEES

Name (Span, Caps)
Nathalie Amiel (1986–2002, 56 caps)
Serge Blanco (1980–91, 93 caps)
André Boniface (1954–66, 48 caps)
Guy Boniface (1960–66, 35 caps)
Marcel Communeau (1906–13, 21 caps)
Pierre de Coubertin (Olympics Games)
Jo Maso (1966–73, 25 caps)
Lucien Mias (1951–59, 29 caps)
Fabien Pelous (1995–2007, 118 caps)
Jean Prat (1945–55, 51 caps)
Jean-Pierre Rives (1975–84, 59 caps)
Philippe Sella (1982–95, 111 caps)

ALL-TIME LEADING TRY-SCORERS: BY POSITION

Position	Player (Span)	Tries
Full-back	Serge Blanco (1980–91)	34
Winger	Vincent Clerc (2002–13)	34
Centre	Philippe Sella (1982–95)	27
Fly-half	Alain Penaud (1992–2000)	10
	Frédéric Michalak (2001–15)	10
Scrum-half	Jerome Gallion (1978–86)	10
	Fabien Galthié (1991–2003)	10
No.8	Imanol Harinordoquy (2002–12)	12
Flanker	Olivier Magne (1997–2007)	14
Lock	Lionel Nallet (2000–12)	9
Prop	Amedée Domenech (1954–63)	8
	Robert Paparemborde (1975–83)	8
Hooker	Raphael Ibanez (1997–2007)	8

FRANCE BLOWN AWAY IN WELLINGTON

A trip to rugby giants New Zealand is not always the best way to prepare for a World Cup campaign and when France travelled to the southern hemisphere to face the All Blacks in June 2007, they returned licking their wounds. If the 42–11 reverse in the first Test at Auckland had been bad, the result of the second Test at Wellington was even worse: France crumbled to a 61–10 loss – the heaviest defeat in their international history.

IF IT ISN'T BROKEN, DON'T FIX IT

France romped to their second-ever grand slam in convincing and record-breaking fashion in the 1977 Five Nations Championship, recording wins over Wales (16–9 in Paris), England (4–3 at Twickenham), Scotland (29–3 in Paris) and Ireland (15–6 in Dublin), but what made their effort all the more laudable was the fact that they used the same 15 players throughout the course of the campaign. It is the only instance of a team remaining unchanged throughout the entire length of the tournament in history.

ABOVE: Philippe Saint-André dazzled on the wing for France in the 1990s, scoring 32 tries – third on the country's all-time try-scoring list. He was national coach from 2011 to 2015.

RIGHT: Fabien Pelous bowed out of international rugby after the 2007 Rugby World Cup semi-final defeat to England as France's most capped player of all time (with 118 caps).

COACHES

Name	Tenure
Jean Prat	1964–68
Fernand Cazenave	1968–73
Jean Desclaux	1973–80
Jacques Fouroux	1981–90
Daniel Dubroca	1990–91
Pierre Berbizier	1991–95
Jean-Claude Skrela	1995–99
Bernard Laporte	1999–2007
Marc Lièvremont	2007–11
Philippe Saint-André	2011–15
Guy Novès	2015–17
Jacques Brunel	2017–present

FRANCE'S MOST CAPPED PLAYER

Fabien Pelous was a formidable line-out jumper and a marauding presence in the loose, who will be remembered as one of the greats of modern rugby. He won his first cap against Romania in 1995 and went on to add another 117 – including a record-equalling 42 appearances as captain – before his retirement following France's Rugby World Cup semi-final defeat against England in 2007. He is the most capped France international of all time.

THE LITTLE CORPORAL INSPIRES FRANCE

Nicknamed the 'Little Corporal' because of his diminutive 5ft 3in (1.6m) stature, what Jacques Fouroux may have lacked in height he more than made up for with brawn and an in-your-face attitude, both on the pitch (where he made 27 appearances for France at scrum-half between 1972 and 1977) and as Les Bleus' coach (between 1981 and 1990). His tactical approach as coach, based on a massive pack, may not have been to everyone's liking – removed as it was from France's traditional, free-flowing game – but it was supremely effective: during Fouroux's tenure, France won the Five Nations Championship six times (with two grand slams) and reached the 1987 Rugby World Cup final. No France coach since has come close to matching his achievements.

RIGHT: One of the finest full-backs in rugby history when he was in full flow, Serge Blanco scored a record 38 tries for France during his 11-year international career.

LEFT: Jacques Fouroux was an inspirational figure for France both as a player and a coach.

BRILLIANT BLANCO SETS ALL-TIME TRY-SCORING MARK

In full flow, Serge Blanco was one of the most majestic sights in rugby history. Born in Venezuela, he grew up in France and made his debut for Les Bleus against South Africa in 1980 on the wing, a testament to the searing turn of pace that would become the hallmark of his career. He eventually switched to full-back and went on to make 93 appearances for his country before his retirement in 1991, scoring a national record 38 tries.

LEFT: Frédéric Michalak had a stop-start 14-year international career with France, but ended it as his country's all-time leading points-scorer, with 436 points.

MOST POINTS: TOP TEN

Pos	Points	Player (Span)
1	436	Frédéric Michalak (2001–15)
2	380	Christophe Lamaison (1996–2001)
3	373	Dimitri Yachvili (2002–12)
4	367	Thierry Lacroix (1989–97)
5	355	Morgan Parra (2008–15)
6	354	Didier Camberabero (1982–93)
7	267	Gerald Merceron (1999–2003)
8	265	Jean-Pierre Romeu (1972–77)
9	252	Thomas Castaignede (1995–2007)
10	233	Serge Blanco (1980–1991)

THE POINTS MACHINE

No French rugby player has divided public opinion in recent times in quite the same manner as Frédérick Michalack. Attacking genius or defensive liability? Maestro or maverick? And a succession of French coaches seemed to go share that opinion or him: after making his international debut in 2001, the Toulouse-born fly-half amassed only 77 caps (25 of those as a replacement) before he bowed out of international rugby following France's defeat to New Zealand in the quarter-finals of the 2015 Rugby World Cup – in contrast, Richie McCaw, whose career spanned the same time, went on to win 148 caps. However, before bowing out of the international game, Michalack did manage to break Christophe Lamaison's long-standing record for the most points (380), taking the record to 436 points – a figure that includes ten tries.

GEORGIA

Georgia gained independence in April 1991 following the break-up of the Soviet Union and the country's development as an international rugby-playing nation is still in its infancy. What Georgia, nicknamed The Lelos, have achieved in such a short space of time, however, has been considerable: they have won the European Nations Cup – the continent's second-tier tournament – on eight occasions and have qualified for five successive Rugby World Cups, in 2003, 2007, 2011, 2015 and 2019.

THE LELOS FIND THEIR FORM

Georgia could not have enjoyed a better build-up to the 2011 Rugby World Cup: they put together the longest winning streak in their history. The run started on 20 November 2010 with an impressive 22–15 home victory over Canada in Tbilisi, included a thumping 60–0 victory over Spain on 12 February 2011 and stretched to eight matches before they suffered a 15–6 defeat to Scotland in their opening game at the 2011 Rugby World Cup.

OVERALL TEAM RECORD

Span	Mat	Won	Lost	Draw	%	For	Aga	Diff	Tries	Conv	Pens	Drop
1989–2018	214	131	73	7	63.74	4956	3766	+1190	593	398	373	28

TRY GLUT FOR GEORGIA AGAINST SORRY CZECHS

Georgia proved their tag as the giants of European second-tier rugby in their Six Nations B clash against the Czech Republic at Tbilisi on 7 April 2007. The Lelos raced into a 57–0 half-time lead and ended the match – in which they scored a staggering 17 tries – as 98–3 winners. It remains the largest victory in Georgia's history.

MAGICAL MERAB

A versatile three-quarter, Merab Kvirikashvili made his debut against Portugal in Lisbon on 16 February 2003, appeared at the 2003 Rugby World Cup (playing at both scrum-half and fly-half) and has been an ever-present in the Lelos' line-up ever since. A veteran of four Rugby World Cups (he also appeared in 2007, 2011 and 2015), he has gone on to amass 840 points (including 17 tries) in 110 appearances for his country. Both are all-time national records.

MR RELIABLE

A rugby rarity, having played for Georgia in both rugby league and rugby union, Merab Kvirikashvili made his debut for the Lelos during the 2003 Rugby World Cup. He became a permanent feature following Paliko Jimsheladze's retirement in 2007. The fly-half took on Jimsheladze's points-scoring mantle and has amassed a national record 840 points in 110 matches.

THE LELOS' LONGEST LOSING STREAK

Georgia's longest losing streak is nine matches. It started with a 19–6 defeat to Romania at Tbilisi on 30 March 2003 and continued with a 33–22 reverse against Italy at Asti on 6 September 2003, defeat in all four 2003 Rugby World Cup matches and a 19–14 loss to Portugal in Tbilisi on 14 February 2003. The sorry record-breaking run came to an end when the Lelos mustered a 6–6 draw against Spain in Tarragona on 22 February 2004.

ABOVE: Merab Kvirikashvili has overtaken Paliko Jimsheladze to become his country's all-time record points-scorer with 840 points.

GEORGIA FREEZE ON THE GAME'S BIGGEST STAGE

Matches against world rugby's more powerful nations have proved difficult for Georgia and their inability to cope with the step up in class was never more painfully evident than when the Lelos faced off against England at Perth in the group stages of the 2003 Rugby World Cup. Trailing 34–3 at the interval, the floodgates opened in the second half as England ran in 12 tries en route to a thumping 84–6 victory. It is Georgia's heaviest defeat in international rugby.

BELOW: Paliko Jimsheladze scored 320 points for Georgia in a 12-year international career.

MOST POINTS: TOP FIVE

Pos	Points	Player (Span)
1	840	Merab Kvirikashvili (2003–18)
2	320	Paliko Jimsheladze (1995–2007)
=	320	Malkhaz Urjukashvili (1997–2011)
4	178	Lasha Malaguradze (2008–18)
5	130	Mamuka Gorgodze (2003–17)

THE LELOS' LONGEST-SERVING CAPTAIN

A bulky but crafty lock, who can also play at No.8, Ilia Zedginidze made his debut for Georgia as a 21-year-old against Ireland on 14 November 1998, but had to wait until 2000 before establishing himself in the Lelos line-up. Appointed national captain in 2002, he had the distinction of leading his side at both the 2003 and 2007 Rugby World Cups, although his experiences on the game's biggest stage were a bittersweet affair, as both were ended prematurely through injury, the latter of which – a broken kneecap against Ireland in 2007 – forced him to announce his retirement from the international game. However, a return to form and fitness saw him back in the Georgia ranks in February 2009 and, although no longer captain, he holds the national record for having led his side on the most occasions (34).

MARVELLOUS MATIASHVILI SETS NEW MARK

Soso Matiashvili was the main architect behind Georgia's impressive 54–22 victory over Canada in Tbilisi on 11 November

ABOVE: Ilia Zedginidze led Georgia at both the 2003 and 2007 Rugby World Cups.

2017. The winger contributed 34 points to the Lelos' cause – two tries, six conversions and four penalties – to set a new national record for the most points by a player in a single match.

MOST TRIES: TOP FIVE

Pos	Tries	Player (Span)
1	26	Mamuka Gorgodze (2003–17)
2	23	Irakli Machkhaneli (2002–14)
=	23	Tedo Zibzibadze (2000–14)
4	22	David Kachavara (2006–18)
5	17	Malkhaz Urjukashvili (1997–2011)
=	17	Merab Kvirikashvili (2003–18)

MOST TRIES IN A MATCH

The Georgia record for the most tries in a match by a player is three, a feat achieved seven times, by seven players (Mamuka Gorgodze has done it twice). Those registering a hat-trick of tries in a match are: Paliko Jimsheladze and Archil Kavtarahvili

(both against Bulgaria in Sofia on 23 March 1995); Gorgodze (against the Czech Republic in Kutaisi on 12 June 2005 and against Spain at Tbilisi on 26 April 2008); David Dadunashvili and Malkhaz Urjukashvili (both against the Czech Republic at Tbilisi on 7 April 2007); Zurab Zhvania against Germany in Heusenstamm on 7 February 2015; and Giorgi Kveseladze against Germany at Offenbach on 17 February 2018.

GEORGIA'S TRY KING

Nicknamed 'Gorgodzilla' because of his imposing 6ft 5in (1.96m) stature, Mamuka Gorgodze made his debut for Georgia as an 18-year-old in March 2003 when he came on as a replacement against Russia. Although he missed out on selection for Georgia's matches at the 2003 Rugby World Cup, he went on to become a cornerstone of the Lelos pack (at either lock or in the back row), making 71 appearances and scoring a national record 26 tries, including three in a match on two occasions – against the Czech Republic (on 12 June 2005) and against Spain (on 26 April 2008).

LEFT: Irakli Machkhaneli's 23 tries leave him second on his country's all-time try-scoring list.

RIGHT: Mamuka Gorgodze adds a giant (and try-scoring) presence at the heart of a powerful Georgia pack.

IRELAND

With only 54,500 registered players in Ireland, one could make a strong case that Ireland has continually over-achieved on the rugby pitch over the years. However, because of the glittering array of talent the country has produced, two grand slam wins in over a century of competition and a failure to progress beyond the quarter-finals of the Rugby World Cup mean that the men from the Emerald Isle are forever labelled with the under-achievers' tag. They are currently ranked second in the World Rugby rankings.

GRAND SLAM GLORY

A crowd of 32,000 gathered at Belfast's Ravenhill stadium on 13 March 1948 to watch a moment of potential history. Having beaten France (13–6), England (11–10) and Scotland (6–0) in their first three matches of the 1948 Five Nations Championship, Ireland had a shot at registering the first grand slam in their history ... and only Wales stood in their way. The home side took the lead when winger Barney Mullan crossed the line; then Welsh centre Bleddyn Williams scored a try of his own to leave the scores locked at 3–3 at half-time and tensions running as high as ever. Then, seven minutes into the second half, came the most famous moment in Ireland's rugby history: prop John Daly crossed the line to hand his side a lead they would never relinquish and Ireland had won their first ever grand slam.

OVERALL TEAM RECORD

Span	Mat	Won	Lost	Draw	%	For	Aga	Diff	Tries	Conv	Pens	Drop	GfM
1875–2018	686	303	348	32	46.70	10194	9634	+560	1261	766	1005	105	3

ENDING THE 61-YEAR DROUGHT

If the Irish rugby-loving public thought that their side's 1948 grand slam success would signal the start of a period of unprecedented success for their team, they were wrong. By the turn of the 21st century, Ireland had won a further seven Five Nations Championship titles (with three triple crowns) but a second grand slam success continued to elude them. That all changed in 2009: having beaten France (30–21), Italy (38–9), England (14–13) and Scotland (22–15), they held their nerve to beat Wales 17–15 in Cardiff and put an end to a frustrating 61-year wait.

ABOVE: Ireland ended 61 years of hurt when they won the Six Nations Championship grand slam in 2009.

LEFT: Denis Hickie is one of three Ireland players to have scored four tries in a match, a feat he achieved in a 2003 Rugby World Cup warm-up match against Italy.

MOST TRIES IN A MATCH

The Ireland record for the most tries in a single match is four, a feat achieved by three players: Brian Robinson (against Zimbabwe at Lansdowne Road on 6 October 1991); Keith Wood (against the United States at Lansdowne Road on 2 October 1999) and Denis Hickie, against Italy at Limerick on 30 August 2003.

MOST TRIES: TOP TEN

Pos	Tries	Player (Span)
1	46	Brian O'Driscoll (1999–2014)
2	30	Tommy Bowe (2004–17)
3	29	Denis Hickie (1997–2007)
4	27	Keith Earls (2008–18)
5	21	Shane Horgan (2000–09)
6	19	Girvan Dempsey (1998–2008)
7	18	Geordan Murphy (2000–11)
8	17	Brendan Mullin (1984–95)
=	17	Andrew Trimble (2005–17)
10	16	Ronan O'Gara (2000–13)

IRELAND'S LONGEST WINNING STREAK

Ireland's longest winning streak is ten consecutive victories. The run started with a 39–8 victory over Romania at Limerick on 7 September 2002 and featured a significant win over Australia (18–9 at Lansdowne Road on 9 November 2002) and Six Nations Championship victories against Scotland (36–6), Italy (37–13), France (15–12) and Wales (25–24) before coming to an abrupt and definitive end in the grand slam decider against England at Lansdowne Road on 30 March 2003, when the visitors took the spoils following a comprehensive 42–6 victory.

HALL OF FAME INDUCTEES

Name	(Span, Caps)
Ronnie Dawson	(1958–64, 27 caps)
Brian O'Driscoll	(1999–2014, 133 caps)
Mike Gibson	(1964–79, 69 caps)
Tom Kiernan	(1960–73, 58 caps)
Jack Kyle	(1947–58, 46 caps)
Willie John McBride	(1962–75, 63 caps)
Basil Maclear	(1905–07, 11 caps)
Syd Millar	(1958–70, 37 caps)
Tony O'Reilly	(1955–70, 29 caps)
Fergus Slattery	(1970–84, 61 caps)
Keith Wood	(1994–2003, 58 caps)

HONOURS

Rugby World Cup:
(best finish) – quarter-finals (1987, 1991, 1995, 2003, 2011)

Six Nations:
winners – 1894#, 1896, 1906*, 1912*, 1926*, 1927*, 1932*, 1935, 1939*, 1948 (GS), 1949#, 1951, 1973*, 1974, 1982#, 1983*, 1985#, 2009 (GS), 2014, 2015, 2018 (GS)

* = shared; (GS) = grand slam; # = triple crown

HAMMERED IN HAMILTON

After putting in a brave performance against the All Blacks a week earlier in a 22–19 defeat, Ireland hoped for more of the same when they faced New Zealand in the last match of their three-Test series at Hamilton on 23 June 2012. Ireland was still seeking their first-ever victory over the world champions (at their 27th attempt). Instead they were crushed: trailing 29–0 at half-time, the Irish could find no answers to the All Blacks' flair and fell to a thumping 60–0 loss – the heaviest defeat in their history.

ENDURING THE WORST OF TIMES

Ireland made an inglorious start to international rugby: they lost their first-ever match – a 20-a-side affair against England at The Oval on 15 February 1875 (by two goals to nil) – and went on to lose their next nine matches, before enjoying the taste of victory for the first time following a two goals to nil victory over Scotland at Belfast on 19 February 1881. Not that the victory sparked an immediate upturn in Irish fortunes: after losing against Wales and drawing against England, they then embarked on an 11-match losing streak – the longest in their history. That was not an isolated case of Irish misery, however: they matched their record-breaking losing streak between 12 October 1991 and 20 February 1993.

ALL-TIME LEADING TRY-SCORERS: BY POSITION

Position	Player (Span)	Tries
Full-back	Girvan Dempsey (1999–2008)	18
Winger	Tommy Bowe (2004–17)	30
Centre	Brian O'Driscoll (1999–2014)	46
Fly-half	Ronan O'Gara (2000–13)	15
Scrum-half	Conor Murray (2011–18)	12
No.8	Jamie Heaslip (2006–17)	13
Flanker	David Wallace (2000–11)	10
Lock	Malcolm O'Kelly (1997–2009)	8
	Paul O'Connell (2002–15)	8
Prop	Marcus Horan (2000–11)	6
Hooker	Keith Wood (1994–2003)	15

MOST CAPS: TOP TEN

Pos	Caps	Player (Span)
1	133	Brian O'Driscoll (1999–2014)
2	128	Ronan O'Gara (2000–13)
3	111	Rory Best (2005–18)
4	108	Paul O'Connell (2002–15)
5	105	John Hayes (2000–11)
6	98	Peter Stringer (2000–11)
7	95	Jamie Heaslip (2006–17)
8	93	Donncha O'Callaghan (2003–13)
9	92	Malcolm O'Kelly (1997–2009)
10	83	Rob Kearney (2007–18)

COOL-HAND O'GARA HITS HEADY HEIGHTS

American-born, but Irish through and through, it took time for Ronan O'Gara to wrestle Ireland's No.10 jersey away from David Humphreys, but by the time the former Under-21 star had established himself in Ireland's senior line-up, he was already a top-level outside-half. An integral part of Ireland's success in the early 2000s, on 20 June 2003 against Samoa in Apia he broke the national record for the most points scored in a match (32), and in Ireland's 2006 Six Nations opener against Italy he overtook Humphreys as his country's all-time leading points-scorer. By the time he made his final appearance in international rugby in 2013, the Munster fly-half had racked up 1,083 international points in 130 appearances (including two caps for the Lions) – only three players in the game's history had scored more.

ABOVE: No international hooker in history has scored more tries than Ireland's Keith Wood (15).

LEFT: Ronan O'Gara is Ireland's all-time time leading points-scorer (1,083), passing the 1,000 points barrier against Wales in the 2011 Six Nations Championship.

WORLD RECORD-BREAKING WOOD

A marauding presence for Ireland for the best part of a decade, hooker Keith Wood made his international debut against Australia in 1994 and went on to win 58 caps for his country (36 of them as captain) before his retirement following the 2003 Rugby World Cup. The inaugural winner of the IRB Player of the Year award in 2001 – he remains the only Irishman to have received the award – he finished his career with 15 international tries to his name, a world record for a hooker.

IRELAND SHOW NO MERCY TO UNCLE SAM

As has become the custom for the game's elite teams in recent years, Ireland used their match against the United States at Manchester, New Hampshire, on 10 June 2000 as a chance to experiment, handing debuts to five players but, regardless of the changes, they still proved far too strong for their hosts. After establishing a 31–3 lead at half-time, the men in green ran riot in the second half en route to a 83–3 victory to record the biggest win in Ireland's history. Ireland ran in a total of 13 tries in the rout.

IN B.O.D. IRELAND ALWAYS TRUSTED

Scintillating in attack and dynamic in defence, the qualities that established Brian O'Driscoll as the greatest centre in the modern game became apparent to an international audience in his tenth game, against France in 2000, when he scored a hat-trick of tries to lead Ireland to their first win in Paris for 28 years. Fourteen years later he had become Ireland's and the world's most capped player (with 133 caps) . A talismanic leader (he led Ireland a record 83 times), he was also his country's all-time leading try-scorer (with 46 tries) when he bowed out of international rugby in 2014.

IRELAND STAR AND BUSINESS MAGNATE

Tony O'Reilly is a unique figure in world rugby. A talented sportsman in his youth and a graduate of University College, Dublin, he excelled at rugby and made his Ireland debut aged 18 against France in 1955. He went on to collect a further 28 caps for his country (and ten for the British and Irish Lions, for whom he scored an all-time record ten tries), with his last outing for Ireland coming in 1970. It is for his successes in the business world, however, that he is better known: he was chairman of Heinz between 1987 and 1998, before going on to establish a media empire and becoming Ireland's first billionaire.

MOST POINTS: TOP TEN

Pos	Points	Player (Span)
1	1083	Ronan O'Gara (2000–13)
2	683	Jonathan Sexton (2009–18)
3	560	David Humphreys (1996–2005)
4	308	Michael Kiernan (1982–91)
5	296	Eric Elwood (1993–99)
6	245	Brian O'Driscoll (1999–2014)
7	217	Ollie Campbell (1976–84)
8	172	Paddy Jackson (2013–17)
9	158	Tom Kiernan (1960–73)
10	150	Tommy Bowe (2004–17)

O'SULLIVAN PROMPTS THE GOOD TIMES

Eddie O'Sullivan first cut his teeth as a rugby coach with Galway club Montivea RFC before earning his spurs as a rugby development officer with the Irish RFU and as coach of the 1996 triple crown-winning Ireland Under-21 side. His appointment as national coach in November 2001 – following the IRFU's controversial decision not to renew Warren Gatland's contract – sparked a hugely successful period in Ireland's rugby history. Under his charge they collected three triple crowns and reached as high as third in the world rankings. He resigned following Ireland's poor 2008 Six Nations campaign, but with 51 wins is the most successful Ireland coach of all time.

COACHES

Name	Tenure
Ronnie Dawson	1969–72
Syd Millar	1972–75
Roly Meates	1975–77
Tom Kiernan	1980–83
Willie John McBride	1983–84
Mick Doyle	1984–87
Jim Davidson	1987–90
Ciaran Fitzgerald	1990–92
Gerry Murphy	1992–95
Murray Kidd	1995–97
Brian Ashton	1997–98
Warren Gatland	1998–2001
Eddie O'Sullivan	2001–08
Declan Kidney	2008–13
Joe Schmidt	2013–present

ITALY

Italy's prize for years of impressive results in the second tier of European rugby was a place in the 2000 Six Nations Championship and a revised status as one of the world's elite rugby-playing nations. It is a billing the Azzurri have struggled to live up to, but there have been many adventures with a string of notable performances (both team and individual) along the way.

20TH TIME LUCKY

By 2007, Italy had recorded three victories in 38 Six Nations matches, but all of them had been at home; an away victory – a result that would have have been a measure of real progress – continued to elude them. That all changed against Scotland at Murrayfield on 24 February 2007.

A fine performance, capped by a 22-point display from Andrea Scanavacca, saw Italy run out comprehensive 37–17 winners to register their first-ever Six Nations away win at their 20th attempt. They have only recorded one Six Nations away win since, 22–19 against Scotland at Murrayfield on 28 February 2015.

LEFT: Sergio Parisse (facing camera) celebrates one of Italy's greatest achievements on a rugby field: an away victory (against Scotland at Murrayfield in 2007) in the Six Nations Championship.

THE SWEET TASTE OF SUCCESS

Italy's last-ever involvement in the European Nations Cup – prior to their elevation to the Six Nations Championship in 2000 – provided them with their one moment of triumph in the competition. Prior to that moment, they had developed a habit of falling at the final hurdle, finishing as runners-up on seven occasions. Until 22 March 1997, that is, when they beat France 42–30 in Grenoble – still their only victory on French soil – to win the trophy for the first time.

KINGS OF SECOND-TIER RUGBY

There is no finer example of why Italy's domination of second-tier European rugby in the mid-1990s prompted a growing clamour for their inclusion in what was the Five Nations Championship than their match against the Czech Republic at Viadana on 18 May 1994. Italy put their hapless opponents to the sword, racing to a 71–0 half-time lead before easing to the biggest win in their history, a 16-try, 104–8 romp.

MOST TRIES IN A MATCH

The Italy record for the most tries by a player in a single match is four, a feat achieved by two players: Renzo Cova, against Belgium at Paris on 10 October 1937; and Ivan Francescato, against Morocco at Carcassonne on 19 June 1993.

BELOW: Ivan Francescato is one of only two Italian players to have scored four tries in a match (against Morocco in June 1993). Tragically he died of a heart attack, aged only 31, in January 1999.

MOST TRIES: TOP TEN

Pos	Tries	Player (Span)
1	25	Marcello Cuttitta (1987–99)
2	22	Paolo Vaccari (1991–2003)
3	21	Carlo Checchinato (1990–2004)
=	21	Manrico Marchetto (1972–81)
5	19	Alessandro Troncon (1994–2007)
6	17	Mirco Bergamasco (2002–12)
=	17	Serafino Ghizzoni (1977–87)
=	17	Massimo Mascioletti (1977–90)
9	16	Ivan Francescato (1990–97)
10	15	Mauro Bergamasco (1998–2015)
=	15	Sergio Parisse (1998–2018)

COACHES

Name	Tenure
Pierre Villepreux	1978–81
Paolo Paladini/ Marco Pulli	1981–85
Marco Bollesan	1985–88
Loreto Cucchiarelli	1988–89
Bertrand Fourcade	1989–93
Georges Coste	1993–99
Massimo Mascioletti	1999–2000
Brad Johnstone	2000–02
John Kirwan	2002–05
Pierre Berbizier	2005–07
Nick Mallett	2007–11
Jacques Brunel	2011–2015
Conor O'Shea	June 2016–

ABOVE: Former Azzurri captain Marco Bollesan held the role as Italy's head coach between 1985 and 1988.

CRUSHED BY LIFE IN THE FAST LANE

Italy had little time to dwell on the considerable positives they could take from their narrow, but highly creditable, 13–12 victory over Argentina in Cordoba on 28 June 2008, because another 511 days would pass before they tasted victory again. During that time, which included a series of autumn Tests against Australia, Argentina and the Pacific Islanders, a disappointing 2009 Six Nations campaign and a daunting tour to Australia and New Zealand, they lost 13 straight matches – the longest losing streak in their history. The miserable run came to an end when they beat Samoa 24–6 at Ascoli on 28 November 2009.

BOKS DISH OUT THE HARSHEST OF RUGBY LESSONS

Just six months before they were due to make their debut appearance in the Six Nations Championship, Italy received the harshest possible reminder of how tough life would be as a top-tier rugby-playing nation. Against South Africa, on 19 June 1999 at Durban, they found themselves on the wrong end of a hammering: 40 down by half-time, they slipped to a humiliating 101–0 whitewash – it remains the heaviest defeat in their history.

RIGHT: An icon of Italian rugby, Mauro Bergamasco scored more tries than any other flanker in his country's history (14).

ITALY GET OFF TO A LOSING START

In the 27 matches played between the two countries, Italy have only ever lost to Spain on three occasions, but the first of those defeats could not have come at a more inopportune moment: in Italy's first-ever match. On 20 May 1929 in Barcelona, it was the hosts who celebrated after Italy slipped to a disappointing 9–0 defeat.

ITALY'S LONGEST WINNING STREAK

Inconsistency is a long-standing feature of Italian rugby and has become a watchword of the national team's performances in recent years: they have never been able to string together a significant run of impressive performances that would truly show they have taken a step up to the next level. In 86 years of international rugby their best winning streak is a mere six consecutive victories, between 12 May 1968 (17–3 against Portugal) and 10 May 1969 (30–0 against Belgium).

ALL-TIME LEADING TRY-SCORERS: BY POSITION

Position	Player (Span)	Tries
Full-back	Paolo Vaccari (1991–2003)	5*
	Luke McLean (2008–16)	5
Winger	Marcello Cuttitta (1987–99)	25
Centre	Ivan Francescato (1990–97)	11
Fly-half	Diego Dominguez (1991–2003)	9
Scrum-half	Alessandro Troncon (1994–2007)	19
No.8	Sergio Parisse (2002–18)	15
Flanker	Mauro Bergamasco (1998–2015)	14
Lock	Carlo Checchinato (1990–2004)	10
Prop	Martin Castrogiovanni (2002–16)	12
Hooker	Alessandro Moscardi (1993–2002)	6

* also scored 17 tries as a winger.

ABOVE: Diego Dominguez is one of only five players in international rugby history to have scored more than 1,000 points.

YOUNGEST AND OLDEST PLAYERS

20 May 1929 was a record-breaking day in Italian rugby: not only was it the Azzurri's first-ever interntional match (a 9–0 defet to Spain in Barcelona), but it also featured Pietro Vinci IV at fly-half, who, at 16 years 176 days old, remains the youngest debutant in Italian international rugby history. Vinci IV went on to make 12 further appearances for Italy, his last coming in 1939. Italy's oldest player is Sergio Lanfranchi. The prop made his international debut for Italy against a French XV in Marseille on 27 March 1949 (a match Italy lost 27–0) and made his final appearance for the Azzurri, his 21st, ten years later, aged 38 years 184 days, during Italy's 12–3 defeat to France at Parma on 29 March 1959.

MOST CAPS: TOP TEN

Pos	Caps	Player (Span)
1	134	Sergio Parisse (2002–2018)
2	119	Martin Castrogoivanni (2002–16)
3	112	Marco Bortolami (2001–15)
4	106	Mauro Bergamasco (1998–2015)
5	104	Alessandro Zanni (2005–18)
6	103	Andrea Lo Cicero Vaina (2000–13)
7	101	Alessandro Troncon (1994–2007)
8	95	Andrea Masi (1999–2015)
9	94	Leonardo Ghiraldini (2006–18)
10	89	Mirco Bergamasco (2002–12)
=	89	Luke McLean (2008–17)

DIEGO'S SUCCESSFUL RETURN TO THE MOTHERLAND

Frustrated by the lack of opportunities in Argentina – although he played two Tests for the country of his birth (scoring 27 points) – Diego Dominguez turned to Italy, his mother's homeland, for the chance to establish himself in international rugby. And what an impact he had on the Azzurri. He made his debut on 2 March 1991 (against France in Rome), went on to collect a further 73 caps and scored 983 points to become Italy's all-time leading points-scorer. He is one of only five players in history (Dan Carter, Jonny Wilkinson, Neil Jenkins and Ronan O'Gara being the others) to have scored more than 1,000 points in international rugby.

RIGHT: With 119 caps, Martin Castrogiovanni is the second most-capped player in Italian rugby history.

MOST SUCCESSFUL CAPTAIN

Fortunate in some respects to have led the Azzurri when they were the dominant force in the second tier of European rugby, Marco Bollesan is the most successful captain in Italy's history. The No.8 was at the helm for 37 matches between 1968 and 1975 and led his country to 15 wins in that time.

OVERALL TEAM RECORD												
Span	Mat	Won	Lost	Draw	%	For	Aga	Diff	Tries	Conv	Pens	Drop
1929–2018	492	182	292	14	38.72	8355	11119	-2764	920	592	922	105

CUTTITTA FINDS HIS TRY-SCORING EDGE

Raised in South Africa by Italian parents and twin brother of prop Massimo (who played for the Azzurri on 60 occasions), Marcello Cuttitta scored a try on his Italy debut, against Portugal in Lisbon on 18 January 1987, and went on to become a regular fixture in the side for the next 12 years. During that time he scored an all-time Italy record 25 tries, including three in a match against Morocco in Casablanca on 19 June 1993.

BETTARELLO FULL HOUSE SEALS BIG ITALY WIN

Stefano Bettarello was the hero of the hour as the Azzurri completed a highly encouraging victory over Canada in Toronto on 1 July 1993. The Rovigo-born fly-half completed the full house, with one try, two conversions, five penalties and two drop goals (for a total of 29 points, an individual record for Italy in a single match) to help his side to a memorable 37–9 victory.

LEFT: Marcello Cuttitta tops Italy's all-time try-scoring list with 25, averaging a try every 2.4 matches.

DOMINGUEZ GETS ITALY OFF TO A FLYER

Italy could not have wished for a better start to life in the top tier of European rugby. On 5 February 2000, in Rome, Diego Dominguez was the hero, kicking an impressive 29 points as Italy thrilled a partisan Stadio Flaminio crowd by securing a memorable 34–20 victory over Scotland In their first-ever Six Nations match.

PARISSE THE PRODIGY

Sergio Parisse was thrown into the deep end when he made his debut for Italy as an 18-year-old against New Zealand in Hamilton on 8 June 2002. Such was the impression he made that he emerged from the 64–10 mauling with his reputation enhanced. It came as no surprise: his supreme handling ability, exceptional line-out skills and a significant presence in both defence and attack – all combined with a supreme work ethic – marked him out as a potentially great player. Appointed captain in 2008 (he has gone on to captain his side a record 71 times), he won his 50th cap in that season's Six Nations and ended the year by becoming the first and, to date, only Italian to be nominated for the IRB Player of the Year award. He won his 100th cap in 2014 and by 2018 had a record 134 caps to his name.

LEFT: Sergio Parisse, a player who would grace any international XV, has been a consistent standout performer in a struggling Italian side since he made his debut as an 18-year-old in June 2002.

MOST POINTS: TOP TEN

Pos	Points	Player (Span)
1	983	Diego Dominguez (1991–2003)
2	483	Stefano Bettarello (1979–88)
3	294	Luigi Troiani (1985–95)
4	260	Ramiro Pez (2000–07)
5	256	Mirco Bergamasco (2002–12)
6	200	Tommaso Allan (2013–18)
7	154	Luciano Orquera (2004–15)
8	147	David Bortolussi (2006–08)
9	133	Ennio Ponzi (1973–77)
10	116	Carlo Canna (2015–18)

PORTUGAL

Portugal lost their first-ever international match, against Spain in April 1935, and had to wait 31 years before recording their first win, but long gone are the days when "Os Lobos" (the Wolves) were considered true minnows of the game. A surprise victory at the 2003–04 European Nations Cup and qualification for the 2007 Rugby World Cup both testify to the team's upsurge in fortunes, and they are a constant presence in the top tier of the European Nations Cup.

EARNING THEIR PLACE IN RUGBY'S BIG TIME

A third-place finish in the 2004–06 European Nations Cup, which doubled as the first round of qualifying for the 2007 Rugby World Cup in France, saw Portugal qualify for a three-match series with Italy and Russia in October 2006, with one place going to the winner. A heavy defeat to Italy (83–0) meant they needed to win their match against Russia to keep their hopes alive: they won 26–23 to enter round six. The Wolves then faced a winner-takes-all, two-legged encounter with Georgia: they lost the first match and drew the second, but there was still a chance – they faced a final repechage round against Uruguay, with the outcome again decided over two legs. Portugal won 12–5 in Lisbon and lost 18–12 in Montevideo, but they had secured the greatest moment in their history: qualification for the Rugby World Cup for the first time, by the slenderest of margins – 24–23 on aggregate.

MOST TRIES: TOP FIVE

Pos	Tries	Player (Span)
1	24	Antonio Aguilar (1999–2014)
2	21	Goncalo Foro (2007–17)
3	15	Diogo Mateus (2000–10)
4	13	Vasco Uva (2003–16)
5	9	Nuno Garvao de Carvalho (2001–05)
=	9	Goncalo Uva (2004–17)

MAJOR CONTRIBUTOR FOR THE LOBOS

A civil engineer away from the rugby field, fly-half Goncalo Malheiro made his debut for the Wolves against Morocco in Casablanca as far back as 25 April 1998, but it wasn't until 2003 that he made the Portugal No.10 jersey his own. Since then he became an integral part of the national team (with two appearances in their Rugby World Cup fixtures in 2007), contributing a Portugal all-time record 279 points in 41 matches.

KING OF THE TRIES

Winger Antonio Aguilar made his Portugal debut against the Netherlands in Amsterdam on 6 March 1999 and scored his first try in his third match (in a 33–24 defeat to Uruguay in the 1999 Rugby World Cup repechage match in Lisbon). An ever-present in the squad ever since, he played in three of Portugal's four matches at the 2007 Rugby World Cup and has scored a record 24 international tries for his country.

ABOVE: Goncalo Malheiro tops the points-scoring chart for Portugal with 279 in 41 matches.

BELOW: Antonio Aguilar is Portugal's all-time leading try-scorer with 24.

MOST TRIES IN A MATCH

The Portugal record for the most tries by one player in a match is three, a feat achieved by three players: Nuno Garvao de Carvalho (against Spain at Ibiza on 21 March 2004), Goncalo Malheiro (against the Barbarians at Lisbon on 10 June 2004 – Portugal awarded caps for the game) and Goncalo Foro (against Germany at Heusenstamm on 27 February 2010).

OVERALL TEAM RECORD

Span	Mat	Won	Lost	Draw	%	For	Aga	Diff	Tries	Conv	Pens	Drop
1935–2018	271	109	149	13	42.61	4674	6019	-1345	348	240	347	25

PORTUGAL HIT THEIR STRIDE

Portugal's Six Nations B match against Germany at Heusenstamm on 27 February 2010, which also doubled as a 2011 Rugby World Cup qualifying match, was one to remember. Leading 31–0 at half-time, the Lobos scored nine tries in the match (a joint national record) – three of them by winger Goncalo Foro – en route to a comfortable 69–0 victory, the biggest win in the country's history.

A NEW LEADER FOR A NEW ERA

Portuguese rugby faced difficult times after the 2007 Rugby World Cup, as several long-standing members of the squad saw the end of the tournament as the perfect time to bring down the curtain on their international careers, and a fifth-place showing in the 2006–08 European Nations Cup (their worst-ever finish) and failure to qualify for the 2011 Rugby World Cup testify to the Lobos' subsequent decline. In 2008, veteran hooker Joao Correia was the man appointed to lead Portuguese rugby into a new era, and although results did not always go his way, Correia went on to break the national record for the most matches as captain (35).

EVERGREEN UVA LEADS THE WAY

Back-row forward Vasco Uva made his debut for Portugal (as a replacement) against Georgia in Lisbon on 16 February 2003. He made his first start a year later against the same opponents, captained his country for the first time (of 20) in 2006 and led Portugal in three of their four matches at the 2007 Rugby World Cup – Os Lobos' only appearance at the tournament. The captain's armband passed on to Joao Correia, but Uva continued to play a huge role for his country, captaining them again in 2015 and has now had amassed a national record 101 caps.

ABOVE: Thiery Teixeira scored a national record 30 points against Georgia at Lisbon in 2000, but still ended up on the losing side.

BELOW: Portugal's most-capped player, back-row forward Vasco Uva (with 101 caps to his name) captained Portugal in three of their four matches at their only ever appearance at the finals of the Rugby World Cup in 2007.

MOST POINTS: TOP FIVE

Pos	Points	Player (Span)
1	279	Goncalo Malheiro (1998–2007)
2	265	Pedro Leal (2004–17)
3	184	Pedro Cabral (2006–11)
4	120	Antonio Aguilar (1999–2014)
5	114	Joe Gardener (2010–12)

LONE RESISTANCE FROM TEIXEIRA

Portugal may have suffered the disappointment of an agonizing 32–30 defeat to Georgia in Lisbon on 8 February 2000, in a Six Nations B match, but it was a personal triumph for Thierry Teixeira. Given the defeat, it might not have provided a great deal of comfort for him, but the fly-half kicked all of the Lobos' points (nine penalties and a drop goal) to break the Portugal record for the most points scored in a match by a single player, 30.

STRUGGLING IN THE BIG TIME

Portugal's reward for beating Uruguay in the final round of qualifying for the 2007 Rugby World Cup was a place in Pool C alongside Italy, New Zealand, Romania and Scotland, and nobody thought much of their chances. They lived up to low expectations when they suffered comprehensive defeats in their opening two matches – 56–10 to Scotland and 108–13 to New Zealand, the biggest reverse in their history. But then, with the pressure off, they started to perform. Victory may have eluded them, but there was honour in defeat: 31–5 to Italy (a considerable improvement on the 83–0 drubbing they had suffered against the same opponents a year earlier) and a battling 14–10 loss to Romania. Their first Rugby World Cup experience was over, but the Wolves had done themselves proud.

ROMANIA

A country with a rich rugby history, Romania have been a major force in second-tier European rugby for decades, so much so that in the 1980s there was talk of them being worthy of a place in what was then the Five Nations. But the collapse of Communism in the early 1990s coincided with a downturn in the country's rugby fortunes, and although they have qualified for every one of the seven Rugby World Cups, the Oaks have still to make the breakthrough to claim a place among the game's elite.

OVERALL TEAM RECORD

Span	Mat	Won	Lost	Draw	%	For	Aga	Diff	Tries	Conv	Pens	Drop	GfM
1919–2018	446	254	177	12	58.69	9941	7939	+2002	853	542	617	70	1

EUROPEAN NATIONS CUP BRINGS ON THE GOOD TIMES

Romania have enjoyed the best moments in their history in the many guises of the European Nations Cup. Between 1936 and 1997, a period of French domination, they won five times (in 1968–69, 1974–75, 1976–77, 1980–81 and 1982–83) and finished runners-up on 12 occasions. And, since 2000, the Oaks have been a dominant force in the current, revamped version of the event, winning second-tier European rugby's biggest prize five times (in 2000, 2001–02, 2004–06, 2010 and 2017).

LEFT: Mihai Macovei has led Romania on 45 occasions between 2012 and 2018 – a national record.

POWERHOUSE LEADER

Another Romania star who has plied his trade in French club rugby (he has played for Colomiers since 2015), Mihai Macovei made his debut for The Oaks against Ukraine at Kiev on 3 June 2006, but missed out on selection for the 2007 Rugby World Cup. However, the powerful flanker has been an ever-present in a powerful Romania pack ever since, played in all four of Romania's matches at the 2011 Rugby World Cup, was appointed captain in 2012 and was his country's standout performer at the 2015 edition of the tournament (notably in Romania's stunning comeback victory against Canada). He has gone on to captain his country on 45 occasions – a national record.

A FAMOUS VICTORY TO SAVOUR

Romania's 64-year wait for a win away against one of the original Five Nations teams finally ended on 10 December 1988 at Cardiff Arms Park. A Gheorghe Ion try and 11 points from fly-half Gelu Ignat stunned Wales and secured a famous 15–9 victory.

VLAICU TOPS POINTS-SCORING LIST

A 6ft 4in, 14-and-a-half stone winger, Florin Vlaicu made a point-scoring debut for Romania as a 19-year-old against Ukraine in June 2006 (scoring four points in a 58–0 victory) and has been a constant source of points for the Oaks ever since, notching up 20-plus points in a match on six occasions. He appeared at the 2007, 2011 and 2015 Rugby World Cups (playing in all four of Romania's matches at the latter) and passed Dan Dumbrava's Romanian record points' haul in the Oaks' match against Argentina A in Bucharest on 12 June 2013. By April 2018, he had amassed 886 points in a record-breaking 111 appearances.

LEFT: Florin Vlaicu is Romania's all-time leading points-scorer with 886 in 111 matches between 2006 and 2018.

MOST POINTS: TOP FIVE

Pos Points Player (Span)

Pos	Points	Player (Span)
1	886	Florin Vlaicu (2006–18)
2	389	Dan Dumbrava (2002–15)
3	339	Petre Mitu (1996–2009)
4	316	Ionut Tofan (1997–2007)
5	233	Valentin Calafeteanu (2004–18)

ROMANIA'S VICTORIES IN RUGBY WORLD CUP MATCHES

Year	Opponent	Result
1987	Zimbabwe	21–20
1991	Fiji	17–15
1999	USA	27–25
2003	Namibia	37–7
2007	Portugal	14–10
2015	Canada	17–15

Note: *Romania have played in 28 Rugby World Cup matches between 1987 and 2015.*

MOST TRIES: TOP FIVE

Pos	Tries	Player (Span)
1	32	Catalin Fercu (2005–18)
2	28	Gabriel Brezoianu (1996–2007)
3	19	Mihai Macovei (2006–18)
4	15	Ovidiu Tonita (2000–16)
5	14	*Three players*

LEFT: Catalin Fercu has crossed the tryline a national record 32 times for Romania in 103 international matches between 2005 and 2018.

FLYING FERCU

Catalin Fercu made a try-scoring debut for Romania in their notable 22–20 victory over Canada in Bucharest on 19 November 2005 and has been one of The Oaks' most impressive performers ever since. He appeared at the 2007 Rugby World Cup, missed the 2011 tournament through injury, but played in all four of Romania's matches at the 2015 edition of the tournament. By April 2018, he had scored a national record 32 tries in 103 matches and, still only 31 years old, there would appear to be plenty more tries to come.

MOST TRIES IN A MATCH

The Romania record for the most tries in a match by a player is five, a feat achieved by three players: Gheorgie Rascanu, against Morocco at Bucharest on 2 May 1972; Cornel Popescu, against Portugal at Birlad on 18 October 1986; and Ionel Rotaru, against Portugal at Bucharest on 13 April 1996.

AN EVER-PRESENT FOR THE OAKS

Cristian Petre's international career with Romania could not have got off to a worse start as he made his debut for the Oaks in their record-breaking 134–0 rout by England at Twickenham on 17 November 2001. However, the 6ft 5in lock kept his place in the national team and became something of a stalwart of the Romanian pack for the next decade. A veteran of three Rugby World Cup campaigns (in 2003, 2007 and 2011), the AS Béziers second row was the first Romanian player to reach the 90-cap milestone. Three of his six career tries for the Oaks came in the space of four matches in early 2007.

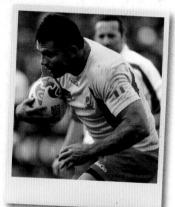

ABOVE: Cristian Petre made 92 appearances for his country between 2001 and 2012.

BELOW: Ionut Tofan (10) scored a Romania record 32 points during his country's 2003 Rugby World Cup qualifying match against Spain in October 2002.

TON UP FOR THE OAKS AGAINST BULGARIA

On 21 September 1976, Romania gave notice of their status as a growing force in the game when they travelled to the Black Sea coastal town of Burgas and proceeded to put their hosts, Bulgaria, to the sword. For the first and only time in their history, they reached three figures, winning the match by the crushing margin of 100–0.

OAKS FELLED AT TWICKENHAM

In 88 matches against the original Five Nations teams (England, France, Ireland, Scotland and Wales), Romania have won only 12 of them, with 11 of those victories coming at home. In short, life on the road in these fixtures has exposed Romanian rugby's greatest weakness over the years: an inability to rise to the challenges posed by a step up in class. And this failing was all too evident when Romania played England at Twickenham on 17 November 2001: they crashed to a thumping 134–0 defeat – the heaviest in their history.

TOFAN'S STAR TURN

Ionut Tofan was the chief architect behind Romania's 67–5 demolition of Spain during the Rugby World Cup qualifying match between the two sides at Iasi on 5 October 2002. The fly-half contributed 32 points to his country's cause – two tries, eight conversions and two penalties – to break the Romania record for the most points scored in a match by one player.

SCOTLAND

One of international rugby's original two, Scotland have enjoyed mixed success on the rugby field. They have won the Home/Five/Six Nations Championship 21 times and in 1991 reached the Rugby World Cup semi-finals, but the years of them punching above their weight appear to be behind them and the glory days (such as the grand slam successes of 1925, 1984 and 1990) are fast becoming a distant memory.

CLASH OF THE TITANS

It is a great sporting occasion at any time, but the Calcutta Cup match of 1990 had added spice: it was the final fixture in that year's Five Nations; both sides were vying for a grand slam; the media hype surrounding the match was unprecedented; and these explosive ingredients combined to produce a classic encounter. It got off to a memorable start: to a chorus of boos, England's players flew out of the tunnel at Murrayfield, confidence oozing after three impressive and comfortable victories; in contrast, the Scots, who had endured a bruising campaign, were greeted by a roar of passionate support as captain David Sole led his team on a slow march towards the pitch. There has perhaps been no stronger statement of intent in sporting history – the Scots, heavy underdogs though they were, were ready for battle. And how they fought. Their 13–7 victory – capped by a Tony Stanger second-half try – remains their most memorable of recent times … and the last grand slam they won.

SCOTLAND OFF TO A WINNING START

The instigators of the world's first rugby international, after a group of their players issued a challenge by letter to their English counterparts in a number of English and Scottish newspapers, Scotland ensured the majority of the 4,000 home crowd went home happy when they beat England by one goal to nil at Raeburn Place in Edinburgh on 27 March 1871. Not that the winning ways continued, however: Scotland would have to wait almost six years before recording their second victory.

SCOTS' GRAND SLAM GLORY

It was the perfect way to start life in their new home: having already beaten France (25–4), Wales (24–14) and Ireland (14–8) in their opening three matches of the 1925 Five Nations campaign, Scotland provided a real sense of occasion for what would be the first-ever match at the new Murrayfield stadium – a shot at a first-ever grand slam, with only arch-rivals England standing in their way. The match lived up to its billing, as tries from James Nelson and Johnnie Wallace were enough to secure a famous, if narrow, 14–11 victory.

HALL OF FAME INDUCTEES

Name (Span, Caps)	
David Bedell-Sivright	(1900–08, 22 caps)
Gordon Brown	(1969–76, 30 caps)
Jim Greenwood	(1952–59, 20 caps)
Ned Haig	Invented rugby sevens
Gavin Hastings	(1986–95, 61 caps)
George MacPherson	(1922–32, 26 caps)
Ian McGeechan	(1972–79, 32 caps)
Bill McLaren	(commentator)
Bill Maclagan	(1878–90, 25 caps)
Andy Irvine	(1972–82, 51 caps)

BELOW: Scotland line up before the start of the most famous match in their recent history: a 13–7 victory over England at Murrayfield in the 1990 Five Nations Championship which gave them their third grand slam.

ABOVE: Stuart Hogg overtook Gavin Hastings as Scotland's leading try-scorer at full-back during the 2018 Six Nations. He has now scored 18 tries in 60 matches for his country.

SLAUGHTERED BY THE SPRINGBOKS

Reigning world champions South Africa taught Scotland a demoralizing rugby lesson at Murrayfield on 6 December 1997. The home side may have put in a worthy stint during the first 40 minutes (they trailed only 14–3 at half-time), but to the disappointment of the home crowd capitulated in sorry fashion in the second half, leaking a total of ten tries on their way to a 68–10 defeat – the heaviest in their history).

ALL-TIME LEADING TRY-SCORERS: BY POSITION

Position	Player (Span)	Tries
Full-back	Stuart Hogg (2012–18)	18
Winger	Ian Smith (1924–33)	24
Centre	Alan Tait (1987–99)	17
Fly-half	Gregor Townsend (1994–2003)	12
Scrum-half	Mike Blair (2002–12)	7
	Roy Laidlaw (1980–88)	7
No.8	Derek White (1988–92)	9
Flanker	John Jeffrey (1984–91)	11
Lock	Damian Cronin (1988–98)	5
	Stuart Grimes (1998–2005)	5
Prop	Tom Smith (1997–2005)	6
Hooker	Ross Ford (2004–17)	5

OVERALL TEAM RECORD

Span	Mat	Won	Lost	Draw	%	For	Aga	Diff	Tries	Conv	Pens	Drop	GfM
1871–2018	685	292	356	32	45.29	9384	10236	-852	1196	698	996	146	3

MOST TRIES: TOP TEN

Pos	Tries	Player (Span)
1	24	Ian Smith (1924–33)
=	24	Tony Stanger (1989–98)
3	22	Chris Paterson (1999–2011)
4	18	Stuart Hogg (2012–18)
5	17	Gavin Hastings (1986–95)
=	17	Alan Tait (1987–99)
=	17	Gregor Townsend (1993–2003)
8	16	Tommy Seymour (2013–18)
9	15	Iwan Tukalo (1985–92)
10	14	Sean Lamont (2004–16)

RIGHT: Tony Stanger shares the record with Ian Smith as Scotland's all-time leading try-scorer. Stanger scored 24 tries in 52 appearances between 1989 and 1998.

HONOURS

Rugby World Cup:
(best finish) – semi-finals (1991)

Six Natio ns:
winners – 1886*, 1887, 1890*, 1891#, 1895#, 1901#, 1903#, 1904, 1907#, 1920*, 1925 (GS), 1926*, 1929, 1933#, 1938#, 1964*, 1973#, 1984 (GS), 1986*, 1990 (GS), 1999

* = shared; (GS) = grand slam; # = triple crown

SCOTS PUT ON A SHOW IN PERTH

A rare home match away from Murrayfield at McDiarmid Park in Perth on 13 November 2004 paid dividends for Scotland when they crushed Japan in front of a thrilled near-capacity 10,200 crowd: 36–8 up by half-time, and in a position of total dominance they went on to run in a total of 15 tries en route to a thumping 100–8 victory, the biggest win in their history.

SCOTLAND'S LONGEST LOSING STREAK

If Scottish fans thought a comfortable 19–0 victory over Wales at Murrayfield on 3 February 1951 would signal the start of a winning run, they were sadly mistaken. Instead, the Scots embarked on the worst run in their history: starting with a slender 6–5 defeat in their next fixture against Ireland at Murrayfield on 24 February, they proceeded to lose their next 17 matches. The sorry sequence finally came to an end when they beat France at Colombes on 8 January 1955.

MOST CAPS: TOP TEN

Pos	Caps	Player (Span)
1	110	Ross Ford (2004–17)
2	109	Chris Paterson (1999–2011)
3	105	Sean Lamont (2004–16)
4	87	Scott Murray (1997–2007)
5	85	Mike Blair (2002–12)
6	82	Gregor Townsend (1993–2003)
7	77	Jason White (2000–09)
=	77	Nathan Hines (2000–11)
9	75	Gordon Bulloch (1997–2005)
10	71	Stuart Grimes (1997–2005)
=	71	John Barclay (2007–18)

MR UTILITY FINALLY FINDS HIS ROLE

Chris Paterson made his debut for Scotland against Spain as long ago as the 1999 Rugby World Cup, but his ability to play in a number of positions – fly-half, full-back or wing – often counted against him in his early years, and it wasn't until he took over the side's kicking duties in 2003 that he showed his true worth to the team. Since then he proved to be a goal-kicker of world-class ability, an essential part of the national side, the first Scotland player to win more than 100 caps (109), and he is his country's all-time leading points-scorer with 809 points.

HASTINGS HITS AN ALL-TIME HIGH

Gavin Hastings was in record-breaking form as he drove Scotland to a comfortable 89–0 victory over minnows Ivory Coast at Rustenberg during the 1995 Rugby World Cup. The veteran full-back, playing in his final tournament for Scotland, scored an all-time national record 44 points in the match, with four tries, nine conversions and two penalties.

ABOVE: In 2017, Ross Ford overtook Chris Paterson to become Scotland's most-capped player, with 110 caps.

LEFT: Chris Paterson is Scotland's all-time leading points-scorer (809).

RIGHT: Bill McLaren was the voice of rugby for more than half a century

RECORD CAPS MARK FOR FORD

Ross Ford made his senior debut when he was just 20 years old, coming on as a replacement during Scotland's 31–14 defeat to Australia at Murrayfield on 6 November 2004. More than a year passed before he made his next appearance but, by 2007, he had made the hooker position his own. He made his only appearance for the British Lions in the third test against South Africa in 2009 and went on to serve Scotland with distinction for the best part of the next decade. By 2018, he had amassed a record 110 caps for his country (eight of them as captain).

MOST POINTS: TOP TEN

Pos	Points	Player (Span)
1	809	Chris Paterson (1999–2011)
2	667	Gavin Hastings (1986–95)
3	623	Greig Laidlaw (2010–18)
4	273	Andy Irvine (1972–82)
5	266	Dan Parks (2004–12)
6	220	Kenny Logan (1992–2003)
7	210	Peter Dods (1983–91)
8	166	Craig Chalmers (1989–99)
9	164	Gregor Townsend (1993–2003)
10	141	Brendan Laney (2001–04)

BILL MCLAREN: THE VOICE OF RUGBY

An incredible attention to detail coupled with a wonderful turn of phrase helped Bill McLaren to become the BBC's voice of rugby for over 50 years. A talented player whose own career was cut short by a bout of tuberculosis, McLaren drifted into broadcasting via journalism and made his first radio broadcast in January 1952. He soon progressed to BBC Television and became a household name and national institution. In November 2001 he became the first non-international to be inducted into the International Rugby Hall of Fame and, such was the affection in which he was held, that when he made his final broadcast – Scotland against Wales in 2002 – he had to do so amid the deafening chorus of 'For he's a jolly good fellow' being sung in his honour by the crowd. He died, aged 86, in March 2011.

BELOW: Greg Laidlaw led Scotland on a record 31 occasions between 2013 and 2017, guiding his side to victory on 14 occasions.

COACHES

Name	Tenure
Bill Dickinson	1971–77
Nairn McEwan	1977–80
Jim Telfer	1980–85
Derrick Grant	1986–88
Ian McGeechan	1988–93
Jim Telfer	1994–99
Ian McGeechan	2000–03
Matt Williams	2003–05
Frank Hadden	2005–09
Andy Robinson	2009–12
Scott Johnson	2013–14
Vern Cotter	2014–17
Gregor Townsend	2017–present

BELOW: Jim Telfer enjoyed two stints as Scotland coach and led them to grand slam glory in 1984.

CAPTAIN FANTASTIC

Greg Laidlaw made his debut for Scotland against New Zealand at Murrayfield in 2010. And his early years in international rugby were hard, as he battled with Mike Blair and Chris Cussiter for the Scotland No.9 jersey. He finally made it his own in 2012 and, the following year, was chosen to lead his country for the first time, against South Africa in Nelspruit (a 30–17 defeat). He held the position for the next four years, until he suffered an injury against France in the 2017 Six Nations. A return to fitness saw him return to the ranks, under John Barclay, but he holds the distinction of having captained Scotland on more occasions (31) than any other player.

SCOTLAND'S LONGEST WINNING STREAK

Scotland's longest winning streak is six matches, which has been achieved on two occasions: between 24 January 1925 and 6 February 1926 and between 28 October 1989 and 17 March 1990. Both runs involved grand slam successes in the then Five Nations Championship.

MOST SUCCESSFUL COACH

A back-row forward whose rugged performances brought him 25 caps for Scotland between 1964 and 1970, eight for the British Lions as well as much praise, Jim Telfer went on to achieve even more fame as a coach. He guided Scotland in two spells (1980–85 and 1994–99) and led them to the grand slam in 1984 and to the Five Nations crown in 1999. With 21 wins, he remains the most successful coach in Scotland's long rugby history.

SPAIN

OVERALL TEAM RECORD

Span	Mat	Won	Lost	Draw	%	For	Aga	Diff	Tries	Conv	Pens	Drop
1927–2018	369	149	205	15	42.41	6817	8109	-1292	469	290	369	20

SPAIN HIT READY HEIGHTS

Not surprisingly for a team who made their debut against Italy in 1927, Spain have established themselves among the world's top-30 ranked rugby-playing nations. Spain have enjoyed some of the most successful moments in their history against Europe's lowest ranked countries, and the Spanish reserved perhaps their finest hour to come during a European Nations Cup match against the Czech Republic in Madrid on 3 April 1995. Having amassed a comfortable 52–0 lead by half-time, they romped to a 90–8 victory – the biggest in their history.

EUROPEAN NATIONS CUP STRUGGLES

Although they have never won the competition in any one of its many guises over the years, Spain have enjoyed some good times in the European Nations Cup. They have finished third on three occasions (in 1973–74, 1977–78 and 2015) and provided cause for cheer when they finished as runners-up (behind Georgia) in the 2012 edition of the event.

MAKING HIS MARK

Born and raised in New Zealand, but qualified to play for Spain through residency, full-back Brad Linklater has made quite an impact on his adopted country since he made his debut against Georgia in Madrid on 28 February 2015, scoring 226 points in 27 matches. His most impressive performance came in Spain's 54–10 victory over Chile at Torrelavega on 21 November 2015, when he scored two tries and seven conversions in the match. His haul of 24 points is a record for a Spain player in a single match.

SPAIN STAR-STRUCK ON THE GAME'S BIGGEST STAGE

Spain's reward for securing qualification for the 1999 Rugby World Cup was a place in Pool 1 alongside defending champions South Africa, Scotland and Uruguay and a firm reminder of the gulf in class that exists between the game's established nations and the developing ones. El XV del Leon lost their opening game against Uruguay (27–15) – realistically their only winnable match – and were swamped by both South Africa (47–3) and Scotland (48–0). They remain the only side in history to have qualified for the Rugby World Cup and then failed to score a single try during the tournament.

BELOW: Qualified to play for Spain through residency, Brad Linklater has scored 226 points in 27 matches for his adopted country.

EL XV DEL LEON'S GOLDEN MOMENT

It may have culminated in the greatest moment in Spain's rugby history, but the path to the prize was a far from simple one: El XV del Leon's quest for a place at the 1999 Rugby World Cup started with a place in Pool 3 in Round B of European qualifying against Andorra on 8 November 1997. They eased to a 62–3 victory, went on to beat the Czech Republic, Germany and Portugal and progressed to the next pool round alongside Scotland and Portugal. With all the matches played at Murrayfield, the Scots were considered firm favourites to win the group, but two of the three teams were granted qualification, which meant that Spain's match against neighbours Portugal on 2 December 1998 was the most important in their history. They came through the tense, high-stakes affair 21–17, with six penalties from fly-half Andrei Kovalenco and a drop goal from centre Fernando Diez Molina. It was mission accomplished, and few recall the 85–3 defeat they suffered against Scotland three days later: Spain had qualified for the Rugby World Cup for the first, and to date only, time in their history and that was all that mattered.

SPAIN'S LONGEST-SERVING CAPTAIN

Longevity is not the word when it comes to captaining the El XV del Leon. The record for the longest-serving captain is a mere 22 matches, held by Jaime Nave de Olano, who has captained the side since 2014.

MOST POINTS: TOP FIVE

Pos	Points	Player (Span)
1	270	Esteban Roque Segovia (2004–07)
2	226	Brad Linklater (2015–18)
3	182	Andrei Kovalenco (1998–2006)
4	177	Cesar Sempere Padilla (2004–14)
5	143	Mathieu Peluchon (2010–18)

LEFT: Andrei Kovalenco (left) is one of only two Spanish players to have scored a point in a Rugby World Cup match.

MAJOR CONTRIBUTOR TO SPAIN'S CAUSE

Drafted into the national squad to bolster the team's qualifying chances for the 2007 Rugby World Cup, Argentina-born fly-half Esteban Roque Segovia made his debut for El XV del Leon against Hungary in Madrid on 20 November 2004 and contributed 23 points towards his team's comfortable 63–9 victory. He remained a steady source of points through what turned out to be a difficult campaign for the Spanish – one that ultimately failed after successive defeats to Romania, Georgia and Portugal. Segovia returned to Argentina in 2007 as Spain's all-time leading points-scorer (with 270, comprising one try, 53 conversions, 52 penalties and one drop-goal).

MR VERSATILE

Jaime Nava de Olana made his senior international debut in Spain's 63–3 demolition of the Netherlands at Murcia on 6 April 2002 and has gone on to become a regular feature of the side. What stands out is his sheer versatility: he has played for his country on the wing, at both centre and fly-half and, more recently, at flanker and No.8 – an extraordinary claim to fame in modern international rugby. One of the few Spanish players to have played club rugby in England (for Plymouth Albion in 2008–09), he was appointed national captain in 2014 and, by 2017, had gone on to become his country's most-capped player, with 71 appearances.

THE PYRENEAN MASSACRE

Of the 23 nations that, along with Spain, have qualified for the Rugby World Cup over the years, Spain have only ever recorded victories against Georgia, Italy, Portugal and Zimbabwe. In short, matches against the world's elite rugby-playing nations have proved to be awkward affairs for the Spanish and none more so than their fixture against a French XV on 4 March 1979 at the small town of Oloron, situated in the Pyrenees in the south-west of France. Spain slumped to a 92–0 defeat: the heaviest loss in their history.

UNIQUE DUO

Fly-half Andrei Kovalenco (15 points against Uruguay) and full-back Ferran Velazco Querol (three points against South Africa) hold a unique place in the annals of Spanish rugby: they are the only two players in their country's history to have scored points in a Rugby World Cup match.

BELOW: A player who has played for his country in a remarkable five positions, Jaime Nava de Olana is Spain's most-capped player, with 71 caps to his name.

MOST TRIES IN A MATCH

The Spanish record for the most tries by one player in a match is three, a feat achieved on five occasions, but only by two players. Ferran Velazco Querol achieved it against the Netherlands at Murcia on 6 April 2002 and Cesar Sempere Padilla did it four times: against Hungary in Madrid on 20 November 2004; Poland in Madrid on 13 November 2005; the Czech Republic in Prague on 5 May 2007; and Ukraine at Alushta on 25 February 2012.

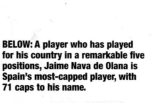

ABOVE: Cesar Sempere Padilla is the only player in Spain's history to have scored three tries in a match on four occasions and he is his country's all-time leading try-scorer with 31.

EL NIÑO PRODIGIO

Perhaps Spain's finest ever player, Cesar Sempere Padilla made his international debut against Hungary in Madrid on 20 November 2004 aged just 20 and got off to an explosive start, scoring three tries during his side's emphatic 63–9 victory. A hard-running full-back, he went on to win 53 caps and sits at the top of Spain's all-time try-scoring list with 31, at the excellent average of 0.58 tries per match.

WALES

Rugby is the national sport of Wales and the hype surrounding the national team is matched only in New Zealand. There have been several golden moments in Welsh rugby – most notably in what is now the Six Nations Championship, which they have won outright on 26 occasions. But there have been plenty of devastating lows, too, such as the time they failed to make it beyond the group stages of the 1991 and 2007 Rugby World Cups.

OVERALL TEAM RECORD

Span	Mat	Won	Lost	Draw	%	For	Aga	Diff	Tries	Conv	Pens	Drop	GfM
1881–2018	714	367	314	29	53.73	12105	10702	+1403	1535	919	1184	129	3

GATLAND LEADS WALES TO GREATNESS

A well-respected coach with both Ireland and London Wasps, Warren Gatland truly made his name as coach of Wales. His direct, physical approach to the game turned Wales into arguably the strongest side in the northern hemisphere and his impact on the Welsh was instantaneous. In 2008, his first season in charge, he led Wales to a 12th grand slam. Three relatively disappointing seasons followed, before Gatland inspired Wales to a fourth-place finish at the 2011 Rugby World Cup and to a 13th Six Nations grand slam the following year. They retained their Six Nations crown in 2013, and although they have not repeated the feat since, Gatland remains their most successful coach in history, with 52 wins in 102 matches.

ABOVE: Wales won the last of their 11 Six Nations grand slams in 2012.

THE FIRST WELSH GOLDEN ERA

When Wales recovered from the 6–3 defeat they had suffered against Scotland to beat Ireland 29–0 in their final match of the 1907 Home Nations Championship to finish second, few would have predicted the greatness that would follow, but the win over Ireland sparked the first golden era in Welsh rugby.

In 1908, the first edition of the Five Nations (following France's inclusion in the tournament), they won the grand slam, a feat they repeated the following year. Following 11 straight victories (still a national record), the magical, 34-month unbeaten run finally came to an end on 15 January 1910, when Wales lost 11–6 to their arch-rivals England at Twickenham.

WALES'S SECOND GOLDEN ERA

The ten-year period between 1969 and 1979 was a period of almost unprecedented success for Wales and a decade during which the names of JPR Williams, Gerald Davies, John Dawes, Barry John, Phil Bennett and Gareth Edwards, among others, would become permanently etched into Welsh folklore. Remarkably during that time, Wales lost only seven matches in the Five Nations Championship, winning the title eight times, with three triple crowns and three grand slams (in 1971, 1976 and 1978). It is known as Wales's second golden era.

LEFT: Warren Gatland has turned Wales into perhaps the strongest side in the northern hemisphere and has amassed the best record of any Wales coach in history, with 52 wins in 102 matches.

MOST TRIES: TOP TEN

Pos	Tries	Player (Span)
1	58	Shane Williams (2000–11)
2	40	Gareth Thomas (1995–2007)
3	33	Ieuan Evans (1987–98)
4	32	George North (2010–18)
5	22	Colin Charvis (1996–2007)
6	20	Gerald Davies (1966–78)
=	20	Gareth Edwards (1967–78)
=	20	Tom Shanklin (2001–10)
9	18	Rhys Williams (2000–05)
10	17	Reggie Gibbs (1906–11)
=	17	Ken Jones (1947–57)
=	17	Johnny Williams (1906–11)

ALL-TIME LEADING TRY-SCORERS: BY POSITION

Position	Player (Span)	Tries
Full-back	Kevin Morgan (1997–2007)	12
Winger	Shane Williams (2000–11)	58
Centre	Tom Shanklin (2002–10)	16
Fly-half	Arwel Thomas (1996–2000)	11
Scrum-half	Gareth Edwards (1967–78)	20
No.8	Scott Quinnell (1994–2002)	11
Flanker	Colin Charvis (1996–2007)	19
Lock	Alun-Wyn Jones (2007–18)	9
Prop	Gethin Jenkins (2002–16)	4
Hooker	Barry Williams (1996–2002)	5

BELOW: In an 11-year career, Colin Charvis scored more tries (22) than any other Wales forward in history, 19 of them as a flanker.

HALL OF FAME INDUCTEES

Name (Span, Caps)

Phil Bennett (1969–78, 29 caps)
Gerald Davies (1966–78, 46 caps)
Mervyn Davies (1969–76, 38 caps)
John Dawes (1964–71, 26 caps)
Gareth Edwards (1967–78, 53 caps)
Ieuan Evans (1987–98, 72 caps)
Arthur Gould (1885–97, 27 caps)
Frank Hancock (1884–86, 4 caps)
Carwyn James (1958, 2 caps)
Barry John (1966–72, 25 caps)
Jack Matthews (1947–51, 17 caps)
Cliff Morgan (1951–58, 29 caps)
Gwyn Nicholls (1896–1906, 24 caps)
Keith Rowlands 1962–65, 5 caps)
Bleddyn Williams (1947–55, 22 caps)
Johnnie Williams (1906–11, 17 caps)
JPR Williams (1969–81, 55 caps)
Shane Williams (2000–11, 87 caps)

WALES FOURTH TO JOIN THE INTERNATIONAL RUGBY CLUB

International rugby between 1871 and 1874 was an exclusive term reserved only for England–Scotland matches, those being the only two countries to have formed national teams. And then Ireland joined the club and the trio continued to play international fixtures against each other for the next seven years. On 19 February 1881, Wales became the fourth international team when they played England at Blackheath. Not that it was a day to remember: Wales lost by eight goals to nil – 82–0 in modern scoring, given that England scored 13 tries, seven conversions and a drop goal.

RETURN OF THE GOOD TIMES FOR WALES

By the start of the 2005 Six Nations the glory days of Welsh rugby were fast becoming a distant memory. Wales had only won the title twice since 1980 (in 1988 and 1994), and such was the lack of faith in the Welsh XV, their pre-tournament odds against winning the grand slam were 50–1. But this was a campaign in which Wales would prove everyone wrong. They got off to a pulsating start when they edged out England 11–9 in their opening match. They then beat Italy (38–8), clawed their way back from being 15–8 down at half-time against France in Paris to win 24–18 and went on to beat Scotland 46–22 at Murrayfield to set up their first chance of a grand slam for 32 years. Only Ireland stood in their way, but Wales won 32–20. It was the first time in Six Nations history that a side had won the grand slam after playing the majority of their games away.

COACHES

Name	Tenure
David Nash	1967
Clive Rowlands	1968–74
John Dawes	1974–79
John Lloyd	1980–82
John Bevan	1982–85
Tony Gray	1985–88
John Ryan	1988–90
Ron Waldron	1990–91
Alan Davies	1991–95
Alex Evans	1995 (caretaker coach)
Kevin Bowring	1995–98
Dennis John	1998 (caretaker coach)
Graham Henry	1998–2002
Lynn Howells	2001 (caretaker coach)
Steve Hansen	2002–04
Mike Ruddock	2004–06
Scott Johnson	2006 (caretaker coach)
Gareth Jenkins	2006–07
Nigel Davies	2007 (caretaker coach)
Warren Gatland	2007–present
Robin McBryde	2009, 2013 (caretaker coach)
Rob Howley	2012–13, 2017 (caretaker coach)

ABOVE: Gareth Edwards was inducted into the World Rugby Hall of Fame in its second year, 2007. The first Welshman to win 50 caps, many consider him to be the greatest scrum-half of all-time.

BOKS TEACH WALES A RUGBY LESSON

Pretoria, 27 June 1998 – the darkest day in Wales's rugby history. A clinical display from South Africa brutally exposed an inexperienced Wales line-up at Loftus Stadium in Pretoria – with fly-half Arwel Thomas the only shining light, scoring all of his side's points – as the visitors, in the face of wave after wave of attack, conceded 15 tries en route to a shattering 96–13 defeat – the heaviest in their history. Welsh rugby had hit rock bottom.

MOST CAPS: TOP TEN

Pos	Caps	Player (Span)
1	129	Gethin Jenkins (2002–16)
2	117	Alun Wyn Jones (2006–18)
3	104	Stephen Jones (1998–2011)
4	100	Gareth Thomas (1995–2007)
=	100	Martyn Williams (1996–2012)
6	95	Adam Jones (2003–14)
7	94	Colin Charvis (1996–2007)
=	94	Mike Phillips (2003–15)
=	94	Jamie Roberts (2008–17)
10	92	Gareth Llewellyn (1989–2004)

ABOVE: Shane Williams proved to be one of the best finishers in world rugby in an 11-year career with Wales, scoring 58 tries.

AS GOOD AS IT GETS FOR WALES

Wales travelled to the inaugural Rugby World Cup in 1987 with low expectations, having finished second from bottom in that year's Five Nations Championship with only one win to their name, but they got off to a morale-boosting start when they beat Ireland 13–6 in their opening game. The tone was set, and Wales went on to beat Tonga (29–16) and Canada (40–9) to finish top of the pool and progress to a quarter-final showdown with England – the only side they had beaten in that year's Five Nations. It was a repeat performance for Wales as they cruised to a comfortable 16–3 victory. The dream ended when they crashed to a 49–6 defeat against New Zealand in the semi-finals, but Wales's 22–21 victory over Australia in the third-place play-off match – thanks to a last-gasp Paul Thorburn touchline conversion – meant they went out of the tournament on a high. It remains Wales's best-ever performance at a Rugby World Cup.

WINGER WILLIAMS STANDS TALL

Shane Williams relied on searing pace, a textbook side-step and an uncanny ability to find space where others could not to silence the many doubters who claimed he was too small to play international rugby and develop into one of the most exciting wingers of modern times. He won his first cap when he came on as a replacement against France on 5 February 2000 and scored his first try on his first full appearance two weeks later, against Italy. He became a constant source of points for Wales from that moment on and by 2011 had scored a national record 58 tries (plus two for the British & Irish Lions – to stand third on international rugby's all-time list. In 2008, he became the first, and to date only, Wales player to win the IRB Player of the Year award.

RIGHT: Gethin Jenkins has been a permanent fixture in the Welsh front row for over a decade and has won a national record 129 caps.

GETHIN THE GREAT

A standout performer in junior and regional rugby, Gethin Jenkins made his debut for Wales aged 22 against Romania at Wrexham on 1 November 2002. He featured in every one of Wales' games at the 2003 Rugby World Cup and by 2005 had forced his way into his country's starting XV. He ended that year's Six Nations campaign in style, scoring his second international try during Wales' grand slam-clinching victory over Ireland at the Millennium Stadium. He played in all three Tests for the British Lions against New Zealand later that year and emerged from the carnage with his reputation intact as being one of the best loose-head forwards in world rugby. But then, perhaps as a result of his workload, injuries struck and his form dipped. He was back to his best in 2007 and started three of Wales' four matches during their disappointing 2007 Rugby World Cup campaign. He captained Wales for the first time (of five) against South Africa later that year. Success has continued to come his way: grand slams in 2008 and 2012, two more Lions tours (in 2009 and 2013) and a further Six Nations title in 2013. By 2017, he had gone on to collect a national record 129 caps.

NATURAL-BORN LEADER

Sam Warburton's initial forays as captain of the Welsh national team ended in disappointment: in his first match as captain, Wales lost 31–28 to the Barbarians, and in his second, a pre-Rugby World Cup warm-up match, they fell 23–19 to England. But the openside flanker showed his leadership credentials when it mattered, at the 2011 Rugby World Cup as Wales progressed to the semi-finals. Under his command, Wales took the Six Nations title in 2012 and 2013 (claiming a grand slam in the former) and, by the time he relinquished the captaincy in 2017 had led his country on a record 49 occasions.

BELOW: Sam Warburton has led Wales in 49 matches – a national record – with 23 victories.

JAPAN SURRENDERS IN CARDIFF

It was as close to a no-contest as you could find in rugby as Wales put on a memorable, try-filled show against Japan at the Millennium Stadium on 26 November 2004. Captain Colin Charvis, leading by example, scored four tries, Tom Shanklin three, while Rhys Williams and Shane Williams grabbed two each and Gareth Cooper, Mefin Davies and Gethin Jenkins one apiece (with 14 conversions from the boot of Gavin Henson) as the home side cantered to a 98–0 victory. It remains their biggest victory of all time, although they have scored more points on one occasion, when they beat Portugal 102–11 in Lisbon in a Rugby World Cup qualifying match on 18 May 1994.

THE WORST OF TIMES

The reality of Wales's many shortcomings during an uncomfortable 32–21 victory over Canada at Cardiff on 16 November 2002 was brutally exposed a week later when New Zealand crushed them 43–17. It sparked a miserable run that saw Wales spiral into an unprecedented freefall. They lost all five of their 2003 Six Nations matches – including a demoralizing 30–22 defeat to Italy in Rome – to collect the tournament's wooden spoon; they then lost both of their matches on a tour to the southern hemisphere – New Zealand (3–55) and Australia (10–30); and proceeded to lose to Ireland (12–35) and England (9–43) in their warm-up matches for the 2003 Rugby World Cup. The hapless ten-match losing streak – the longest in Wales's history – spanning a desperate 272 days, finally came to an end when they beat Romania 54–8 in Wrexham on 27 August 2003.

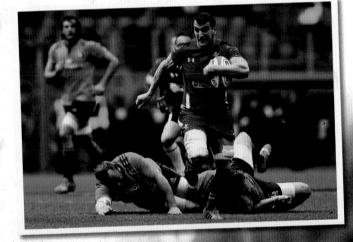

RIGHT: Neil Jenkins was the first player in international rugby history to break the 1,000-point barrier and is still Wales's leading points-scorer with a total of 1,049.

MOST POINTS: TOP TEN

Pos	Points	Player (Span)
1	1049	Neil Jenkins (1991–2002)
2	917	Stephen Jones (1998–2011)
3	696	Leigh Halfpenny (2008–18)
4	352	James Hook (2006–15)
5	304	Paul Thorburn (1985–91)
6	295	Dan Biggar (2008–18)
7	290	Shane Williams (2000–11)
8	211	Arwel Thomas (1996–2000)
9	200	Gareth Thomas (1995–2007)
10	166	Phil Bennett (1969–78)

OTHER EUROPEAN TEAMS

Rugby has flourished more in Europe than on any other continent on earth: of the 105 teams that appear in the current IRB rankings, 39 of them – including Israel – are European. This section looks at the best of the rest from Europe (from Andorra to the Ukraine), those countries outside of the game's elite, whose aspirations, for the time being at least (Russia apart), are restricted to the second and third tiers of world rugby and who contest the earliest rounds of Rugby World Cup qualifying matches.

KNOCKING ON THE RUGBY WORLD CUP DOOR

They may never have appeared at a Rugby World Cup, but the Netherlands have won more qualifying matches than any other country in Europe (30 between 1989 and 2017). And the Dutch have come mighty close to appearing on the game's greatest stage over the years, falling at the final qualifying hurdle in 1991, 1995 and 1999.

FIFTH TIME LUCKY FOR RUSSIA

Until recently, Rugby World Cup qualification had become the sore point of Russian rugby: a 30–0 defeat to Romania ended their hopes in 1995; they fell at the final hurdle in 1999; suffered the embarrassment of expulsion in 2003 (for fielding ineligible players); and lost a winner-takes-all showdown with Portugal in 2007 (losing 26–23). It took a change in format to trigger an upturn in Russia's fortunes. Qualification for the 2011 Rugby World Cup would begin with the 2008–10 European Nations Cup, with automatic places given to the top two teams. Russia, playing the best rugby in their history, won seven and drew one of their ten games to finish second and earned a place on world rugby's biggest stage for the first time in their history.

BELOW: 2010 was a great year for Russian rugby. The team qualified for its first ever Rugby World Cup, then won the Bowl final of the Churchill Cup.

BEST OF THE REST: WORLD RANKINGS

Russia (19); Belgium (25); Netherlands (27); Germany (28); Czech Republic (32); Switzerland (33); Lithuania (35); Poland (36); Malta (37); Ukraine (38); Moldova (45); Croatia (55); Latvia (57); Israel (59); Sweden (60); Luxembourg (63); Hungary (68); Andorra (69); Bosnia & Herzegovina (70); Austria (75); Slovenia (77); Denmark (82); Serbia (84); Uzbekistan (89); Bulgaria (95); Norway (96); Finland (98); Monaco (102); Greece (103)

Ranking correct as of 17 March 2018.

SWEDEN AND GERMANY TRY-FESTS

The earliest rounds of Rugby World Cup qualifying in Europe have seen a plethora of one-sided results, but none more so than Sweden's 116–3 away victory over Luxembourg on 5 May 2001 and Germany's 108–0 home win over Serbia and Montenegro on 12 November 2005: both Sweden and Germany ran in 18 tries during their impressive triumphs.

RUGBY WORLD CUP QUALIFYING WOE FOR BELGIUM

Of all the teams never to have qualified for the Rugby World Cup finals, Belgium hold the European zone record for the most qualifying round defeats. They have lost 32 of 53 RWC qualifying matches between 1989 and 2018.

WINS OVER SIX NATIONS TEAMS

Team	Result	Opponent	Venue	Date
Germany	17–16	France	Frankfurt	15 May 1927
Germany	19–8	Italy	Berlin	14 May 1936
Germany	6–3	Italy	Milan	1 Jan 1937
Germany	10–0	Italy	Stuttgart	6 Mar 1938
Germany	3–0	France	Frankfurt	27 Mar 1938
Germany	12–3	Italy	Milan	11 Feb 1939
Czechoslovakia	14–6	Italy	Prague	22 May 1949
Poland	12–6	Italy	Warsaw	23 Oct 1977
Russia	11–9	Italy	Rome	18 Nov 1978
Russia	9–0	Italy	Moscow	28 Oct 1979
Russia	4–3	Italy	Rovigo	2 Nov 1980
Russia	12–6	France XV	Merignac	1 Nov 1982
Russia	16–7	Italy	Kiev	30 Oct 1983
Russia	15–13	Italy	Moscow	10 Nov 1985
Russia	16–14	Italy	Genova	16 Nov 1986
Russia	12–9	Italy	Kishinev	7 Nov 1987
Russia	17–10	France XV	Kutaisi	22 May 1988
Russia	18–12	Italy	Treviso	5 Nov 1988
Russia	15–12	Italy	Moscow	5 Nov 1989

A DAY TO REMEMBER FOR THE CZECHS

Five successive failed Rugby World Cup qualifying campaigns, coupled with a long-established position among the third-tier teams in world rugby, mean that Czech fans have had little reason to celebrate over the years, but they certainly had something to shout about on 22 May 1949. In what still ranks as the most notable victory in Czech rugby history (and their only win over a Six Nations opponent), they beat Italy 14–6 in Prague.

BACK IN THE BIG TIME

When Ukraine lost all ten of their matches in the 2004–06 European Nations Cup (with a sorry points difference of –499) and suffered the ignominy of relegation to the second division of the competition (essentially the third tier of European rugby), it could have triggered a collapse in the country's rugby fortunes; instead, it triggered a mini-revival, albeit a slow one. In 2006–08, they finished second from bottom in Division 2A, narrowly missing out on a second successive relegation. In the following competition (2008–10), however, they won five out of eight games to gain promotion (as Division 2A champions) back into the top tier of continental European rugby. It remains the greatest achievement in Ukraine's rugby history.

CROATIAN BLOOD COURSES THROUGH THEIR VEINS

Croatia are currently the 56th ranked team in international rugby and have never qualified for the Rugby World Cup. However, over the years, there have been several players with ancestral links to the country (and thus were qualified to play for it) but who appeared on the international stage for other countries. Most notable is England winger Dan Luger (38 caps), whose father was the head of Croatia's rugby federation. Frano Botica, who won seven caps for New Zealand, had grandparents from Croatia, while New Zealanders Sean Fitzpatrick (92 caps), Mark Carter (seven caps) and Mike Brewer (32 caps) and Australian Matthew Cooper (seven caps) all have Croatian heritage.

GERMAN RUGBY'S GLORY DAYS

German rugby was at its strongest between the two World Wars. Between 1927 and 1938 – a period during which they recorded regular victories over Italy (including a 6–3 win in Milan on 1 January 1937) and enjoyed two defeats of France (17–16 in Frankfurt on 15 May 1927 and 3–0 in Frankfurt on 27 March 1938) – they established themselves among the best of continental Europe's teams.

ONE MOMENT OF TRUE RUGBY GLORY

Poland may not have set international rugby alight in the 59 years that have passed since they played their first match – against East Germany in 1958 – but for a period in the 1970s, a surge in form saw them arouse a degree of interest. During that time they recorded wins over the Netherlands, Morocco, Czechoslovakia and the Soviet Union; suffered narrow defeats to a France XV and Italy; and went on to record the greatest win in Poland's rugby history: a 12–6 victory over Italy in Warsaw on 23 October 1977. Sadly, they have not hit such heights since.

BELOW: Former England winger Dan Luger (carrying the ball against Uruguay in the 2003 Rugby World Cup) is the son of the former head of the Croatian rugby federation, but he is just one of numerous international rugby stars who have links to the Balkan state.

ONWARDS AND UPWARDS FOR LITHUANIA

Although rugby is still very much a minority sport in Lithuania, playing second and third fiddle to football and basketball, the performances of its national team in recent years has made people sit up and take notice. In the 2006–08 European Nations Cup they won all eight of their Division 3B matches to win promotion to Division 3A. In 2008–10 they recorded their second successive 100 per cent campaign – with seven wins out of seven – to gain promotion to Division 2. Currently ranked 35th in the world, Lithuania are a team undeniably on the up.

LIFE AT THE BOTTOM FOR GREECE

Greece are relative newcomers to international rugby. They played their first match on 14 May 2006, against Finland in Athens, and lost 17–12. Two weeks later, they travelled to Helsinki to play the same opponents and ended up falling to a 27–0 defeat. They beat Azerbaijan in Baku in October of that year (20–5), and played sporadically through to 2014, at which point they had won 15 of the 32 matches they had played. They hold the unwanted distinction of being the lowest-ranked team in Europe (103rd).

SCORED 100 POINTS OR MORE IN A MATCH

Team	Opponent	Result	Venue	Date
Sweden	Luxembourg	116–3	Luxembourg City	5 May 2001
Germany	Serbia & Mon	108–0	Heidelberg	12 Nov 2005
Russia	Denmark	104–7	Copenhagen	13 May 2000
Denmark	Finland	100–0	Eskilistuna	10 Oct 1987

ASIA AND OCEANIA

Oceania is home to two of the powerhouses of the world game: Australia, the two-time Rugby World Cup winners, who have a rugby heritage dating back to the 1860s; and three-time Rugby World Cup winners New Zealand, home of the legendary All Blacks, the team that captures the essence of the game more than any other. European settlers took rugby with them to the Pacific Islands and Fiji, Samoa and Tonga were all playing international rugby by 1924. Rugby has yet to achieve lift-off in Asia, although Japan, the kings of Asian rugby, have appeared in all eight Rugby World Cups.

BELOW: Samoa, like many of the South Pacific teams, perform a war dance before the start of a match. Theirs is called the "Siva Tau".

AUSTRALIA

Rugby has a rich heritage in Australia, but although the Wallabies have been playing international rugby since the 1880s, it wasn't until the 1980s – and in particular a grand-slam winning tour to the British Isles in 1984 – that they became established as a truly dominant force in the world game, a position they have maintained ever since. They won the Rugby World Cup in 1991 and became the first team to win the trophy for a second time when they triumphed in 1999.

WALLABIES CONFIRM STATUS AS WORLD'S NO.1

Australia lost their first-ever Tri-Nations match, against New Zealand in Wellington on 6 July 1996, 43–6, and the heavy defeat seemed to set the tone for the Wallabies' struggles in the competition in its earliest years: they finished bottom in 1996 and 1997 and second in 1998 and 1999. As such, the newly crowned world champions had a point to prove going into the 2000 campaign, but got off to the worst possible start when they lost a thrilling match against New Zealand (39–35). They rallied a fortnight later in Brisbane to beat South Africa (26–6), and edged out the All Blacks in Wellington (24–23). It meant that victory in their final match, against South Africa in Durban, would bring the Wallabies their first-ever Tri-Nations crown: they lived up to their billing as the best team in the world when they won a gripping match 19–18.

OVERALL TEAM RECORD

Span	Mat	Won	Lost	Draw	%	For	Against	Diff	Tries	Conv	Pens	Drop	GfM
1899–2018	625	316	283	19	52.66	13025	10790	+2235	1624	992	1209	82	2

WALLABIES' RECORD-BREAKING STATEMENT OF INTENT

Australia's crushing 142–0 win over Namibia at Adelaide in the 2003 Rugby World Cup will always be remembered as a classic example of the massive gulf in class that exists between the game's haves and have-nots rather than the hard-hitting statement of intent from a team playing at the top of its game – form that would take them to the final – that it was. The Wallabies ran in 22 tries – five of them by Chris Latham (an all-time national record) – en route to the biggest-ever win in a Rugby World Cup match. It was their largest victory of all time and the only time in their history that they have scored 100 points in a match.

ABOVE: Bob Dwyer masterminded Australia's victory at the 1991 Rugby World Cup.

BELOW: Mat Rogers runs in one of Australia's 22 tries against the minnows of Namibia at the 2003 Rugby World Cup.

DEFYING THE ODDS FOR RUGBY WORLD CUP GLORY

Australia's 2–1 series defeat to the British and Irish Lions in 1989 was a moment of revelation for their coach Bob Dwyer: it made him recognize the absolute importance of a dominant pack, and he set about addressing what, in truth, had been an Australian weakness for years. The results were encouraging if not spectacular and the Wallabies travelled to the 1991 Rugby World Cup as nobody's pick to win the tournament. They struggled through the group stages, winning all three games but in less than spectacular fashion, and survived a huge scare in the quarter-finals in Dublin before a last-gasp Michael Lynagh try saw off the spirited Irish 19–18. Two tries from David Campese and another from Lynagh inspired them to a 16–6 semi-final win over New Zealand and only England stood in the way of an unlikely victory. And it was a resilient pack that won the day for Australia in the final at Twickenham on 2 November. Tony Daley's first-half try, coupled with heroic defence – repelling wave after wave of England attacks – helped the Wallabies to a 12–6 victory and the first Rugby World Cup win in their history.

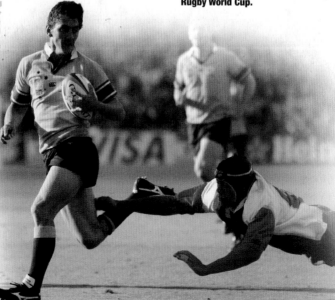

TAKING THEIR TIME TO TAME THE LIONS

Between 1899 and 1989, Australia had played 17 matches against the British and Irish Lions and had won only three of them. What's more, no Australia side had ever recorded a series victory over the northern-hemisphere tourists. That all changed in 2001, even though the Wallabies got off to the worst of starts, losing 29–13 in the opening Test in Brisbane. The defending world champions bounced back in style a week later in Melbourne, winning 35–14 before making history on 14 July 2001, when they edged a tense deciding Test in Sydney, 29–23.

UNDERDOGS MAKE RUGBY WORLD CUP HISTORY

Few fancied Australia's chances of success at the 1999 Rugby World Cup, but he Wallabies silenced the doubters in style. They cruised through Pool 5, beating Romania (57–9), Ireland (23–3) and the United States (55–19), battled to an efficient if not convincing 24–9 victory over hosts Wales in the quarter-final in Cardiff, and edged a tense semi-final against South Africa to reach the Rugby World Cup final for a second time. On 6 November 1999, at the Millennium Stadium in Cardiff, Australia proved too

LEFT: Australia's players celebrate on the pitch at Sydney in July 2001 following the 29–23 victory that gave the Wallabies their first-ever series victory over the British & Irish Lions.

COACHES

Name	Tenure
Bob Dwyer	1982–84
Alan Jones	1984–87
Bob Dwyer	1988–96
Greg Smith	1996–97
Rod Macqueen	1997–2001
Eddie Jones	2001–05
John Connolly	2006–07
Robbie Deans	2007–13
Ewen McKenzie	2013–14
Michael Chieka	2014–present

MOST TRIES: TOP TEN

Pos	Tries	Player (Span)
1	64	David Campese (1982–96)
2	40	Chris Latham (1998–2007)
3	37	Adam Ashely-Cooper (2005–16)
4	34	Drew Mitchell (2005–16)
5	32	Israel Folau (2013–17)
6	30	Tim Horan (1989–2000)
=	30	Joe Roff (1995–2004)
=	30	Lote Tuqiri (2003–08)
=	30	Matt Giteau (2002–16)
10	29	Matt Burke (1993–2004)
=	29	Stirling Mortlock (2000–09)

strong for France and won the match 35–12 to become the first team to lift the Webb Ellis Cup for a second time.

BELOW: Mark Ella is one of 16 Australian inductees into the World Rugby Hall of Fame.

HALL OF FAME INDUCTEES

Name	(Span, Caps)
David Campese	(1982–96, 101 caps)
Daniel Carroll	(1908–12, 2 caps)
Ken Catchpole	(1961–68, 27 caps)
Bob Dwyer	(coach, 1988–96)
John Eales	(1991–2001, 86 caps)
Mark Ella	(1980–84, 25 caps)
Nick Farr-Jones	(1984–93, 63 caps)
George Gregan	(1994–2007, 139 caps)
Tim Horan	(1989–2000, 80 caps)
Thomas Lawton	(1920–32, 14 caps)
Michael Lynagh	(1984–95, 72 caps)
Rod Macqueen	(coach, 1997–2001)
Tom Richards	(1908–12, 3 caps)
Nicholas Shehadie	(1947–58, 30 caps)
John Thornett	(1955–67, 37 caps)
Roger Vanderfield	(referee)

SPRINGBOKS HAND AUSTRALIA RECORD-BREAKING DEFEAT

Australia's fine start to the 2008 Tri-Nations campaign – they had won three of their opening four games (against South Africa in Perth, 16–9, and Durban, 27–15, and against New Zealand in Sydney, 34–19) – came to a crashing and record-breaking

end on 30 August 2008 against a Springbok side who lived up to their world-champion status in front of a passionate home crowd in Johannesburg. The Boks ran riot, scoring eight tries (five of them converted) and a penalty to win 53–8. It remains Australia's biggest-ever defeat.

LONGEST WINNING STREAK

Australia's longest winning streak is ten matches, a feat achieved on three occasions: between 4 October 1991 and 19 July 1992 (a period that included the Wallabies' first Rugby World Cup success); between 29 August 1998 and 24 July 1999; and between 28 August 1999 and 8 July 2000 (a period that saw them lift the Webb Ellis trophy for the second time).

LEFT: A Rugby World Cup winner in 1991, Michael Lynagh sits at the top of Australia's all-time points-scoring list with 911.

AUSTRALIA'S MR RELIABLE

Michael Lynagh made his debut for Australia at inside-centre against Fiji at Suva on 9 June 1984 and did enough in the match – he slotted three penalties – to retain his place in the Wallabies' line-up for the forthcoming tour of Britain and Ireland, going on to play a full part in his team's grand slam success (scoring 42 points in the four Test matches). He switched to fly-half after the tour and directed operations for the Wallabies for the next decade, guiding them to Rugby World Cup success in 1991. When he retired, after 72 appearances, in 1995 – following the Wallabies' Rugby World Cup quarter-final defeat to England – he did so as the world's all-time leading points-scorer (with 911 points). That mark has since been overtaken by others, but Lynagh remains Australia's leading points-scorer of all time.

LONGEST LOSING STREAK

Australia's longest losing run is ten matches, a feat achieved on two occasions: between 22 July 1889 and 3 August 1907 (when the game was still in its infancy in the country); and between 26 June 1937 and 14 June 1947 (when the game of rugby took a back seat in the country before, during and after the Second World War).

SECOND TIME LUCKY FOR DWYER

Bob Dwyer's two stints as Australia coach could not have been more different. The first ended after a disappointing two years when Alan Jones replaced him in February 1984. The second (1988–96), on the other hand, coincided with arguably the greatest period in Australia's rugby history, notably the Wallabies' Rugby World Cup win in 1991. When he left his post in 1996, this time of his own volition, he did so with a sky-high global reputation and as Australia's most successful coach of all time.

BELOW: Chris Latham in record-breaking form against Namibia at the 2003 Rugby World Cup. The full-back ran in five tries during the 142–0 victory, a record for Australia.

MOST CAPS: TOP TEN

Pos	Caps	Player (Span)
1	139	George Gregan (1994–2007)
2	129	Stephen Moore (2005–17)
3	116	Nathan Sharpe (2002–12)
=	116	Adam Ashley-Cooper (2005–16)
5	111	George Smith (2000–13)
6	103	Matt Giteau (2002–16)
7	102	Stephen Larkham (1996–2007)
8	101	David Campese (1982–96)
9	91	Sekope Kefu (2008–17)
10	88	Will Genia (2009–17)

MOST POINTS: TOP TEN

Pos	Points	Player (Span)
1	911	Michael Lynagh (1984–95)
2	878	Matt Burke (1993–2004)
3	698	Matt Giteau (2002–16)
4	543	Bernard Foley (2013–17)
5	489	Stirling Mortlock (2000–09)
6	315	David Campese (1982–96)
7	260	Paul McLean (1974–82)
8	244	Joe Roff (1995–2004)
9	223	James O'Connor (2008–13)
10	200	Chris Latham (1998–2007)
=	200	Berrick Barnes (2007–13)

ALL-TIME LEADING TRY-SCORERS: BY POSITION

Position	Player (Span)	Tries
Full-back	Chris Latham (1998–2007)	36
Winger	David Campese (1982–96)	52
Centre	Tim Horan (1989–2000)	26
Fly-half	Stephen Larkham (1998–2007)	20
Scrum-half	George Gregan (1994–2007)	18
No.8	Toutai Kefu (1997–2003)	10
Flanker	Michael Hooper (2012–17)	15
Lock	Nathan Sharpe (2002–12)	8
Prop	Ben Alexander (2008–12)	4
	Tony Daly (1989–95)	4
	Sekope Kefu (2008–17)	4
Hooker	Jeremy Paul (1998–2006)	14

HUNTING A HISTORIC GRAND SLAM

When Alan Jones became Australia coach in February 1984, he did so with the intention of taking the Wallabies to the pinnacle of world rugby. A Bledisloe Cup defeat to New Zealand may not have signalled the best of starts, but Jones knew the upcoming tour to Britain and Ireland in late autumn 1984 presented his young charges with a fantastic opportunity to become the first Australian team in history to win all four tour matches. They opened up with a 19–3 victory over England at Twickenham on 3 November; beat Ireland 16–9 in Dublin a week later; eased past Wales 28–9 at Cardiff on 24 November and rounded off the tour in style with a commanding 37–12 victory over Scotland at Murrayfield. They had won the grand slam, and in some style: fly-half Mark Ella scored a try in each match and the Wallabies had become the first side in history to score more than 100 Test points on a tour to Britain and Ireland.

BELOW: George Gregan shone for Australia in a 13-year career that saw him amass a then world-record 139 international caps. Ireland's Brian O'Driscoll set a new mark in 2014.

SHOWSTOPPER CAMPESE IS THE WALLABIES' TRY KING

Although he amassed as many critics as admirers over the years (for his brashness off the field rather than his skills on it), there is little doubt that David Campese is the finest player Australia has ever produced. He made a try-scoring debut against New Zealand in 1982 and crossed the line again in his second match. He made his name on the Wallabies' 1984 grand-slam winning tour to Britain and Ireland, thrilling the crowd with a magnificent solo try against the Barbarians. The highlight of his career came at the 1991 Rugby World Cup, when his six tries saw him voted Player of the Tournament. He retired in 1996 with 101 caps and a then world record 64 tries.

GREGAN IN FOR THE LONG HAUL

In 1994, his first full season with the Wallabies, George Gregan became a part of Australia's rugby folklore when he pulled off one of the greatest try-saving tackles of all time – against the All Blacks' Jeff Wilson – to help his side to a famous Bledisloe Cup win. He appeared in the first of three Rugby World Cups in 1995, with the tournament ending in the disappointment of a quarter-final defeat to England. As vice-captain, the Lusaka-born scrum-half enjoyed better fortune during Australia's victorious 1999 Rugby World Cup campaign, scoring a try against Wales in the quarter-finals. He inherited the captaincy in 2001, led his country to the Rugby World Cup final in 2003, won his 100th cap in 2005 and passed Jason Leonard's all-time appearance record in 2006. He won the last of his international record 139 caps during the 2007 Rugby World Cup.

ABOVE: David Campese's outstanding talents on a rugby pitch saw him notch up an Australian record 64 tries in 101 appearances from 1982 to 1996. He was the first Australian player to reach the 100-cap mark.

BELOW: Australia's most successful captain, John Eales, shows off the Rugby World Cup in 1999.

MOST SUCCESSFUL CAPTAIN

John Eales is the most successful captain in the history of Australian rugby, leading his country to 41 wins in 55 matches as captain between 1996 and 2001. One of only six players in the game's history to have won the Rugby World Cup on two occasions, he ended his career in eighth place on Australia's all-time points-scoring list (a phenomenal achievement for a lock forward). He made his debut in 1991 as a 21-year-old and played a full part in his side's Rugby World Cup victory that year. Five years later he was made Australia's captain and fought his way back from a serious shoulder injury to lead his side to a second Rugby World Cup success in 1999.

FIJI

There are few countries with as much passion for the game of rugby as Fiji and the national team, currently ranked tenth in the world, has enjoyed considerable success over the years. They won the South Pacific Championship (the forerunner of the Pacific Nations Cup) on four occasions, have reached the Rugby World Cup quarter-finals twice (in 1987 and 2007) and, what's more, have stuck to their principles of playing a thrilling brand of attacking rugby.

BIG PERFORMANCES ON THE BIGGEST STAGE

It is Fiji's record in the Rugby World Cup over the years, and the attacking brand of rugby they have brought to the tournament, that mark the islanders out as being the most thrilling and spectacular of the Pacific Island nations' teams. In the inaugural event in 1987, a 28–9 opening game win over Argentina proved enough to see them through a tough group completed by Italy and New Zealand, although the dream ended following a 31–16 quarter-final defeat to France. Tough years then followed, including failing to qualify for the 1995 Rugby World Cup, but they were back in the quarter-finals in 2007 – thanks in no small part to a pulsating 38–34 victory over Wales in Nantes – only to lose yet again, this time 37–20 to South Africa.

RIGHT: Waisale Serevi, a legend on the Sevens circuit, performed with distinction for Fiji in the 15-a-side game, too, scoring 221 points in 38 Tests between 1989 and 2003.

OVERALL TEAM RECORD

Span	Mat	Won	Lost	Draw	%	For	Aga	Diff	Tries	Conv	Pens	Drop
1924–2018	335	161	161	10	50.00	7077	6910	+167	995	597	502	37

FIJI DUMP WALES OUT OF THE RUGBY WORLD CUP

Victories over Japan (35–31) and Canada (29–16) followed by an expected defeat to Australia (55–12) meant that Fiji's final 2007 Rugby World Cup Pool B match against Wales – who had produced an identical record – at Nantes on 29 September had become a straight knockout clash for a quarter-final place. Fiji raced into a 25–10 lead at half-time; Wales rallied in the second half and reclaimed the lead with minutes remaining; and then came the most famous moment in Fiji's rugby history. In the final throes of the game, prop Graham Dewes bundled his way over the line and Fiji secured a memorable 38–34 victory.

ABOVE: Severo Koroduadua Waqanibau notched an all-time Fiji best 36 points during the country's record-breaking 120–4 rout of Nieu Island in 1983.

TOUGH TIMES AGAINST THE ALL BLACKS

Fiji have endured some difficult times in matches against New Zealand. In the ten matches they have played against the All Blacks, they have lost them all, scored just 75 points (7.5 per match) and conceded a mighty 519 (51.9 per match). Their heaviest defeat against New Zealand – and the worst in Fiji's history – came at North Shore City on 10 June 2005, when the All Blacks cruised to a 91–0 win.

FIJI'S RECORD-BREAKING WIN

Fiji's match against Niue Island, a tiny Polynesian nation with a population of 1,398, at the South Pacific Games (the tournament first took place in 1963 and, like the Olympic Games, is staged every four years) at Apia (Samoa's capital) on 10 September 1983, was as one-sided a game of rugby as you'll ever find. Fiji scored 20 tries in the match on the way to a crushing 120–4 victory – the largest win in their history – with full-back Severo Koroduadua Waqanibau contributing a national record 36 points to Fiji's cause.

MOST POINTS: TOP FIVE

Pos	Pts	Player (Span)
1	670	Nicky Little (1996–2011)
2	321	Seremaia Baikeinuku (2000–16)
3	268	Severo Koroduadua Waqanibau (1982–91)
4	221	Waisale Serevi (1989–2003)
5	217	Nemani Nadolo (2010–17)

MOST TRIES: TOP FIVE

Pos	Tries	Player (Span)
1	69	Daisuke Ohata (1996–2006)
2	55	Hirotoki Onozawa (2001–13)
3	32	Takashi Kikutani (2005–14)
4	29	Terunori Masuho (1991–2001)
5	26	Yoshikazu Fujita (2012–17)

LEFT: Takuro Miuchi, a former Oxford Blue, was an inspired leader for Japan in 45 Tests between 2002 and his retirement in 2008. Under his charge, the Cherry Blossoms recorded 17 victories, 27 defeats and one draw.

RUGBY'S MOST PROLIFIC TRY-SCORER

Japan may not be one of the superpowers of world rugby, but they possess the most prolific try-scorer ever to have played international rugby. On 14 May 2006, Daisuke Ohata scored three tries in Japan's victory over Georgia to take his tally to 65 tries in 55 Tests and past David Campese's world record which had stood for a decade. He broke on to the scene at the 1999 Hong Kong Sevens, a spawning ground for the game's biggest names, and was voted the tournament's most valuable player – an accolade once afforded to Campese. By the time he retired in 2006 after 58 matches, Ohata had stretched his world record try tally to 69.

KURIHARA SETS NEW WORLD-BEST MARK

On 7 July 2002, Japan hammered Chinese Taipei 155–3 in Tokyo – their 152-point winning margin is the joint highest in international rugby history. Two weeks later, they travelled to Tainan for the reverse fixture and romped to not only another comfortable victory but also a record-breaking one: winger Toru Kurihara, with six tries and 15 conversions, scored 60 points in the match to break Eduardo Morgan's long-standing all-time record (50 points for Argentina against Paraguay in October 1973) for the most points scored by a single player in an international match.

WAITING FOR THE RUGBY WORLD CUP PARTY TO BEGIN

Even though Japan were considered to have the stronger bid, they suffered the disappointment of losing out to New Zealand for the right to host the 2011 Rugby World Cup, but the IRB could not ignore the Cherry Blossoms' strong claims to host the tournament for long. Having successfully co-hosted the 2002 FIFA World Cup, they possessed both the experience and infrastructure to hold an event of such magnitude. In July 2007, the IRB announced that England would host the 2015 Rugby World Cup and that Japan would become the tournament's first Asian hosts in 2019. The countdown has already started.

HALL OF FAME INDUCTEE

Name
Yoshihiro Sakata

WINNING AND LOSING STREAK RECORDS

Throughout history, the start of a Japanese losing streak tends to coincide with the moment they play a team from world rugby's top tier and their winning ways re-emerge the instant they return to the comfort of Asian rugby or to other internationals against second-tier nations. So, it is little surprise that Japan's longest-ever losing streak came when they played a host of touring teams at home between 1952 and 1958 – they lost 11 straight matches. Their longest winning run – six matches between 16 November 2008 and 23 May 2009 – came during two Tests against the United States and a 100 per cent qualifying campaign for the 2011 Rugby World Cup.

GOROMARU SEIZES HIS CHANCE

Ayumu Goromaru was aged just 19 years when he made his international debut for the Cherry Blossoms (against Uruguay in April 2005). The full-back made three further appearances that year before he was jettisoned from the squad following a change of coach – and had to wait four years before making his next appearance. Goromaru seized the opportunity with both hands, became an integral part of the Cherry Blossoms' set-up and, by 2016, had scored 708 points (in 56 matches) to become the leading points-scorer in Japan's history.

LEFT: Ayumu Goromaru is top of Japan's all-time points-scoring list with 708, garnered in 56 matches between 2005 and 2016.

MIUCHI'S LEADERSHIP QUALITIES

A former Oxford Blue, Takuro Miuchi made his debut for Japan as a flanker during the Cherry Blossoms' 59–19 victory over Romania at Tokyo on 19 May 2002. Remarkably, he was appointed national captain in only his second Test appearance, but soon settled into the role and led Japan to the 2003 Rugby World Cup and beyond. Controversially, new coach Jean-Pierre Elissalde relieved him of the captaincy in February 2006, but Miuchi's stint among the ranks was a short one: John Kirwan reappointed him as captain the moment he took over the coaching reins on 1 January 2007. By the time of his final appearance, against Samoa at Apia on 5 July 2008, Miuchi had led his country on 45 occasions, an all-time record for Japan.

LEFT: Toru Kurihara amassed a breathtaking 60 points (six tries and 15 conversions) for Japan against Chinese Taipei in Tainan on 21 July 2002 to break a world record that had stood since 1973. Japan won the Rugby World Cup qualifier 120–3.

NEW ZEALAND

New Zealand are to rugby what Brazil are to football: they capture the very heart and soul of the game. Like Brazil, the All Blacks start every competition among the pre-tournament favourites; but unlike their South American football counterparts, New Zealand have not translated year-on-year dominance into regular Rugby World Cup success: the 14-time Tri-Nations/The Rugby Championship winners have claimed the game's greatest prize on three occasions in eight attempts.

SECOND STRING ALL BLACKS PUT ON A RECORD SHOW

Given that victory in the group had all but been assured following convincing opening wins over Ireland (43–19) and Wales (34–9), New Zealand made 11 changes to their side for their final Pool C fixture at the 1995 Rugby World Cup – against Japan at Bloemfontein on 4 June. The results were explosive: finally given an opportunity to display their talent, what was essentially a second-string All Blacks XV blew Japan apart, scoring 21 tries – with winger Marc Ellis scoring six tries and fly-half Simon Culhane slotting 45 points (both All Blacks records) – on the way to a stunning 145–17 victory. It is the largest win in New Zealand's history.

OVERALL TEAM RECORD

Span	Mat	Won	Lost	Draw	%	For	Aga	Diff	Tries	Conv	Pens	Drop	GfM
1903–2018	577	437	109	20	78.97	15425	7454	+7971	2010	1327	1178	91	5

ALL BLACKS TAME THE LIONS

New Zealand won their first-ever match against a touring team from Britain – 9–3 in a one-off encounter at Wellington on 13 August 1904 – and have maintained the upper hand over the men from the northern hemisphere ever since. In 38 matches against the British and Irish Lions, the All Blacks have won 29 of them and have collected nine series wins in the 11 contested, with one drawn and one lost (in 1971). Most recently, in 2017, New Zealand drew 1–1 with the Lions.

BIGGEST DEFEAT

Of their 577 international matches – the first being a 22–3 win over Australia at Sydney on 15 August 1903 – New Zealand have only ever lost 109 and, remarkably, only one of them by more than 20 points. The heaviest defeat in New Zealand's history came against Australia at Sydney on 28 August 1999, when they slipped to a 28–7 reverse.

AGAINST-THE-ODDS RUGBY WORLD CUP SUCCESS

New Zealand rugby was in turmoil in the build-up to the inaugural Rugby World Cup in 1987. The year before, a rebel tour to South Africa had resulted in several star players being banned. This shook the All Blacks to their very core and, disenfranchised, the country's passionate supporters were starting to turn their backs on the national team in their droves. The 1987 Rugby World Cup provided the All Blacks with an opportunity to win back those supporters … and they did it in some style. They won their pool comfortably, beat Scotland 30–3 in the quarter-finals and thumped Wales 49–6 in the semi-finals to take their place in the final against France in front of an adoring crowd at Eden Park, Auckland. Then, in what remains one of the New Zealand's greatest days in rugby, they ran in three tries to France's one to win the match 29–9 and claim the game's greatest prize for the first time in their history.

ABOVE: One of the finest ever All Blacks, Richie McCaw led his team to Rugby World Cup glory in 2011 and 2015.

BELOW LEFT: Marc Ellis scored a New Zealand record six tries in the 145–17 dismantling of Japan at the 1995 Rugby World Cup.

THE LONG WAIT ENDS

In 2011, New Zealand finally brought an end to 24 years of deep Rugby World Cup frustration and often misery. The All Blacks, tournament hosts and – as often before – hot favourites for the title, romped to the top of their first round pool with comfortable victories over Tonga (41–10), Japan (83–7), France (37–17) and Canada (79–15), outlasted Argentina in the quarter-finals (33–10), outclassed Australia in the semi-finals (20–6) and edged to the narrowest of victories (8–7) over France in a tense final at Eden Park, Auckland, to lift the Webb Ellis trophy for a second time.

Name	(Span, Caps)
Fred Allen	(1946–49, 6 caps)
Don Clarke	(1956–64, 31 caps)
Sean Fitzpatrick	(1986–97, 92 caps)
Grant Fox	(1985–93, 46 caps)
David Gallaher	(1903–06, 6 caps)
Michael Jones	(1986–98, 56 caps)
Ian Kirkpatrick	(1967–77, 39 caps)
David Kirk	(1983–87, 17 caps)
John Kirwan	(1984–94, 63 caps)
Dick Littlejohn	(manager, co-founder of Rugby World Cup)
Brian Lochore	(1964–71, 25 caps)
Jonah Lomu	(1994–2002, 63 caps)
Terry McLean	(journalist)
Colin Meads	(1957–71, 55 caps)
Graham Mourie	(1977–82, 21 caps)
George Nepia	(1924–30, 9 caps)
Fiona Palmer	(1998–2006, 35 caps)
Anna Richards	(1991–2010, 49 caps)
Gordon Tietjens	(Sevens)
Joe Warbrick	(1884, 7 caps)
Wilson Whineray	(1957–65, 32 caps)

TRI-NATIONS/RUGBY CHAMPIONSHIP GLORY

Their electric form in The Rugby Championship (formerly the Tri-Nations – international rugby's toughest annual competition), established New Zealand's credentials as the world game's No.1. They won the inaugural competition in 1996 with a 100 per cent record, repeated the feat the following year and now have won 15 of the 20 tournaments contested, most recently in 2017.

ABOVE: New Zealand have won the Rugby Championship on 15 occasions, most recently in 2017.

MOST TRIES: TOP TEN

Pos	Tries	Player (Span)
1	49	Doug Howlett (2000–07)
2	46	Christian Cullen (1996–2002)
=	46	Joe Rokocoko (2003–10)
=	46	Julian Savea (2012–17)
5	44	Jeff Wilson (1993–2001)
6	37	Jonah Lomu (1994–2002)
7	36	Tana Umaga (1997–2005)
8	35	John Kirwan (1984–94)
9	34	Mils Muliaina (2003–11)
10	31	Ma'a Nonu (2003–15)

RIGHT: Kieran Read has scored 23 international tries since making his debut in 2008 – a record for an All Black No.8.

THE ALL BLACKS' WINNING WAYS

New Zealand tasted victory in all of their first six internationals (between 1903 and 1905) and have gone on to win three of every four matches played and record a remarkable win percentage of 78.79. There have been plenty of lengthy winning streaks along the way, but the longest stretched to 18 matches from August 2015 to October 2016 and came to an end following a 40–29 defeat to Ireland in Chi. The All Blacks' longest unbeaten streak is 23 matches: the run of wins, which started with a 70–6 victory over Italy at Auckland on 22 May 1987 and included the country's first, and to date only, Rugby World Cup win, ended at ten after a 19–19 draw against Australia at Brisbane on 16 July 1988. But the unbeaten run stretched a further 12 games before New Zealand lost 21–9 to Australia at Wellington on 18 August 1990.

BACK-TO-BACK SUCCESS FOR THE ALL BLACKS

New Zealand arrived at the 2015 Rugby World Cup as the firm favourites to lift the trophy. And, on this occasion, it was a tag they seemed comfortable with. They romped through the pool stages, beating Argentina (26–16), Namibia (58–14), Georgia (43–10) and Tonga (47–9), destroyed France in the quarter-finals (62–13), survived a few scares to edge past South Africa in the semi-finals (20–18) and produced a vintage performance in the final to beat Australia (34–17). Victory saw them become the first team in the tournament's history to defend the Rugby World Cup crown.

ALL-TIME LEADING TRY-SCORERS: BY POSITION

Position	Player (Span)	Tries
Full-back	Christian Cullen* (1996–2002)	41*
Winger	Doug Howlett (2000–07)	47
Centre	Ma'a Nonu (2003–15)	30
Fly-half	Dan Carter (2003–15)	25
Scrum-half	Justin Marshall (1995–2005)	24
No.8	Kieran Read (2008–17)	23
Flanker	Richie McCaw (2001–15)	26
Lock	Ian Jones (1990–99)	9
Prop	Kees Meeuws (1998–2004)	10
	Tony Woodcock (2002–15)	10
Hooker	Sean Fitzpatrick (1986–97)	12
	Keven Mealamu (2002–15)	12

* scored five tries as a centre or wing.

A LEADING LIGHT FOR NEW ZEALAND

One of the finest players ever to emerge from the land of the long white cloud, hooker Sean Fitzpatrick experienced both the highs and lows of New Zealand's rugby fortunes. His swift rise to international rugby – he made his debut against France at Christchurch in June 1986, shortly after his 23rd birthday – had been accelerated by the blanket ban imposed on New Zealand players who had appeared in the 1986 rebel tour to South Africa, and Fitzpatrick became part of the 'Baby Blacks' – a new generation of players charged with restoring the All Blacks' fortunes and with winning over an increasingly frustrated New Zealand rugby public. An integral part of the 1987 Rugby World Cup-winning team, he was appointed captain in 1992 and took his side to the 1995 Rugby World Cup final against South Africa – only to suffer the anguish of defeat. By the time he bowed out of international rugby in 1997 after his 92nd cap, he was New Zealand's most capped player – a record that stood until 2010.

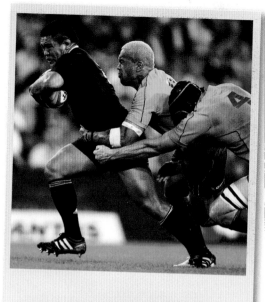

MOST CAPS: TOP TEN

Pos	Caps	Player (Span)
1	148	Richie McCaw (2001–15)
2	132	Keven Mealamu (2002–15)
3	118	Tony Woodcock (2002–15)
4	112	Dan Carter (2003–15)
5	109	Kieran Read (2008–17)
6	103	Ma'a Nonu (2003–15)
7	100	Mils Muliaina (2003–11)
8	96	Sam Whitelock (2010–17)
9	95	Owen Franks (2009–17)
10	94	Conrad Smith (2004–15)

LEFT: With 132 caps to his name, Keven Mealamu as the second-most capped All Black in history and the most-capped hooker in the world game.

DAN'S THE MAIN MAN FOR NEW ZEALAND

A player whose reputation transcends both hemispheres, Dan Carter made his debut for New Zealand aged 21 against Wales at Hamilton on 21 June 2003 and scored 20 points in the match (one try, six conversions and a penalty). But it took a disastrous Rugby World Cup campaign in 2003 – in which New Zealand lost 22–10 to Australia in the semi-finals, with Carter watching on from the sidelines – before he was given a chance to establish himself as the All Blacks' first-choice No.10. Showing raw speed, a natural side-step, huge defensive strength and a metronomic left boot, he grabbed the opportunity with both hands, played a starring role in New Zealand's 3–0 series victory over the British Lions in 2005 and has gone on to become arguably the most complete fly-half in the game's history. By 2016, a winner of 112 caps, he has scored 1,598 international points (with 29 tries) to become the all-time leading points-scorer in international rugby.

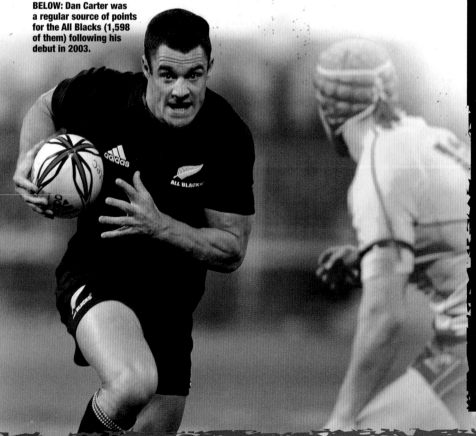

BELOW: Dan Carter was a regular source of points for the All Blacks (1,598 of them) following his debut in 2003.

COACHES

Name	Tenure
Alex McDonald	1949
Tom Morrison	1950
Len Clode	1951
Arthur Marslin	1953–54
Tom Morrison	1955–56
Dick Everest	1957
Jack Sullivan	1958–60
Neil McPhail	1961–65
Ron Bush	1962
Fred Allen	1966–68
Ivan Vodanovich	1969–71
Bob Duff	1972–73
John Stewart	1974–76
Jack Gleeson	1977–78
Eric Watson	1979–80
Peter Burke	1981–82
Bryce Rope	1983–84
Sir Brian Lochore	1985–87
Alex Wyllie	1988–91
Laurie Mains	1992–95
John Hart	1996–99
Wayne Smith	2000–01
John Mitchell	2002–03
Graham Henry	2004–11
Steve Hansen	2012–present

DEADLY DOUG HITS NEW HEIGHTS

A player blessed with searing pace (he once clocked 10.68 for the 100m in his youth), Doug Howlett made his first appearance for New Zealand, as a replacement, against Tonga in June 2000 and helped himself to two tries – the first just 20 seconds after coming on to the pitch. Remarkably, he went on to score a try in each of his next six internationals setting the tone for the rest of his successful career: he was a try-scoring regular in the All Blacks line-up and appeared at both the 2003 and 2007 Rugby World Cups. By the time he was sensationally dropped from the squad, after causing alleged criminal damage during a drunken night out in Cardiff (for which he issued a grovelling apology), he had scored 49 tries in 62 matches to become New Zealand's leading try-scorer of all time. Howlett's international career may have ended on a sour note, but he will always be remembered as one of the greatest finishers in rugby history.

BELOW: Three-time IRB International Player of the Year, flanker Richie McCaw is not only New Zealand's longest-serving captain, he is also the nation's most successful skipper, lifting the Rugby World Cup on two occasions, in 2011 and 2015.

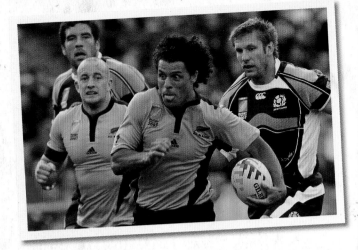

ABOVE: Doug Howlett was New Zealand's supreme finisher, scoring a national record 49 tries in 62 Tests between 2000 and 2007.

MAGICAL McCAW LEADS THE WAY

When Richie McCaw burst on to the international scene in 2001 aged 20 there was immediate talk that New Zealand had unearthed another potential legend. Super strong in both attack and defence, he fulfilled those heady expectations to become the best active openside flanker in the world and, maybe, the best of all time. He is the only player ever to win the IRB Player of the Year award three times (in 2006, 2009 and 2010). McCaw was appointed New Zealand captain in 2004 and enjoyed a highly successful stint at the helm, leading the All Blacks in 112 matches, winning 97, including the Rugby World Cup finals in both 2011 and 2015.

ABOVE: Graham Henry's record of 88 wins in 103 matches is the best of any New Zealand coach in history. The most important of those wins came in the 2011 Rugby World Cup final.

HENRY LEADS ALL BLACKS TO GAME'S HOLY GRAIL

When Graham Henry was appointed New Zealand coach in 2004, following the country's disastrous semi-final collapse at the 2003 Rugby World Cup, he was charged with the task of bringing back the Webb Ellis trophy to the land of the long white cloud for the first time since 1987. And although New Zealand enjoyed plenty of good times under Henry, notably five Tri-Nations triumphs, Rugby World Cup glory eluded them for 20 years. The task was completed in 2011. Once again overwhelming pre-tournament favourites, especially as New Zealand were the hosts, Henry guided the All Blacks to the top of their pool, and victories over Argentina (33–10), Australia (20–6) and France in the final (8–7) to leave an indelible mark on his country's rugby history.

MOST POINTS: TOP TEN

Pos	Points	Player (Span)
1	1,598	Dan Carter (2003–15)
2	967	Andrew Mehrtens (1995–2004)
3	645	Grant Fox (1985–93)
4	465	Beauden Barrett (2012–17)
5	322	Aaron Cruden (2010–17)
6	291	Carlos Spencer (1997–2004)
7	245	Doug Howlett (2000–07)
8	236	Christian Cullen (1996–2002)
9	234	Jeff Wilson (1993–2001)
10	230	Joe Rokocoko (2003–10)

PACIFIC ISLANDERS

Born out of the formation of the Pacific Islands Rugby Alliance (PIRA) in 2003 and created to ease the considerable financial constraints under which teams from the South Pacific operate, the Pacific Islanders, made up, initially, of players from Fiji, Samoa and Tonga, played their first international match in 2004. An oddity in rugby because they do not appear at the Rugby World Cup – in which each individual nation represents itself – they have not played a match since November 2008.

ENDING THE LONG WAIT FOR VICTORY

The Pacific Islanders endured a torrid start to life in international rugby, losing each of their first eight matches, but their ninth fixture, against Italy at Reggio Emilia on 22 November 2008, finally presented them with a realistic chance of success. They went on to take it with both hands: two tries from winger Vilimoni Delesau and one from full-back Kameli Ratuvou were enough to see them to a slender 25–17 victory – the first, and to date only, win in their history.

OVERALL TEAM RECORD

Span	Mat	Won	Lost	Draw	%	For	Aga	Diff	Tries	Conv	Pens	Drop
2004–08	9	1	8	0	11.11	178	339	-161	25	13	9	0

A SORRY SWANSONG FOR THE ISLANDERS

The Pacific Islanders' match against Ireland at Dublin on 26 November 2006 will principally be remembered for being the last international played at Lansdowne Road before the stadium underwent extensive redevelopment, but for the Pacific Islanders it will go down as the worst performance in their short history. Ireland swamped them, running in eight tries en route to a comprehensive 61–17 victory.

BELOW: Seremaia Baikeinuku is the Pacific Islanders' all-time leading scorer with 35 points.

RIGHT: Sitiveni Sivivatu starred for the Pacific Islanders before playing for New Zealand.

CROSSING THE DIVIDE

One of the PIRA's intentions when setting up the Pacific Islanders team was to safeguard the region's players against the prying eyes of the southern hemisphere's biggest rugby nations and to provide them with financial incentives to abstain from the temptation of the Australia or New Zealand dollar. Instead of protecting the players, however, Pacific Islanders matches have, in two instances, merely showcased them. Both previously uncapped, Fiji's Sitiveni Sivivatu and Tonga's Sione Lauaki made their international debuts for the Islanders in July 2004 and impressed, with winger Sivivatu scoring two tries against both New Zealand and South Africa and Lauaki putting together a string of solid performances at No.8. Soon after, the All Blacks came calling and Sivivatu and Lauaki made their New Zealand debuts in June 2005.

BAI A NATURAL PICK AT NO.10

Seremaia Baikeinuku – otherwise known as 'Bai' – made his international debut when he came on as a replacement during Fiji's 47–22 victory over Japan in Tokyo on 20 May 2000, and soon became a first-choice selection for his national side (at either fly-half or centre). He was also a natural choice to wear the No.10 jersey in the Pacific Islanders' first-ever match, against Australia at Adelaide on 3 July 2004, contributing four points during the 29–14 defeat. He played in the Islanders' next seven matches and is both their all-time leading points-scorer, with 35, and the record holder for the most points in a match by a single player – 12 (four penalties) against France at Sochaux-Montbéliard on 15 November 2008

MOST POINTS: TOP FIVE

Pos Points Player (Span)

Pos	Points	Player (Span)
1	35	Seremaia Baikeinuku (2004–08)
2	20	Kameli Ratuvou (2006–08)
=	20	Sitiveni Sivivatu (2004)
4	19	Seru Rabeni (2004–08)
5	15	Sione Lauaki (2004)

PACIFIC ISLANDERS REPRESENTATION

Country	No. of Players
Samoa	20
Fiji	19
Tonga	17
Cook Islands	1

THE EVER-PRESENTS

Centre Seru Rabeni and scrum-half Moses Rauluni (both from Fiji) are the only two players to have played in all nine of the Pacific Islanders' internationals.

MOST TRIES

Two players hold the record for the most tries by a Pacific Islanders player: Kameli Ratuvou, with four tries in six matches between 2006 and 2008; and Sitiveni Sivivatu, with four tries in three matches in 2004.

ABOVE: Fijian centre Seru Rabeni (white shirt) is one of only two players to have appeared in all nine of the Pacific Islanders' matches.

LEFT: Another Fijian, Kameli Ratuvou (with ball), tops the Pacific Islanders' all-time try-scoring list (alongside compatriot Sitiveni Sivivatu) with four, in six matches between 2006 and 2008.

MOST TRIES: TOP FIVE

Pos	Tries	Player (Span)
1	4	Kameli Ratuvou (2006–08)
=	4	Sitiveni Sivivatu (2004)
3	3	Sione Lauaki (2004)
=	3	Seru Rabeni (2004–08)
5	2	Sireli Bobo (2004)
=	2	Vilimoni Delasau (2008)

IN AT THE DEEP END

The Pacific Islanders could not have chosen three tougher opponents for their first-ever internationals: three matches in three weeks against Australia, New Zealand and South Africa. And although they lost all three, they put in a trio of commendable performances in defeat, losing 29–14 to the Wallabies, 41–26 to the All Blacks and 38–24 to the Springboks. It may not have been a winning start to international rugby life for the Islanders, but it had been a worthy one.

NORTHERN HEMISPHERE BLUES

Many believed the Pacific Islanders' second tour – to Wales, Scotland and Ireland, their first to the northern hemisphere, in November 2006 – would bring with it their first victory. Instead the Islanders struggled, losing 38–20 to Wales and 34–22 to Scotland before suffering a 61–17 collapse against Ireland. The Pacific Islanders' record now stood at played six lost six, and the long wait for that elusive victory continued.

LONGEST-SERVING CAPTAIN

Tonga lock forward Inoke Afeaki holds the distinction of having captained the Pacific Islanders in their first-ever outing in international rugby, against Australia in July 2004. He also holds the record as the Islanders' longest-serving captain (three matches) along with Fiji lock Simon Raiwalui, who led them on their tour to the northern hemisphere in 2006.

FROM THREE TO TWO

In July 2009, following the International Rugby Board's announcement that they would only sanction a Pacific Islanders' tour every four years rather than every two, Samoa quit PIRA claiming that the union had failed to bring the expected financial rewards. As of March 2011, plans for the Islanders' fourth tour have yet to be announced and the future of the Pacific Islanders as a team remains in doubt.

SAMOA

Known as 'Manu Samoa' in their own land, after a famous warrior, Samoa can justifiably lay claim to being the best of the Pacific island rugby-playing nations. Their hard-hitting, physical style has brought them plenty of success over the years: nine Pacific Tri-Nations championships, the Pacific Nations Cup in 2010, 2012 and 2014, qualification for every Rugby World Cup for which they were eligible and a place in the last eight of the game's biggest tournament in 1991 and 1995.

PNG PULPED IN APIA

Samoa's punishment for what by their standards had been a disappointing 2007 Rugby World Cup campaign – they lost three of their four matches – was to pass through the Oceania qualifying section and earn a place at the 2011 tournament. Not that this presented Samoa with too difficult a hurdle: qualification, it transpired, hinged on a winner-takes-all, home-and-away tie against Papua New Guinea. It was a no-contest: in the first match, at Apia on 11 July 2009, Samoa ran in 17 tries with Gavin Williams scoring a national record 30 points during a thumping 115–7 victory – the biggest in their history – and they went on to win the tie 188–19 on aggregate.

OVERALL TEAM RECORD

Span	Mat	Won	Lost	Draw	%	For	Aga	Diff	Tries	Conv	Pens	Drop
1924–2017	228	99	120	9	45.39	4574	5083	-509	476	304	369	12

TOUGH TIMES AGAINST THE ALL BLACKS

Given the close, albeit tense, association between the two countries, it seems strange that Samoa and New Zealand have only ever contested seven Tests over the years and, for Samoa, the results make disappointing reading. They have lost all seven, conceded 50 points or more in five of them and, on 3 September 2008 at New Plymouth, the two sides' fifth encounter, crashed to a sorry 101–14 away defeat – the heaviest in their history.

BELOW: Gavin Williams contributed 30 points in Samoa's 115–7 rout of Papua New Guinea in July 2009.

POLICY CHANGE REAPS REWARDS FOR SAMOA

Qualification for the 1991 Rugby World Cup ultimately triggered an upturn in fortunes for Samoa, but not before they had embarked on a radical change of policy. Back in the 1960s and 1970s, there had been a mass migration of Samoans to New Zealand; 20 years later, and the offspring of these migrants were starting to make waves in New Zealand domestic rugby, and the Samoan coaching staff spotted an opportunity to call on the island's lost sons to play for their homeland. In came New Zealand-born players such as Pat Lam, Stephen Bachop, Frank Bunce and Apollo Perelini, and the improvement was instantaneous. In 1991, thanks in no small part to a stunning 16–13 opening victory over Wales in Cardiff, Samoa reached the quarter-finals; they repeated the feat in 1995, but since then – and the advent of professionalism – it has become harder for them to attract such players, and they have failed to progress beyond the group stages at the last five Rugby World Cups.

SUCCESS ON THE HOME FRONT

Samoa have enjoyed considerable success in the Pacific Tri-Nations championship over the years, winning the annual event against Fiji and Tonga 12 times in 22 attempts between 1982 and 2005. When the tournament evolved into the Pacific Five Nations Championship the following year, Samoa finished a creditable second behind the Junior All Blacks. It remained their best result in the expanded competition until 2010, when they won the renamed Pacific Nations Cup for the first time and took the title again in 2012 and 2014.

NOTABLE SAMOA VICTORIES

Team	Score	Venue	Date
Wales	16–13	Cardiff	6 Oct 1991 (RWC)
Argentina	35–12	Pontypridd	13 Oct 1991 (RWC)
Wales	34–9	Moamoa	25 Jun 1994
Ireland	40–25	Dublin	12 Nov 1996
Wales	38–31	Cardiff	14 Oct 1999 (RWC)
Argentina	28–12	Buenos Aires	3 Dec 2005
Australia	32–23	Sydney	17 Jul 2011
Wales	26–19	Cardiff	16 Nov 2012
Scotland	27–17	Durban	8 Jun 2013
Italy	39–10	Nelspruit	15 Jun 2013
Italy	15–0	Apia	14 Jun 2014

SAMOA SHOCK IRELAND IN DUBLIN

Samoa have not reserved the champagne moments of their rugby history – the victories against top-tier nations – exclusively for the Rugby World Cup. On 12 November 1996 (just three months after losing 60–0 to Fiji), at Lansdowne Road, Dublin, they outscored Ireland by five tries to one to record a stunning 40–25 victory. During what was perhaps the most notable result in their history, they had put 40 points past a top-tier opponent for the first, and to date only, time in their history.

LEADING POINTS-SCORER

Something of a rugby nomad (he has played club rugby in New Zealand, France, Japan and England), fly-half Tusi Pisi made three appearances for the now-defunct Pacific Islanders in 2006 and had to wait five years before making his first appearance for Samoa, against Japan in Tokyo on 2 July 2011. He has been one of his country's most consistent performers ever since, appearing at the Rugby World Cup in both 2011 and 2015, and going on to score a national record 219 points in 30 matches.

MOST TRIES: TOP FIVE

Pos	Tries	Player (Span)
1	29	Brian Lima (1991–2007)
2	18	Alesana Tuilagi (2002–15)
3	17	Semo Sititi (1999–2009)
4	15	Afato So'oalo (1996–2001)
5	14	Lome Fa'atau (2000–07)

THE CHIROPRACTOR STARS FOR SAMOA

Nicknamed 'The Chiropractor' because of his bone-crunching tackles, Brian Lima's formidable defence became the stuff of rugby legend – just ask South Africa's Derick Hougaard. Lima legitimately flattened him during the 2003 Rugby World Cup and left the Springbok fly-half visibly dazed for several minutes, prompting one commentator to describe the scene as a 'car crash'. But Lima has brought much more to Samoa rugby than defensive brawn: an incisive runner, he made his debut as a 19-year-old against Tonga in May 1991, went on to appear in every one of his country's Rugby World Cup appearances (and is the only player in the game's history to appear in the tournament five times) and bowed out of international rugby in 2007 as his country's most capped player (64 caps) and leading try-scorer (29 tries).

ABOVE: Brian Lima was a standout performer for Samoa for more than a decade and a half and he scored a national record 29 tries in his 64 appearances.

LONG-TIME LEADER

A back-row forward who is equally comfortable on the flank or at No.8, Semo Sititi made his Samoa debut against Japan at Apia in May 1999 and did enough in his first few internationals to earn a place in the 1999 Rugby World Cup squad – he was the only Samoa-based player to do so. He took over the captaincy following Pat Lam's retirement after the Rugby World Cup and led the islanders a record 39 times, until 2007, at which point he relinquished the leadership and returned to the playing ranks until his retirement later that year.

CHANGING SIDES

The rugby relationship between Samoa and New Zealand is a thorny and complex one, with the standard argument being that New Zealand feasts upon the islands for rugby talent. The situation, however, is far from that simple. Born out of politics (and a mass migration of Samoans to New Zealand in the 1960s and 1970s), by the early 1990s a new generation of New Zealand-born Samoans were starting to make waves in domestic rugby and, quite naturally, both Samoa and New Zealand laid claim to them. The choice for the players was straightforward: an easier path into international rugby with Samoa or the chance to pull on the famous All Black jersey. Unfortunately, to the detriment of Samoa rugby (and making a mockery of the IRB's player qualification rules), some did both. Over the years Samoa has lost quality players such as Michael Jones, Frank Bunce, Ofisa Junior Tonu'u, Va'aiga Tuigamala, Stephen Bachop, Alama Ieremia, Pat Lam, John Schuster and Andrew Blowers to the All Blacks.

MOST TRIES IN ONE MATCH BY A PLAYER

The Samoa record for most individual tries in a match is four, achieved by four players, all since 2000, and the first three in the capital, Apia: Elvis Seveali'i, against Japan, on 10 June 2000; Alesana Tuilagi, against Tonga, on 2 July 2005; Esera Lauina, against Papua New Guinea, on 11 July 2009; and Robert Lilomaiava, against Canada, at Colwyn Bay, Wales, on 9 November 2012.

LEFT: Tusi Pisi is Samoa's all-time record points-scorer, with 219 points in 30 matches.

MOST POINTS: TOP FIVE

Pos	Points	Player (Span)
1	219	Tusi Pisi (2006–17)
2	174	Earl Va'a (1996–2003)
3	145	Silao Leaegailesolo (1997–2002)
4	140	Brian Lima (1991–2007)
5	137	Darren Kellett (1993–95)

TONGA

Missionaries brought rugby to Tonga in the early twentieth century and the islanders were playing international matches by 1924. Their early games were restricted to fixtures against South Pacific neighbours Fiji and Samoa and were often brutal affairs, which goes some way to explaining the physicality for which the Sea Eagles have become renowned. Tonga's uncompromising style may have its critics, but it has brought them two Pacific Tri-Nations titles and seven Rugby World Cup appearances.

TONGA REACH RUGBY WORLD CUP IN RECORD-BREAKING STYLE

With a place at the 2003 Rugby World Cup all but assured following their 75–0 away victory in the first leg of their repechage showdown with Korea, Tonga gave their fans even more reason to celebrate when they produced a record-breaking performance in the return fixture at Nuku A'lofa on 22 March 2003. The Sea Eagles raced into a 56–0 half-time lead and went on to register 17 tries in the one-sided match (four of them from No.8 Benhur Kivalu and two from fly-half Pierre Hola, who also slotted 17 conversions – his 44 points in the match is a national record) en route to a 119–0 victory – the biggest in their history.

OVERALL TEAM RECORD

Span	Mat	Won	Lost	Draw	%	For	Aga	Diff	Tries	Conv	Pens	Drop
1924–2018	274	104	159	7	39.81	4907	6083	-1176	583	349	332	8

OUT OF THEIR DEPTH

Tonga have played five matches against the All Blacks and have lost all of them, scoring only 35 points and conceding a mighty 326. The heaviest of those defeats – and the heaviest in the Sea Eagles' history – came at North Shore City, Auckland, on 16 June 2000, when they were crushed 102–0.

BELOW: Tonga's record points-scorer (with 317) Pierre Hola shone for the Sea Eagles for more than a decade.

SORRY TIMES FOR TROUBLED TONGA

Their first match at the 2003 Rugby World Cup triggered the most miserable run of form in Tonga's history. The Sea Eagles slumped to a 36–12 defeat to Italy and went on to lose all four games. The barren spell continued when they endured disappointing Pacific Tri-Nations campaigns in 2004 and 2005 (they lost all six matches) and a difficult tour to the northern hemisphere that saw them lose to Italy (48–0) and France (43–8). The sorry losing streak, stretching to 12 matches, finally came to an end when the Sea Eagles beat Japan 57–16 at Fukuoka on 4 June 2006 – two years and eight months after it had started.

LACK OF CONSISTENCY KEY TO STILTED PROGRESS

The ability to put together a string of consistent performances has eluded Tonga over the years. In 265 internationals played since 1924, they have only won three consecutive matches on six occasions and four consecutive matches three times: a pair of victories over both the New Zealand Maoris and Samoa in 1969; between 30 November 2002 and 22 March 2003; and between July 2015 and September 2015.

BELOW: Tonga captain Nili Latu tries to break through the Samoa defence during the Sea Eagles' 19–15 2003 Rugby World Cup victory.

MOST POINTS: TOP FIVE

Pos	Points	Player (Span)
1	338	Kurt Morath (2009–15)
2	317	Pierre Hola (1998–2009)
3	190	Sateki Tuipulotu (1993–2003)
4	147	Fangatapu 'Apikotoa (2004–14)
5	135	Tane Takulua (2014–17)

TONGA'S TRIUMPHS

The golden times in Tonga's rugby history are hard to find, but the Pacific Tri-Nations tournament provided the Sea Eagles with their greatest moments: victory in 1983 and 1986 – during the latter they won both of their matches (31–13 against Samoa and 13–6 against Fiji) for the only time in their history. Their best performance in the expanded Pacific Nations Cup came in 2011, when they finished second to Japan on points-difference

MAGICAL MORATH

Born in North Shore, New Zealand, Kurt Morath was a former New Zealand Under-21 international who seemed destined to become one of the game's journeymen (he played club rugby in New Zealand, Britain, Spain and Australia) before making his debut for Tonga against Portugal in Lisbon on 28 November 2009. And the fly-half immediately proved his worth to his adopted nation, coming on as a replacement and scoring 11 points in a narrow 24–19 victory. He has been a permanent fixture in the Tonga side ever since, appearing at the 2011 and 2015 Rugby World Cups, and amassing a national record 338 points.

TONGA'S BEST PERFORMANCE AT THE RUGBY WORLD CUP

Tonga have appeared in six of the first seven Rugby World Cups (failing to qualify only in 1991). But they have struggled to make a serious breakthrough on rugby's biggest stage, never progressing beyond the group stages and winning only six of 21 matches. However, the Sea Eagles' performances appear to be on the up: they won twice at the tournament for the first time in 2007 and repeated the feat in New Zealand in 2011, including a 19–14 victory over France – arguably the most famous victory in the team's 90-year history.

FLYING FETU'U

A winger known for his explosive ball-carrying abilities, Fetu'u Vainikolo made his name by scoring five tries in ten minutes on debut for Northland in the 2007 New Zealand Cup to earn himself a Super Rugby contract with the Highlanders. He moved to the west coast of Ireland for the 2011–12 season, and produced some standout performances for Connacht, before joining Exeter Chiefs in England's top-flight league in 2013. He has also excelled in international rugby. He made his debut for Tonga in a 27–12 defeat to Fiji at Lautoka on 13 August 2011, scored his first international try in a 32–20 victory over the same opponents and the same venue six days later, and went on to make two appearances at the 2011 Rugby World Cup, scoring one try in Tonga's 31–18 victory over Japan. Now one of the first names on Tonga's team sheet, the tries have continued to flow for the dynamic winger. By the time of his last international appearance in 2016, he had scored 17 tries in 28 appearances – an all-time record for Tonga.

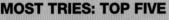

MOST TRIES: TOP FIVE

Pos	Tries	Player (Span)
1	17	Fetu'u Vainikolo (2011–16)
2	14	Josh Taumalolo (1996–2007)
3	12	Vunga Lilo (2007–15)
4	11	Pierre Hola (1998–2009)
5	10	Fepiku Tatafu (1996–2002)

ABOVE: Fetu'u Vainikolo, Tonga's all-time leading try-scorer, developed a reputation as being one of the most destructive finishers in world rugby.

LEADING BY EXAMPLE

Nili Latu began his rugby-playing career in New Zealand and soon developed a reputation as being one of the most ferocious tacklers in world rugby. He made his debut for Tonga in June 2006, captained his country for the first time in only his third international appearance and went on to lead Tonga at the 2007 Rugby World Cup. He went on to lead Tonga at both the 2011 and 2015 Rugby World Cups, and went on to captain his country on 42 occasions and had won 46 caps – both all-time records for Tonga.

LEFT: Tonga celebrate after their 19–14 defeat of France at the 2011 Rugby World Cup.

OTHER ASIA AND OCEANIA TEAMS

Rugby in Asia and Oceania may be dominated by the gargantuan presence of Australia and New Zealand (on the global scene) and Japan (in Asia), but rugby life beneath those top-tier teams is alive and kicking in both regions, each of which stages its own Rugby World Cup qualifying tournament. In Asia, teams also compete in the various divisions of the Asia Five Nations Championship; in Oceania, second-tier teams and below compete for the Oceania Cup.

RECORDS SHATTERED IN KUALA LUMPUR

Hong Kong's greatest moment on a rugby field came against Singapore at Kuala Lumpur, Malaysia, in an Asia Pool 2 Rugby World Cup qualifying match on 27 October 1994. They won the match 164–13 to break the all-time record for the most points scored in an international match and set a new mark for the most tries scored with 27; their full-back, Ashley Billington, scored ten of them – another international all-time record for a player in a single match.

KOREA'S RUGBY WORLD CUP QUALIFYING WOES

It may be due to their regular forays into the latter stages of the tournament, but Korea have lost more Rugby World Cup qualifying matches (28) than any other nation and some of those defeats have been particularly painful: against Japan in the qualification final for the 2005 tournament and against Tonga in three repechage matches (for the 1999, 2003 and 2007 tournaments).

A RUGBY WORLD CUP WORST FOR VANUATU

Vanuatu, currently 104th in the world rankings, hold the unenviable record of having played in the most Rugby World Cup qualifying matches without ever recording a win. Their record reads: played five, lost five, points for 40, points against 246. And there have been some hefty defeats along the way, the worst of which came at Port Moresby on 20 August 2005 when they lost 97–3 to Papua New Guinea.

LEFT: Ashley Billington's ten tries for Hong Kong against Singapore in 1994 is a world record.

ABOVE: Korea's 21–17 defeat of Japan in the final of the 1998 Asian Games in Bangkok was one of the country's finest moments on a rugby field. They repeated their success on home soil in 2002.

CHINESE TAIPEI TROUNCED IN TOKYO

The vast difference between Asian rugby's haves and have-nots is best shown when one of the region's second-tier nations pays a visit to Japan, the undisputed kings of Asian rugby – they are the only team from the continent to play in the Rugby World Cup and have not lost a home qualifying match against an Asian opponent in 13 attempts. On 1 May 2002, in Tokyo, Chinese Taipei became Japan's latest victims, losing 155–3; the 152-point losing margin is the joint highest in international rugby history (matched only by Paraguay's miserable 152–0 defeat to Argentina in Mendoza on 1 May 2002).

GOLDEN MOMENTS FOR KOREA

Korea's finest rugby moments both came at the Asian Games. In 1998, in Bangkok, they beat arch-rivals Japan 21–17 in the final to take gold; four years later, in Busan, South Korea, they overcame Japan in the semi-finals (24–7) before going on to beat Chinese Taipei 33–21 in the final to retain their crown. These are the only two occasions a 15-a-side tournament was contested at the event.

100-PLUS POINTS SCORED IN A MATCH

Team	Opponent	Result	Venue	Date
Hong Kong	Singapore	164–13	Kuala Lumpur	27 Oct 1994
Korea	Malaysia	135–3	Hong Kong	20 Sep 1992
Korea	Chinese Taipei	119–7	Seoul	30 Jun 2002
Hong Kong	Chinese Taipei	114–12	Taipei	9 Nov 1996
Korea	Malaysia	112–5	Taipei	5 Nov 1996
Hong Kong	Sri Lanka	108–0	Taipei	9 Nov 1980
Hong Kong	Philippines	108–0	Hong Kong	26 Apr 2014
Hong Kong	Malaysia	103–5	Taipei	3 Nov 1996
Korea	Malaysia	102–0	Hong Kong	12 Nov 1988
Philippines	Brunei	101–0	Guam	2 July 1988

ASIA RUGBY CHAMPIONSHIP

Year	Top div	Div 1	Div 2	3E	3WC	3W
2015	Japan	Sri Lanka	Malaysia	Guam	Uzbekistan	Lebanon
2016	Japan	Malaysia	Uzbekistan	Laos	Qatar	Jordan
2017	Japan	Malaysia	Singapore	-	-	Lebanon

KEY: E = East; WC = West Central; W = West
Note: The 2017 3 East tournament was cancelled due to availability of both Guam and Indonesia

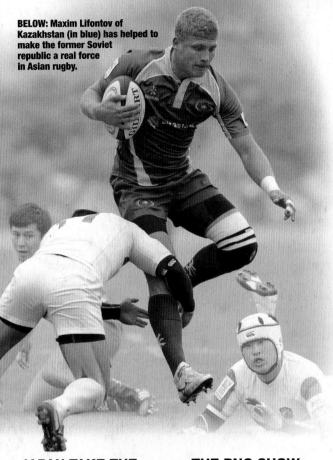

BELOW: Maxim Lifontov of Kazakhstan (in blue) has helped to make the former Soviet republic a real force in Asian rugby.

KAZAKHS ON THE UP

With the exception of Georgia, Kazakhstan are the most successful of the ex-Soviet nations and one of the fastest rising teams in world rugby. They finished runners-up in both the 2009 and 2010 Asia Five Nations Championship – won, convincingly, on both occasions by Japan – to stake their further claim (backed up by their current world ranking of 61) to being among the best teams in Asia.

YO-YO TIMES FOR SINGAPORE

Singapore, currently 56th in the IRB world rankings, have struggled to cross the divide between the first and second tier of Asian rugby. The 2008 Asia Five Nations Division 1 champions earned promotion to the top flight of the championship, but lost all four of their matches the following year and were relegated back to Division 1. They were the first promoted team in the tournament's brief history to lose their top-flight status.

Best of the rest: world rankings

Hong Kong (22); Korea (29); Sri Lanka (42); Malaysia (48); Cook Islands (54); Singapore (56); Philippines (58); Kazakhstan (61); Chinese Taipei (65); Papua New Guinea (66); United Arab Emirates (71); Guam (72); Thailand (74); India (79); Tahiti (85); China (87); Pakistan (92); Indonesia (97); Niue Island (99); Solomon Islands (101); Vanuatu (104); American Samoa (105).

MAGIC MOMENT FOR TAHITI

Renowned more for the stunning beauty of its location and its appeal to tourists, rather than for its rugby-playing ability, Tahiti, currently ranked 85th in the world, had no rich tradition of tournament success. But that all changed in the 2017 Oceania Cup. Benefitting in no small part from Papua New Guinea's withdrawal, the beat the Cook Islands 13–9 on 4 August 2017 to collect their first international trophy.

LEFT: Japan collected the Asia Rugby Championships trophy for the fourth consecutive year in 2017.

JAPAN TAKE THE SPOILS ... AGAIN

Renamed and contested for the first time in 2015, the Asia Rugby Championship was a rebranded version of the tournament known as the Asian Five Nations. There were few surprises: Japan had dominated the event in its former guises, winning 14 of the previous 15 editions of it, and did so again, beating South Korea both home and away (66–10 in Fukuoka and 56–30 in Incheon) and Hong Kong at home (41–0 in Tokyo) before the reverse fixture in Hong Kong was abandoned after 20 minutes due to adverse weather conditions. They took the title again in 2016 and 2017, winning all of their matches, to confirm their status as the undoubted kings of Asian rugby.

THE PNG SHOW

The Federation of Oceania Rugby Unions Cup, otherwise known as the FORU Oceania Cup, was contested for the first time in 2007. It is contested between teams from nine nations or territories: American Samoa, the Cook Islands, New Caledonia, Niue Island, Papua New Guinea, Solomon Islands, Vanuatu and Wallis and Fortuna. There is no doubt about who have been the stars of the show: Papua New Guinea have collected the title four times: in 2007, 2009, 2011 and 2015).

Oceania Cup winners

Team	Winners
2005	Cook Islands
2007	Papua New Guinea
2008	Niue Island
2009	Papua New Guinea
2011	Papua New Guinea
2013	Cook Islands
2015	Papua New Guinea
2017	Tahiti

AFRICA

Although rugby had been around in Africa since the 1850s, it wasn't until 1891 – when Governor Cecil Rhodes's preference for the sport over football prompted him to invite a British touring team to South Africa – that interest in the game started to grow in southern Africa and, helped by the presence of troops in the various colonies, it did not take long before the rugby gospel was spread to the far corners of the continent. Not that everyone listened: of Africa's 54 countries, only 18 of them are listed in the current world rankings.

BELOW: Comfortably Africa's strongest team, South Africa have won the Rugby World Cup twice, most recently in 2007.

IVORY COAST

The Federation Ivoirienne de Rugby was formed as recently as March 1990, so it came as a huge surprise when the Ivory Coast qualified for the Rugby World Cup for the first time in their history in 1995. The tournament itself, however, was a disaster. The Elephants lost all three matches, endured the agony of seeing one of their players horrifically injured and have not qualified for the event since. In recent times, they have played in the continent's annual Africa Cup competition.

TOUGH START FOR THE ELEPHANTS

The Ivory Coast's first recognized match in international rugby came against Zimbabwe at Harare on 5 May 1990 in a Rugby World Cup qualifying match: they lost 22–9. Two further defeats over the next seven days (12–7 against Tunisia on 8 May and 11–4 against Morocco on 12 May) left their Rugby World Cup dreams in tatters and a further three years would pass before the Elephants contested another international fixture.

HOME COMFORTS

The Ivory Coast national team may only be a relative newcomer to the international rugby scene, but the Elephants have already established an impressive home record, winning 11, drawing two and losing just three of the 16 fixtures they have played. Of those victories, the most impressive came against Tunisia on 12 May 2001, when they won the African CAR Championship match 46–0.

THE LONG ROAD TO SOUTH AFRICA

The Ivory Coast's third international match – three years after their second – would lead them on the path towards the greatest moment of their short rugby history. A 19–16 Rugby World Cup qualifying round one victory over Tunisia in Tunis on 26 October 1993 (their first-ever win) virtually assured them of a safe passage to the next round, a position that was confirmed four days later following a comfortable 25–3 win over Morocco (who had also beaten Tunisia). The Elephants progressed into the final qualifying group, containing Morocco, Namibia and Zimbabwe, with the winner of the round-robin tournament, staged in Casablanca in June 1994, earning qualification to the 1995 Rugby World Cup. The Ivory Coast got off to the worst of starts, losing 17–9 to a Morocco side revitalized by playing in front of their home crowd. Instead of capitulating, the Elephants rallied in style, beating Namibia (13–12) and Zimbabwe (17–10) to top the group and win one of the biggest prizes in the game – a coveted place at the sport's biggest event – the Rugby World Cup.

HARD TIMES FOR THE IVORY COAST

A major consolation for the Ivory Coast was that their Rugby World Cup appearance in 1995 guaranteed them a place in the final round of qualifying for the 1999 tournament (a group of four teams). They lost all three matches to finish bottom and have endured nothing but Rugby World Cup disappointment since. They failed to make it beyond the initial group stages in 2003 and fell in the second round in 2007. There was a glimmer of hope in June 2009 when they advanced to the semi-finals of the 2011 qualification tournament, but that was soon extinguished following a 67–27 aggregate defeat to Namibia.

ABOVE: Max Brito's tragic story is the darkest spot on the Rugby World Cup's history.

THE RUGBY WORLD CUP'S DARKEST MOMENT

Max Brito, who played club rugby in south-west France, was 24 years old when he travelled to South Africa to play in the 1995 Rugby World Cup. A committed winger, he made his debut in the Ivory Coast's opening-game against Scotland (an 89–0 defeat), coming on as a replacement, and played a full part in the Elephants' much improved performance against France (a 54–18 defeat). In the third minute of the Ivory Coast's final group match, against Tonga, Brito made an impressive defensive catch on the run and advanced towards the massed Tonga defence. Disaster struck: he was tackled, ended up at the bottom of a ruck and was left motionless on the ground, paralyzed from the neck down: 3 June 1995 remains the darkest day in Rugby World Cup history.

CHASTENED ON THE BIG STAGE

The Ivory Coast's reward for securing qualification for the 1995 Rugby World Cup in South Africa was a place in Pool D alongside France, Scotland and Tonga. It proved too tough a proposition for the Elephants. In their opening match they crashed to an 89–0 defeat against Scotland in their opening match (still the biggest defeat in their history). They fared a little better against France, scoring two tries in a 54–18 reversal, then battled to a 29–11 defeat to Tonga (scoring one try in the match) to finish bottom of the group. The Ivory Coast's only Rugby World Cup experience had been a chastening one.

ABOVE: The Ivory Coast came up short against Scotland at the 1995 Rugby World Cup, especially against line-out jumpers such as Doddie Weir.

NAMIBIA

Rugby has been played in Namibia since 1916, when South African soldiers invaded the German colony, but the country did not play its first international match until 1990, when it gained independence. Since then, the Namibia national team – known as the Welwitschias – has gone on to establish itself as one of Africa's strongest second-tier sides: they have qualified for the Rugby World Cup on five occasions and have won the Africa Cup seven times, most recently in 2017.

OFF TO A FLYER

There have been several newcomers to the world rugby fold since the early 1990s and Namibia, hardened by years of playing in South Africa's domestic Currie Cup competition (as Southwest Africa), were the most prepared to cope with the rigours of the international game. Between March 1990 and May 1992, the Welwitschias won 16 of their first 18 internationals, which included recording a memorable pair of home victories over Italy (17–7 and 33–19) and Ireland (15–6 and 25–15).

BELOW: The most famous name in Namibia rugby, Gerhard Mans captained the Weltwitschias in their first-ever international and scored a national record 27 tries in 26 matches between 1990 and 1994.

THIRD TIME LUCKY FOR NAMIBIA

Independence came too late for Namibia to participate in the qualifying tournament of the 1991 Rugby World Cup and they fell at the final hurdle in 1995, losing to the Ivory Coast (13–12) and drawing with Morocco (16–16), but they finally found the winning formula at the third time of asking. They progressed to the final round of the 1999 qualifying tournament on points difference (following a surprise 20–17 defeat to Tunisia), but went on to win all three of their round-robin matches – against the Ivory Coast (22–10), Morocco (17–8) and Zimbabwe (39–14) – to earn a place on the game's biggest stage for the first time. They have qualified for every Rugby World Cup since.

A VICTORY TO REMEMBER

Namibia have become the kings of African Rugby World Cup qualifying tournaments over the years, winning all but nine of 34 matches and progressing through the various rounds of the competition to qualify for 1999, 2003, 2007, 2011 and 2015 editions. There have been some thumping victories along the way, but none more so than their 18-try, 112–0 romp against Madagascar at Windhoek on 15 June 2002 – the biggest win in the Welwitschias' history.

STRUGGLING ON THE BIG STAGE

Namibia may have discovered the knack of qualifying for the Rugby World Cup, but once they have get there they struggle. The Weltwischias have played 19 matches on rugby's biggest stage (in five separate tournaments) and lost every single one of them, including eight by 50 points or more. The worst of those defeats came on 25 October 2003, when they lost 142–0 to Australia in Adelaide – the heaviest defeat in both Namibia's and the tournament's history.

NAMIBIA'S AFRICA CUP SUCCESS

Namibia have enjoyed considerable success in the Africa Cup, which has been played on an annual basis since 2000. In 2002, the Welwitschias won the competition on tries scored following their 43–43 aggregate tie against Tunisia in the two-legged final. They lost to Morocco in the final the following year (27–7), but gained revenge over the North Africans in the 2004 final, winning 39–22 to claim the cup for a second time. They claimed the title for the third time in 2008–09 with a 40–23 aggregate victory over Tunisia in the final, and won the event for the fourth, fifth, sixth and seventh times in their history in 2014, 2015, 2016 and 2017 respectively.

ABOVE: Theuns Kotze's 430 points is a record total for a Namibian player.

KOTZE SETS TONGUES WAGGING

After making his debut for Namibia against Portugal in Bucharest on 15 June 2011, Theuns Kotze made a name for himself at the Rugby World Cup held in New Zealand later that year. In Namibia's match against Fiji, he nailed three drop goals (to become only the fourth player in the tournament's history to achieve the feat) to set tongues wagging. He may not have gone on to live up to the early hype, but he has scored 430 points in 40 matches – an all-time record for Namibia.

LEGEND MANS LEADS TRY-SCORING LIST

Gerhard Mans is a legend in Namibia rugby. A winger with deadly finishing skills, he was a leading member of the South West Africa side that defied the odds to finish third in the 1988 Currie Cup. He was captain of Namibia in their first post-independence international, against Zimbabwe on 24 March 1990 (he scored a try in the 33–18 victory), and carried on playing until 1994, by which time he had scored an impressive 27 tries (a national record) in 27 matches.

SOUTH AFRICA

In 1891, South Africa became the first team from the southern hemisphere to play international rugby and it was not long before the Springboks became established as one of the world's leading sides. Barred from competing in IRB-sanctioned matches between 1984 and 1992 as a result of their government's apartheid policy, they returned to the world stage as a dominant force, winning the Rugby World Cup in 1995 and 2007 and the Tri-Nations/The Rugby Championship in 1999, 2004 and 2009.

THE BOKS AGAINST THE LIONS

British representative sides have been touring South Africa since 1891, providing the opposition for the Springboks when they played their first-ever international match (at Port Elizabeth on 30 July 1891) and recorded their first-ever win (5–0 at Cape Town on 5 September 1896), but it wasn't until 1955 that a representative team dubbed the British Lions came to town. The Boks won the final match 22–8 to level the series … and a legendary rivalry was born. Of the six series played since then, South Africa have won four of them (in 1962, 1968, 1980 and, most recently, 2009) and lost only two (in 1980 and 1997).

HONOURS

Rugby World Cup:
(best finish) – champions (1995, 2007)
Tri Nations/Rugby Championship:
(best finish) – champions (1998, 2004, 2009)

RIGHT: South Africa's inspired Rugby World Cup victory on home turf in 1995 is the proudest moment in the country's rugby history.

OVERALL TEAM RECORD

Span	Mat	Won	Lost	Draw	%	For	Aga	Diff	Tries	Conv	Pens	Drop	GfM
1891–2018	486	298	156	23	64.88	11059	7664	+3395	1339	892	977	105	1

THE BOKS BECOME A WORLD FORCE

If South Africa's first tour to the northern hemisphere in 1906–07 had been a political attempt to ease the strained relations that prevailed in the aftermath of the Boer War, then the Springboks' second tour to Britain, France and Ireland in 1912–13 was about showing the world what a true rugby force they had become. They won all five matches – against Scotland (16–0), Ireland (38–0), Wales (3–0), England (9–3) and France (38–5) to achieve the northern hemisphere grand slam for the first time in their history.

SPRINGBOKS BATTER URUGUAY IN EAST LONDON

Nobody had expected Uruguay to pose South Africa too many problems when the two sides met in a one-off Test in East London on 11 June 2005, but few could have predicted the abject capitulation that followed. The Springboks raced into a 56–3 half-time lead and continued to run riot in the second half, scoring a total of 21 tries in the match – Tonderai Chavhanga scored six of them (a national record) – on the way to completing a crushing 134–3 victory – the biggest in their history.

SOUTH AFRICA'S WILDERNESS YEARS

The murmurs of dissatisfaction directed towards South Africa's national rugby team as a result of the country's apartheid policy had been growing into a worldwide clamour for more than a decade and a half (the Gleneagles Treaty discouraging sporting contact with South Africa had been signed by Commonwealth-member countries as early as 1976), but South Africa continued to play in IRB-sanctioned international matches until 1984. And then came the wilderness years, when the Springboks were restricted to playing matches against rebel touring teams. Their first match back in the international fold came against New Zealand at Johannesburg on 15 August 1992 – they lost a thriller 27–24.

ABOVE: Tonderai Chavhanga scored a national record six tries against Uruguay on 11 June 2005.

SOUTH AFRICA HIT ROCK BOTTOM

Having won two and drawn one of their opening three games of the 2017 Rugby Championship, South Africa must have been quietly confident of producing a performance of note in their fourth match of the tournament, against New Zealand at North Shore City on 16 September 2017. Instead, they were walloped, crashing to a 57–0 defeat. It the heaviest reverse in their history, only the 13th time in 486 matches that they had failed to score a single point in the match, and the first time they had failed to do so for nine years.

UNITING THE RAINBOW NATION

The 1995 Rugby World Cup provided the world with one of the greatest moments of modern times and one of the most iconic images in sporting history. The tournament was the first major sporting event to take place in post-apartheid South Africa and the first Rugby World Cup in which the hosts had competed. The Springboks got off to a blistering start, beating defending champions Australia 27–18 in their opening match, and when they followed that up with hard-fought victories over Romania (21–8) and Canada (20–0) an entire nation started to believe. Fuelled by an increasingly vociferous support, the Boks beat Samoa 42–15 in the quarter-finals and defied appalling conditions in Durban to see off France in the semis (19–15). All that stood between them and rugby immortality was a powerful New Zealand side playing at the peak its powers and brimming with confidence following a 45–29 demolition of England in the last four. It was a final nobody expected South Africa to win, but they succeeded in stifling All Black giant Jonah Lomu, where others had failed and, thanks to the boot of Joel Stransky, secured a 15–12 victory after extra-time. Few who saw it will forget the moment when Nelson Mandela, wearing a No.6 Springbok shirt (so often the symbol of white supremacy in the country), handed the Rugby World Cup trophy to Francois Pienaar and, moments later, as the Webb Ellis trophy was hoisted aloft, an entire nation danced in the streets.

ABOVE: The most iconic moment in rugby's rich history as Nelson Mandela hands the Webb Ellis Trophy to Francois Pienaar after South Africa's 1995 Rugby World Cup final victory over New Zealand at Ellis Park, Johannesburg.

PARADISE IN PARIS FOR SOUTH AFRICA

South Africa had won only two of their previous five matches (against Namibia and Scotland) going into the 2007 Rugby World Cup in France and few thought they had any chance of winning the trophy for a second time. The Springboks, however, quickly found their stride, beating Samoa (59–7), England (36–0), Tonga (30–25) and the USA (64–15) to win their pool with ease. They then beat Fiji in the quarter-finals (37–20) and downed Argentina in the last four (37–13) before ending England's spirited title defence with a 15–6 victory in the final in Paris. South Africa had joined Australia as a two-time world champion.

ON A RECORD-BREAKING ROLL

A 61–12 demolition of Australia in Pretoria on 23 August 1997 sparked the richest vein of form in the Springboks' history. They travelled to the northern hemisphere three months later and won all five matches; they beat Ireland, Wales and England in matches at home; they went on to record a 100 per cent record in the 1998 Tri-Nations; and travelled to Britain and Ireland off the back of 14 consecutive wins. The record-breaking winning streak ended at 17 matches following a 13–7 defeat to England at Twickenham on 5 December 1998.

LEFT: (left to right) Bryan Habana, Jake White and John Smit celebrate South Africa's 2007 Rugby World Cup triumph.

THE BOKS' LONGEST LOSING STREAK

For a period of 13 months in the mid-1960s South Africa could not buy a win. The slump began with an 8–6 home defeat against France at Springs on 25 July 1964 and continued with away defeats to Ireland (9–6) and Scotland (8–5) in 1965. The Springboks lost four further Tests – two apiece to Australia and New Zealand – before ending the longest losing run in their history at seven matches when they beat the All Blacks 19–16 in the third Test at Christchurch on 4 September 1965.

SPRINGBOKS ROMP TO TRI-NATIONS GLORY

New Zealand had grabbed the headlines in the opening years of the Tri-Nations, winning the first editions of the tournament (in 1996 and 1997) without losing a single match. In 1998, however, it was South Africa's turn to steal the glory. The Springboks, who had ended the first two series as runners-up to the All Blacks, opened their 1998 campaign with a tense 14–13 victory over Australia in Sydney on 18 July, beat the All Blacks 13–3 in Wellington a week later (to record their first win on New Zealand soil since 1981), edged a nervy encounter against New Zealand in Durban on 15 August (24–23) and beat Australia 29–15 in their final match at Johannesburg a week later to win the Tri-Nations crown for the first time in their history. The Springboks won the trophy for a second time in 2004 and again in 2009.

HALL OF FAME INDUCTEES

Name	(Span, Caps)
Naas Botha	(1980–92, 28 caps)
Kitch Christie	(coach)
Danie Craven	(1931–38, 16 caps)
Morne du Plessis	(1971–80, 22 caps)
Frik du Preez	(1961–71, 38 caps)
Danie Gerber	(1980–92, 24 caps)
Barry Heatlie	(1896–1903, 6 caps)
Nelson Mandela	(politician)
Hennie Muller	(1949–53, 13 caps)
Benny Osler	(1924–33, 17 caps)
Francois Pienaar	(1993–96, 29 caps)
John Smit	(2000–11, 111 caps)
Joost van der Westhuizen	(1993–2003, 89 caps)
Jake White	(coach)

MONTGOMERY SETS THE BOKS' ALL-TIME POINTS MILESTONE

Namibia-born Percy Montgomery made his debut for South Africa (at centre) during the Boks' series-losing 18–15 defeat to the British and Irish Lions at Durban on 28 June 1997, scoring one of his side's three tries in the match. An incisive runner with a steady boot, he switched to full-back later in the year and went on to make the Springbok No.15 jersey his own for the best part of a decade (although he did make a handful of appearances at fly-half or centre). A veteran of three Rugby World Cups, he bowed out of international rugby in August 2008 after 102 caps (he was the first South African in history to pass the 100-cap landmark) as South Africa's all-time leading points-scorer (with 893). He also holds the South Africa record for the most points in a match (35 – one try, 12 conversions and a penalty – against Namibia at Cape Town on 15 August 2007).

BELOW: Percy Montgomery, South Africa's all-time leading points scorer, in full flow. He scored 893 points and was the first player from his country to earn 100 caps.

MOST CAPS: TOP TEN

Pos	Caps	Player (Span)
1	127	Victor Matfield (2001–15)
2	124	Bryan Habana (2004–16)
3	111	John Smit (2000–11)
4	109	Jean de Villiers (2002–15)
5	102	Percy Montgomery (1997–2008)
6	98	Tendai Mtawarira (2008–17)
7	89	Joost van der Westhuizen (1993–2003)
8	88	Ruan Pienaar (2006–15)
9	86	Schalk Burger (2003–15)
10	85	Bakkies Botha (2002–14)

INSPIRATIONAL LEADER

John Smit won his first cap (at hooker) for South Africa against Canada on 10 June 2000 at the age of 22, but it wasn't until coach Jake White made him captain in 2004 that he truly established himself as a real force in the team and proved his true worth to his country. Smit was an inspirational choice as captain, and by 2011 had led South Africa on 83 occasions and to some of the greatest moments in the Springboks' history: two Tri-Nations wins (in 2004 and 2009), a memorable series victory over the British Lions (in 2009) and, most notably, to the Rugby World Cup crown in 2007. By the time he retired in 2011, he was South Africa's most-capped player, with 111 – a record since broken by Victor Matfield.

ABOVE: South Africa's hooker and captain John Smit was a talismanic leader for his country. He led the Springboks to the second Rugby World Cup triumph in their history in France in 2007 and when he retired in 2011 did so having led his country on a record 83 occasions.

ALL-TIME LEADING TRY-SCORERS: BY POSITION

Position	Player (Span)	Tries
Full-back	Percy Montgomery (1997–2008)	18
Winger	Bryan Habana (2004–16)	66
Centre	Jaque Fourie (2003–13)	28
Fly-half	Morne Steyn (2009–16)	8
Scrum-half	Joost van der Westhuizen (1993–2003)	38
No.8	Pierre Spies (2006–13)	7
Flanker	Schalk Burger (2003–15)	14
Lock	Mark Andrews (1994–2001)	12
Prop	Gurthro Steenkamp (2004–14)	6
Hooker	Bismarck du Plessis (2007–15)	11

MOST POINTS: TOP TEN

Pos	Points	Player (Span)
1	893	Percy Montgomery (1997–2008)
2	736	Morne Steyn (2009–16)
3	335	Bryan Habana (2004–16)
4	312	Naas Botha (1980–92)
5	240	Joel Stransky (1993–96)
6	221	Braam van Straaten (1999–2001)
7	218	Handre Pollard (2014–17)
8	203	Elton Jantjies (2012–17)
9	190	Joost van der Westhuizen (1993–2003)
10	181	Jannie de Beer (1997–99)

THE COACH WHO COAXED THE BOKS TO RUGBY WORLD CUP SUCCESS

It is hard to argue against Kitch Christie's claims to be the most successful coach in South Africa's rugby history. Appointed to the position in mid-1994, following the Springboks' 2–0 series defeat against New Zealand, the former Transvaal coach was charged with turning a team that had won just four of its previous ten internationals into serious challengers for the following year's Rugby World Cup, which South Africa was hosting. He did just that: the Springboks won every one of their 14 matches under Christie's charge, including the Rugby World Cup, before ill-health forced him to step down from the position in March 1996. Tragically, he died two years later, aged 58.

THE LINEOUT KING

Victor Matfield was a standout performer in South African domestic rugby before he was called up to the senior Springbok side in 2001. A powerful lock, he developed into arguably the best lineout jumper in world rugby, and was a cornerstone of a powerful pack that helped the Springboks land the Tri-Nations title in 2004 and the Rugby World Cup in 2007. In 2008, he captained the Springboks to victory over the all Blacks in New Zealand (the first

captain to do so since England's Martin Johnson in 2003). He enjoyed further Tri-Nations success in 2009 and initially bowed out of international rugby following South Africa's quarter-final exit (to Australia) at the 2011 Rugby World Cup. Two-and-a half-years later, aged 37, he was back, and by the time he retired after the 2015 Rugby World Cup had gone on to become his country's most capped player, with 127 caps.

COACHES

Name	Tenure
Danie Craven	1949–56
Basil Kenyon	1958
Hennie Muller	1960–61, 1963, 1965
Boy Louw	1960–61, 1965
Izak van Heerden	1962
Felix du Plessis	1964
Ian Kirkpatrick	1967, 1974
Avril Malan	1969–70
Johan Claassen	1964, 1970–74
Nelie Smith	1980–81
Cecil Moss	1982–89
John Williams	1992
Ian McIntosh	1993–94
Kitch Christie	1994–96
Andre Markgraaff	1996
Carel du Plessis	1997
Nick Mallett	1997–2000
Harry Viljoen	2000–02
Rudolph Straeuli	2002–03
Jake White	2004–07
Peter de Villiers	2008–11
Heyneke Meyer	2012–15
Allister Coetzee	2016–present

ABOVE: A scintillating finisher, Bryan Habana scored more tries than any other South African in international rugby history – 67.

MOST TRIES: TOP TEN

Pos	Tries	Player (Span)
1	67	Bryan Habana (2004–16)
2	38	Joost van der Westhuizen (1993–2003)
3	32	Jaque Fourie (2003–13)
4	27	Jean de Villiers (2002–15)
5	26	Breyton Paulse (1999–2007)
6	25	Percy Montgomery (1997–2008)
7	24	J.P. Pietersen (2006–16)
8	21	Pieter Rossouw (1997–2003)
9	20	James Small (1992–97)
10	19	Danie Gerber (1980–92)
=	19	Stefan Terblanche (1998–2003)

FLYING HABANA SHOWS A LETHAL TRY-SCORING TOUCH

A player blessed with an electric turn of pace (he once clocked a time of 10.2 for the 100m), Bryan Habana was a star of the IRB Under-21 World Championship in 2004 (in which South Africa finished third) and went on to make his senior debut against England at Twickenham on 20 November later that year, sensationally scoring a try with his first touch of the ball. His reputation as one of the most

lethal finishers in the game's history was cemented at the 2007 Rugby World Cup, in which his eight tries in seven matches did much to lead South Africa to the country's second title; he ended the season as the IRB's Player of the Year. By the time he retired from international rugby in 2017, he had made 124 appearances for his country and scored a South Africa record 67 tries, 29 more than previous mark, set by 1995 Rugby World Cup winning scrum-half Joost van der Westhuizen.

ABOVE: A World Cup winner in 2011, Victor Matfield came out of retirement in 2014 and went on to break John Smit's record as South Africa's most-capped player.

ZIMBABWE

Zimbabwe has a long rugby history dating back to the 1890s, when British soldiers first brought the game to the country (which was then known as Rhodesia). Nicknamed the Sables, they have competed as Zimbabwe since 1981 and participated in the first two Rugby World Cups, 1987 and 1991, without winning a single match. The nation's political problems saw a downturn in fortunes on the rugby pitch until 2012, when they won the Africa Cup for the first time in their history.

SABLES HIT THE HEIGHTS

Zimbabwe produced the best performance in their history when Botswana came to Bulawayo on 7 September 1996: the Sables won the match 130–10 to record the biggest victory in their history and the only time they have won a match by more than 100 points.

BELOW: Kenny Tsimba made only six appearances for Zimbabwe before turning his back on international rugby to forge a successful career on South Africa's domestic circuit.

OVERALL TEAM RECORD

Span	Mat	Won	Lost	Draw	%	For	Aga	Diff	Tries	Conv	Pens	Drop
1981–2017	157	59	98	0	37.57	3667	4277	-610	321	179	243	12

WALLOPED IN WINDHOEK

Back in 1987, Zimbabwe's national rugby team was considered strong enough to receive one of the 16 invitations to the inaugural Rugby World Cup; less than two decades later, however, their fortunes had spiralled downwards to such an extent that they were considered one of world rugby's third-tier nations. A measure of just how far they had fallen came in their Africa Cup match against near neighbours Namibia in Windhoek on 15 August 2015: they crashed to a 80–6 defeat – the heaviest in their history.

SABLES' LONGEST WINNING STREAK

Victories have been hard to come by for the Sables – of the 146 internationals they have played since the formation of the Zimbabwe Rugby Union in 1981 they have won just 57 of them. Their longest winning streak during that time is seven matches, achieved during their march to the African Cup triumph in 2012 – the highlight being a 49–0 victory over Madagascar in Kampala on 15 June 2011.

THE ONE THAT GOT AWAY

Once considered one of the most promising No.10s in world rugby, Kennedy Tsimba made only six appearances for the Sables between 1997 and 1998 – scoring a national record 72 points – before he turned his back on Zimbabwe rugby at the age of 24 to pursue a domestic career in South Africa, where he further enhanced his reputation with a string of stirring performances for the Free State Cheetahs in the Currie Cup.

ZIM'S LONGEST LOSING STREAK

Zimbabwe used a five-match home-and-away series of games against Namibia as preparation for the 1991 Rugby World Cup. It was a disaster: they lost all five matches, went winless in the Rugby World Cup (losing all three fixtures) and then lost three two-match series against a France XV (42–15 and 37–16), Namibia (55–23 and 69–26) and Wales (35–14 and 42–13). The Sables' miserable 13-game losing streak – stretching over two years – finally came to an end on 3 July 1993 when they beat Kenya 42–7 at Nairobi.

RUGBY WORLD CUP WOE FOR ZIMBABWE

Zimbabwe received one of the 16 invitations to appear in the inaugural Rugby World Cup in 1987 and, although the Sables got off to a commendable start – losing only narrowly to Romania (21–20) – the remainder of the tournament proved a chastening experience as they suffered heavy defeats to Scotland (60–21) and France (70–12). They qualified for the tournament in 1991, but suffered three consecutive defeats for a second time – against Ireland (55–11), Scotland (51–12) and, disappointingly, against Japan (52–8). Zimbabwe have not competed at a Rugby World Cup since.

MOST POINTS: TOP FIVE

Pos	Points	Player (Span)
1	72	Kennedy Tsimba (1997–98)
2	66	Ian Noble (1993–96)
3	61	Marthinus Grobler (1987–94)
4	54	Andy Ferreira (1987–91)
5	48	Anthony Papenfus (1997–98)

MOST TRIES: TOP FIVE

Pos	Tries	Player (Span)
1	8	Victor Olonga (1993–98)
2	7	Shaun Landman (1993–98)
3	4	Kennedy Tsimba (1997–98)
4	3	Brendon Dawson (1990–98)
=	3	Aaron Jani (1994–97)
=	3	Ian Noble (1993–94)
=	3	Anthony Papenfus (1997–98)
=	3	Doug Trivella (1997–98)
=	3	Richard Tsimba (1987–91)

ZIMBABWE'S ALL-TIME LEADING TRY-SCORER

Victor Olonga – the older brother of Henry, who, at the 2003 Cricket World Cup, famously wore a black armband to mourn the death of democracy in Zimbabwe (and was subsequently forced into hiding) – made a try-scoring debut for the Sables during their 35–14 defeat to Wales in Bulawayo on 22 May 1993. A diminutive 5ft 8in (1.73m) full-back, he went on to make a further 13 appearances for his country (the last coming against Namibia in Casablanca on 19 September 1998) and scored a national record eight tries.

RIGHT: Victor Olonga, brother of former international cricketer Henry, tops the Sables' all-time try-scorers list with eight.

GENEROUS HOSTS

From 1910, the Zimbabwe national team (playing under its former name Rhodesia) hosted touring sides from Britain and Ireland, but with little success. They lost every one of the eight matches played (the last in 1974), scoring a total of 83 points and conceding a mighty 265.

BELOW: Andy Ferreira scored 54 points in his Zimbabwe international career which ended against Ireland in the 1991 Rugby World Cup.

EXODUS OF PLAYERS

Presented with ever-decreasing opportunities to further their careers in their homeland, thanks to an increasingly fraught political situation and a general lack of money, a growing number of players have left Zimbabwe to pursue their rugby careers in other countries. Among the most notable of these exiles are Bobby Skinstad, Tonderai Chavange, Tendai Mtawarira (who went on to play for South Africa), and David Pocock (who has gone on to achieve great success with Australia).

ON THEIR WAY BACK

Political upheaval in the country has undoubtedly played its part, but Zimbabwe have enjoyed little success on the field since the last of their two appearances at the Rugby World Cup in 1991. There was some cause for joy in 2012: they won the Africa Cup for the first time ever, beating Uganda 22–18 in the final.

BELOW: Zimbabwe-born Tendai Mtawarira has gone on to make 98 appearances for South Africa since his debut in 2008.

OTHER AFRICA TEAMS

Of all the African nations (17) to appear in the IRB world rankings, only two-time world champions South Africa could be considered as a force in the world game. There is, however, an increasingly active rugby scene on the continent, with the lesser nations competing on a four-year basis for Africa's one available Rugby World Cup qualification spot and on an annual basis for the Africa Cup, organized by the Confederation of African Rugby (CAR) and contested since 2000.

100 POINTS UP FOR KENYA

Kenya are an emerging side in world rugby, and currently stand 30th in the World Rugby rankings. And they found their form in eye-catching style in their African CAR Championship match against Tunisia in Nairobi on 8 July 2017. The Kenyans ran in 13 tries – including a hat-trick for Mukidza Kinyang and two tries apiece for Jacob Ojee and Eric Kerre – as they routed the hapless Tunisians 100–10. This was the first time in their history that they had notched up 100 points in a Test match, but it wasn't the biggest victory in their history. That came when they beat Nigeria 96–3 in Nairobi on 10 August 1987 – a winning margin of 93 points (as opposed to the 90-point margin in their 2017 victory over Tunisia.

SOUTH AFRICA AMATEURS A MAJOR AFRICA CUP FORCE

South Africa may have sent an amateur side to compete in the Africa Cup to promote a level of fairness, but they have still proved the team to beat in the tournament, emerging victorious in 2000 (beating Morocco 44–14 in the final), 2001 (beating Morocco 36–20 in the final) and again in 2006 (when they beat Namibia 29–27 in the final to become the competition's first three-time winners).

NEAR MISSES FOR MADAGASCAR

It's been a case of almost but not quite for Madagascar in the Africa Cup. In 2005, they enjoyed a commendable 33–31 victory over perennial challengers South Africa Amateurs in the semi-final, only to lose out to Morocco in the final in Paris (43–6). It was a similar story in 2007: they beat the Ivory Coast 32–25 in the semi-final and, despite having home advantage in the final, lost out to Uganda (32–22).

AFRICA CUP

Year	Winner	Runners-up
2000	South Africa Amateurs	Morocco
2001	South Africa Amateurs	Morocco
2002	Namibia	Tunisia
2003	Morocco	Namibia
2004	Namibia	Morocco
2005	Morocco	Madagascar
2006	South Africa Amateurs	Namibia
2007	Uganda	Madagascar
2008–09	Namibia	Tunisia
2010	*Tournament cancelled*	
2011	Kenya	Tunisia
2012	Zimbabwe	Uganda
2013	Kenya	Zimbabwe
2014	Namibia	Zimbabwe
2015	Namibia	Zimbabwe
2016	Namibia	Kenya
2017	Namibia	Kenya

MOROCCO ONCE MAD FOR THE AFRICA CUP

Once the highest ranked African team not to have appeared at a Rugby World Cup – Kenya, currently ranked 23rd in the World Rugby rankings now hold that honour – Morocco (currently ranked 49 in the world) have reserved their best rugby moments for the Africa Cup. They finished as runners-up to South Africa Amateurs in 2000 and 2001, beat Namibia in the 2003 final (27–7) to win the trophy for the first time, lost out 39–22 to the same opponents in the 2004 final (to finish runners-up for a record third time) and enjoyed their second tournament victory in 2005 following a comprehensive 43–6 victory over Madagascar in the final. Unfortunately, the Moroccan rugby team has struggled considerably since then.

Best of the rest: world rankings

Kenya (30); Uganda (34); Morocco (39); Tunisia (43); Madagascar (46); Senegal (49); Botswana (67); Nigeria (73); Zambia (78); Swaziland (88); Mauritius (90); Rwanda (91); Ghana (93); Cameroon (100).

Correct as of 17 March 2018

RIGHT: Namibia are the Africa Cup's most successful team, winning the tournament on seven occasions, most recently in 2017 when they beat Kenya in the final.

CAR DEVELOPMENT TROPHY WINNERS

Year	North section winners	South section winners
2004	Mali	Botswana
2005	Burkina Faso	Mauritius
2006	Niger	Tanzania
2007	Nigeria	Botswana
2008	Niger	Réunion

RIGHT: Uganda (with Allan Musoke Senkindu in black) had to wait a long time for recognition on the contintental stage.

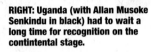

LEFT: Benoit Nicolas wins a line-out for Morocco. The North Africans won the Africa Cup in 2003 and 2005, and are a country with a rich rugby tradition. They currently stand 39th in the World Rugby rankings.

90 AND OVER POINTS SCORED IN A MATCH

Team	Opponent	Result	Venue	Date
Mauritius	Swaziland	134–0	Gaberone	21 Jun 2014
Zambia	Rwanda	107–9	Lusaka	9 Sep 2003
Uganda	Burundi	100–0	Lusaka	9 Sep 2003
Kenya	Tunisia	100–10	Nairobi	8 Jul 2017
Kenya	Nigeria	96–3	Nairobi	10 Aug 1987
Zambia	Rwanda	92–3	Lusaka	29 Apr 2017

NEAR MISSES FOR TUNISIA

Tunisia contested their first international match against the Netherlands on 1 July 1979; they lost 12–0, and it would take three years before they tasted success for the first time (beating Portugal 16–13 on 17 April 1982). Since then, they have become one of the most improved rugby nations on the planet and are currently ranked 43rd in the world. Yet to qualify for the Rugby World Cup, their best moments have been reserved for the Africa Cup, where they have reached the final four times. They have twice lost in the in the final to Namibia (in 2002 and 2008–09); and in 2011, Kenya defeated them. Tunisia is the only nation to have appeared in three Africa Cup finals without ever winning the competition.

THE CRANES HIT NEW HEIGHTS

A member of the international rugby brotherhood since 1958 (when they played their first match, against Kenya), Uganda – nicknamed the Cranes – had to wait 44 years before they enjoyed any significant success, when they won the second division of the Africa Cup. Five years later, in 2007, they were the toast of the continent after beating Madagascar 42–11 in the final to win the Africa Cup proper for the first time in their history.

TWO-TIME WINNERS

Established in 2004 to help develop the game among Africa's lesser nations, the CAR Development Trophy, which is split into two sections (north and south), is essentially the second division of the Africa Cup. Each of the sections has produced a two-time winner: Botswana (2004 and 2007) in the south; and Niger (2006 and 2008) in the north.

OVER 100 POINTS CONCEDED

Team	Opponent	Result	Venue	Date
Swaziland	Mauritius	0–134	Gaberone	21 Jun 2014
Botswana	Zimbabwe	10–130	Bulawayo	7 Sep 1996
Madagascar	Namibia	0–116	Windhoek	15 Jun 2002
Nigeria	Zimbabwe	12–111	Bulawayo	7 Sep 1996
Tunisia	France XV	3–104	Split	18 Sep 1979
Tunisia	Kenya	10–100	Nairobi	8 Jul 2017

THE AMERICAS

Rugby has been played in the Americas since the late nineteenth century, but, perhaps more than in any other part of the world, has struggled to establish itself in the face of the passion felt for other sports, notably American football, baseball, basketball and ice hockey in the North and football in the South. Nevertheless the game remains in good health in the region: Argentina and Canada have been ever-presents at each of the eight Rugby World Cups (with the Pumas reaching the semi-finals in 2007 and 2015, and the Canucks reaching the quarter-finals in 1991) and there are annual competitions staged in both the North and the South.

BELOW: Argentina may have finished bottom of the table in the 2016 Rugby Championship, but they savoured their 26–24 victory over South Africa in Salta.

ARGENTINA

Although rugby in Argentina has long been overshadowed by the country's passion for football, the Pumas have achieved considerable success on the rugby pitch over the years. In recent times, they have developed into a real force on the world stage, with their tough, forward-dominated game taking them to the Rugby World Cup semi-finals in 2007 and once again in 2015. Their entry into the Rugby Championship has seen their game improve enormously.

PUMAS GET OFF TO A LOSING START

Argentina's first international fixture came against a Great Britain touring side at Flores on 12 June 1910, but it was a disappointing day for the Pumas as the tourists ran out 28–3 winners. Argentina did not contest another international fixture for 17 years and had to wait until September 1936 (their ninth match – the eight-match losing streak is the longest in Argentina's history) before registering their first victory – 29–0, away against Chile at Valparaiso.

OVERALL TEAM RECORD

Span	Mat	Won	Lost	Draw	%	For	Aga	Diff	Tries	Conv	Pens	Drop	GfM
1910–2018	441	228	195	10	53.81	12519	8679	+3840	1626	1050	894	102	1

THE MENDOZA MASSACRE

Argentina may have fielded a virtual second-string side in their South American Championship clash against Paraguay at Mendoza on 1 May 2002 – of the 15 who played in the match only two would line up for the Pumas in their opening match of the 2003 Rugby World Cup – but they still proved far too strong for their near neighbours. They ran in 24 tries in the match to complete a crushing 152–0 victory, the joint-highest winning margin in international rugby history (equalled by Japan when they beat Chinese Taipei 155–3 in Tokyo on 7 July 2002).

WELLINGTON WOE FOR THE PUMAS

Argentina have endured some torrid times against New Zealand over the years. Of the 24 official matches played between the countries (the first in Buenos Aires in October 1985), they have lost 23 of them and drawn one. Of those defeats, the heaviest – the biggest reverse in their history – came at Wellington on 21 June 1987, when the All Blacks ran in 14 tries en route to a thumping 93–8 victory.

BELOW: Only England and South Africa did better than Argentina at the 2007 Rugby World Cup. The Pumas lost 37–13 to the Springboks in their first-ever semi-final, but they went on to win their third-place playoff against France.

PUMAS SHOCK LES BLEUS

The stage was set. Tournament hosts France, playing in front of an expectant public, were favourites to beat Argentina in the opening match of the 2007 Rugby World Cup in the Stade de France in Paris. The only problem was that Argentina hadn't read the script. The Pumas, dominating an error-strewn French side, led 17–9 at half-time – thanks to an Ignacio Corleto try and four Felipe Contepomi penalties – and held on to win 17–12 and record the most sensational result in their history. It was only the second time in the Rugby World Cup that the tournament hosts failed to win their opening game (England lost to New Zealand in 1991).

DOMINATING THE AMERICAS' SCENE

The Pumas confirmed their status as the Americas' no.1 team with their performances in the Pan-American Championship, a tournament staged on five occasions between 1995 and 2003 and contested against Canada, the United States and Uruguay. Argentina won the event every time it was held (1995, 1996, 1998, 2001 and 2003).

HONOURS

Rugby World Cup:
(best finish) – third (2007)
S American Championship:
(best finish) – champions (1951, 1958, 1961, 1964, 1967, 1969, 1971, 1973, 1975, 1977, 1979, 1983, 1985, 1987, 1989, 1991, 1993, 1995, 1998, 2000, 2001, 2002, 2003, 2004, 2005, 2006, 2007, 2008, 2009, 2010, 2011, 2012, 2013)
Pan-American Championship:
(best finish) – champions (1995, 1996, 1998, 2001, 2003)
Rugby Championship:
(best) – third (2015)

SOUTH AMERICAN GIANTS

Argentina are the undisputed kings of South American rugby, winning the South American Championship 34 out of the 35 times they contested it. The only occasion they did not win the competition was in 1981 – it was the only time they did not take part in the tournament.

MOST POINTS: TOP TEN

Pos	Points	Player (Span)
1	651	Felipe Contepomi (1998–2013)
2	603	Nicolas Sanchez (2010–17)
3	590	Hugo Porta (1971–99)
4	486	Gonzalo Quesada (1996–2003)
5	365	Santiago Meson (1987–97)
6	256	Federico Todeschini (1998–2008)
7	188	Lisandro Arbizu (1990–2005)
8	176	Juan Martin Hernandez (2003–17)
9	158	Juan Fernandez Miranda (1997–2007)
10	145	Jose Nunez Piossek (2001–08)

ARGENTINA'S GREATEST OF ALL TIME

Argentina's rise in world rugby can be attributed to the deeds of one man: Hugo Porta. A fly-half with a deadly boot – perhaps the deadliest of all time – he made his debut against Chile on 10 October 1970 (aged 20) and, phenomenally, went on to enjoy a 16-year stint as his country's first choice fly-half. There were plenty of highlights along the way: in October 1979, he kicked all of the Pumas' points in their 24–13 victory over Australia in Buenos Aires – the greatest result in their history to that point; six years later, he kicked all of the Pumas' points in their historic 21–21 draw against the All Blacks. He retired after Argentina's 1987 Rugby World Cup campaign but returned, briefly, in 1990 and for one match against a World XV in 1999. He is his country's all-time leading points-scorer (with 590 points) and was the first player from Argentina to be inducted into the World Rugby Hall of Fame.

THE PUMAS SILENCE THEIR CRITICS

Argentina's many critics were left to eat their words as Argentina produced some stunning performances at the 2015 Rugby World Cup. The Pumas showed their intent in their opening match, losing narrowly to New Zealand (26–16), but then eased past Georgia (54–9), Tonga (45–16) and Namibia (64–19) in their remaining pool matches and crushed Ireland (43–20) in the quarter-finals before losing to Australia (29–15) in the semi-finals. They lost to South Africa (24–13) in the third-place playoff, but had proved their worth as the fourth-best team in world rugby.

PUMAS TAME THE WALLABIES

This was the moment the rugby world sat up and took notice of Argentina. Five weeks after beating a star-studded World XV (containing David Campese and Mark Ella) 28–20 in Buenos Aires, the Pumas travelled to Brisbane on 31 July 1983 to play Australia. Their 18–3 victory – thanks to tries from Buenaventura Minguez and Tomas Petersen, coupled with ten points from the boot of Hugo Porta – marked the moment Argentina emerged as a true force in international rugby and remains their most famous away victory of all time.

RECORD-BREAKING TIMES AGAINST PARAGUAY

Argentina have played Paraguay on 16 occasions and have won every one of the matches – scoring 1,311 points (with 225 tries) and conceding a mere 58. And what's more, the Pumas have reserved some of their record-breaking moments for the fixture, including their largest ever victory (152–0) and the most points in a match by one player: 50 by Eduardo Morgan (six tries and 13 conversions) in the South American Championship clash at Sao Paulo, Brazil, on 14 October 1973.

BELOW: Jose Nunez Piossek notched a national record 29 tries in 28 appearances for Argentina between 2001 and 2008.

PIOSSEK TOPS THE PUMAS' ALL-TIME TRY-SCORING LIST

Winger Jose Nunez Piossek made a try-scoring debut for the Pumas in their 32–27 victory over Uruguay in their Pan-American Championship match at Kingston, Jamaica, on 19 May 2001. He finally established himself in the Argentina side in 2003 – a year that saw him score nine tries in a match against Paraguay in Montevideo (a record for an Argentina player in a single match) and win a place in his country's Rugby World Cup squad for the tournament in Australia (in which he played all three matches). He made his 28th and final appearance for the Pumas on 9 August 2008 (a 63–9 loss toSouth Africa in Johannesburg) and bowed out of international rugby as his country's all-time leading try-scorer, with 29 tries.

MOST CAPS: TOP TEN

Pos	Caps	Player (Span)
1	87	Felipe Contepomi (1998–2013)
2	86	Lisandro Arbizu (1990–2005)
=	86	Rolando Martin (1994–2003)
4	84	Mario Ledesma Arocena (1996–2011)
5	82	Juan Manuel Leguizamon (2005–17)
6	78	Pedro Sporleder (1990–2003)
=	78	Martin Landajo (2008–17)
8	74	Juan Martin Hernandez (2003–17)
9	73	Federico Mendez Azpillaga (1990–2004)
10	71	Agustin Pichot (1995–2007)
=	71	Juan Martin Fernandez Lobbe (2004–15)
=	71	Agustin Creevy (2005–17)

ABOVE: Lisandro Arbizu led his side on a record 48 occasions between 1992 and 2005 and won 86 caps for the Pumas.

LONG-TIME LEADER

Lisandro Arbizu brought a dash of flair and invention to Argentina's back division for 15 years. Equally comfortable at fly-half or centre, he made his international debut aged 19 when he came on as a replacement during the Pumas' slender 20–18 defeat to Ireland at Lansdowne Road on 27 October 1990. He appeared at the 1991 Rugby World Cup (the first of his three appearances in the tournament) and became his country's youngest-ever captain (aged 21) when he led the Pumas to a 38–10 victory over Spain in September 1992. He went on to captain Argentina on 48 occasions (a national record) and retired from international rugby in June 2005 after collecting his 86th cap (having equalled the national record with long-serving flanker Rolando Martin).

MOST TRIES: TOP TEN

Pos	Tries	Player (Span)
1	29	Jose Nunez Piossek (2001–08)
2	28	Diego Cuesta Silva (1983–95)
3	24	Gustavo Jorge (1989–94)
4	21	Juan Imhoff (2009–15)
5	18	Rolando Martin (1994–2003)
=	18	Facundo Soler (1996–2002)
7	17	Lisandro Arbizu (1990–2005)
=	17	Hernan Senillosa (2002–07)
9	16	Felipe Contepomi (1998–2013)
=	16	Manuel Montero (2012–17)
=	16	Joaquin Tuculet (2012–17)

LOFFREDA LEADS THE PUMAS TO DIZZY NEW HEIGHTS

Marcelo Loffreda won 46 caps for Argentina between 1978 and 1994 (12 of them as captain) – playing at centre outside legendary fly-half Hugo Porta – and switched to coaching when his playing career ended. Appointed coach of the national side in 2000, he led the Pumas to five South American Championship titles, to prestigious series victories over France (in 2003) and Wales (in 2006), to a first-ever victory over England at Twickenham (25–18 on 11 November 2006) and to within a whisker of his country's first-ever victories over South Africa (33–37 on 12 November 2000) and New Zealand (20–24 on 1 December 2001). His crowning moment, however, came when he led the Pumas to an unexpected third place at the 2007 Rugby World Cup. He left his role after the tournament to take up a coaching position with Leicester Tigers, but will be remembered as Argentina's greatest coach of all time.

RIGHT: An outstanding player, Marcelo Loffreda achieved even more fame as a coach when he led Argentina to third place at the 2007 Rugby World Cup, a run that saw two spectacular victories over hosts France.

PICHOT: THE PUMAS' LITTLE MASTER

Though small in stature, at 5ft 9in (1.75m), Agustin Pichot was a giant for Argentina on the rugby pitch for over a decade. A talented scrum-half capable of sniping runs through the smallest of gaps, he made his debut against Australia in April 1996, was appointed captain in 2000 and led the Pumas to some of the greatest moments in their history, culminating in a third-place finish at the 2007 Rugby World Cup. He retired from international rugby in 2008, and in the same year received the IRB Special Merit award for his role in leading the Pumas towards the top of the world game. He is the only Argentina player in history to be presented with such an award from the IRB.

BELOW: Scrum-half Agustin Pichot's 71-match, 12-year career did much to propel Argentina to an all-time high third in the world rankings.

CLASSY CONTEPOMI

Argentina's most accomplished player since Hugo Porta, Felipe Contepomi made his international debut against Chile in 1998 and appeared at the 1999 Rugby World Cup. Playing at either inside-centre or fly-half, he was an integral part of Argentina's march up the world rankings (he contributed 91 points to the Pumas' sensational march to the 2007 Rugby World Cup semi-finals). He retired in 2013 having scored a national record 651 points in 87 matches – the latter is also an all-time record for an Argentina player.

BELOW: Argentina's best player in recent times, Felipe Contepomi is the Pumas most-capped player (89) and record points-scorer (651).

ALL-TIME LEADING TRY-SCORERS: BY POSITION

Position	Player (Span)	Tries
Full-back	Joaquin Tuculet (2012–17)	15
Winger	Jose Nunez Piossek (2001–08)	29
Centre	Diego Cuesta Silva (1983–95)	21
Fly-half	Hugo Porta (1971–90)	11
Scrum-half	Tomas Cubelli (2010–17)	13
No.8	Pablo Camerlinckx (1989–99)	8
Flanker	Rolando Martin (1994–2003)	18
Lock	Pedro Sporleder (1990–2003)	14
Prop	Martin Scelzo (1996–2011)	10
Hooker	Federico Mendez Azpillaga (1994–2004)	10

CANADA

One of only 12 nations to have competed at every one of the eight Rugby World Cups (they reached the quarter-finals in 1991), Canada has a rich rugby history dating back to the late nineteenth century, although the Canucks did not contest their first international fixture until 1932. Considered one of the game's second-tier nations (they are currently ranked 21st in the world), they are the fourth strongest team in the Americas, behind Argentina, the United States and Uruguay.

CANUCKS COAST TO RECORD-BREAKING VICTORY

Canada eased past Barbados in their Rugby World Cup qualifying match at Bridgetown on 24 June 2006 in record-breaking style. They led 45–0 at half-time and ran in a total of 11 tries in the match on the way to a comprehensive 69–3 victory. The 66-point winning margin is the best in their history, although they have scored more points on one occasion – when they beat Namibia 72–11 in Toulouse during the pool stages of the 1999 Rugby World Cup.

HALL OF FAME INDUCTEES

Name (Span, Caps)
Heather Moyse
(2006–10, 22 caps)
Gareth Rees
(1986–99, 55 caps)

RIGHT: Aaron Carpenter has notched up a record-breaking 80 appearances for Canada between 2005 and 2017.

THUMPED AT TWICKENHAM

Canada have only ever tasted victory once against England in 11 attempts, 15–12 at Burnaby Lake on 29 May 1993, but that was against England's second-string XV. Matches against a full-strength England side have proved altogether tougher affairs, and none more so than at Twickenham on 13 November 2004. England ran in 12 tries – three of them by Jason Robinson – to complete a 70–0 drubbing. It remains the heaviest defeat in Canada's history.

CANADA STUN WALES IN CARDIFF

Trailing by nine points to six at half-time during their match against Wales at Cardiff on 10 November 1993, most expected Canada to fall to yet another defeat against their loftier opponents. But the Canucks had other ideas: second-half tries from Al Charron and Scott Stewart, both converted by Gareth Rees (who also added three penalties), saw them march to a surprise 26–24 win. It was Canada's first-ever victory over one of rugby's top-tier nations fielding a full-strength side.

RECORD-BREAKING RUN OF DEFEATS

Ironically, Canada's bid to break their record for the most consecutive wins ended not only in defeat but also triggered their longest ever losing streak. The Canucks played Argentina in Buenos Aires on 22 August 1998 seeking a record-breaking seventh successive win, but lost 54–28. They then lost to Japan (23–21), Samoa (17–13), the USA (18–17) and Tonga (18–10) before embarking on an unsuccessful tour to Britain that saw them lose both matches – against Wales (33–19) and England (36–11). It was far from ideal preparation for the 1999 Rugby World Cup, and Canada lost their opening two games – to France (33–20) and Fiji (38–22) – before bringing their record-breaking losing streak to an end at ten matches when they beat Namibia 72–11 in their final group game.

LAST EIGHT AS GOOD AS IT GETS FOR CANADA

Canada were one of the 16 teams invited to take part in the inaugural Rugby World Cup in 1987, but an opening-game victory over Tonga in Napier (37–4) was as good as it got for the Canucks as subsequent defeats to Ireland (46–19) and Wales (40–9) saw them fail to progress beyond the group stages. They qualified for the 1991 tournament and got off to a flyer, beating Fiji 13–3 in their opening match and following up with a hard-fought 19–11 victory over Romania. A narrow 19–13 defeat to France mattered little: Canada had qualified for the quarter-finals. But that is where their journey ended: the All Blacks proved too strong for the Canucks and ran out 29–13 winners in Lille. It still ranks as Canada's best-ever performance at a Rugby World Cup: they failed to progress beyond the group stages in 1995, 1999, 2003, 2007, 2011 and 2015 and did not win more than one game in any tournament.

OVERALL TEAM RECORD

Span	Mat	Won	Lost	Draw	%	For	Aga	Diff	Tries	Conv	Pens	Drop
1932–2018	262	103	152	6	40.61	5424	6714	-1290	568	380	572	36

MOST POINTS: TOP FIVE

Pos	Points	Player (Span)
1	607	James Pritchard (2003–15)
2	491	Gareth Rees (1986–99)
3	419	Bobby Ross (1989–2003)
4	234	Mark Wyatt (1982–91)
5	226	Jared Barker (2000–04)

LEFT: James Prichard adds more points to his all-time Canadian record haul of 607.

CANADA'S LONGEST WINNING STREAK

Winning hasn't come easily to Canada over the years and they got off to the worst of starts: it took them until 1977 (45 years and 12 matches after they had played their first international) before they recorded their first victory and a further six years before they won back-to-back games for the first time. The Canucks' longest winning streak is six matches, a feat achieved on two occasions – between 16 June 1990 and 9 October 1991 and between 23 May 1998 and 18 August 1998.

MOST CAPS FOR CARPENTER

Versatility was the key to Aaron Carpenter's longevity as a player: he had the rare ability to play either as a hooker or anywhere in the back row. He made his debut for the Cannucks against the United States in May 2005 and cemented himself in the side, playing in all four of Canada's matches at the 2007 Rugby World Cup. A second World Cup followed in 2011 and he captained his country for the first time (of 12) the following year. He made his third appearance at a Rugby World Cup in England in 2015 (during which Canada lost all four of their matches), but was forced to retire in January 2018 following a string of head injuries – by which time had notched up a record 80 appearances for his country.

PERFECT PRITCHARD

A former rugby league player in his native Australia, James Pritchard switched codes in 1999 at the age of 19. Equally adept at full-back or on the wing, he joined English club side Bedford Blues in 2001. He was an instant hit, scoring a division-record 374 points in his second season. His performances caught the eye of Canada's international rugby scouts, for whom he qualified via a Canada-born grandfather. He made his debut for the Canucks against the New Zealand Maoris in July 2003 and made two appearances at that year's IRB Rugby World Cup. A three-year absence followed, but Pritchard grabbed his second chance with both hands after he was recalled for the 2006 Churchill Cup, scoring 23 points in two matches. He has not looked back since: he scored a national record 36 points against the United States on 12 August 2006 and played at the 2007, 2011 and 2015 Rugby World Cups. He retired as Canada's all-time leading points-scorer with 607 points.

MOST TRIES: TOP FIVE

Pos	Tries	Player (Span)
1	32	D.T.H. van der Merwe (2006–18)
2	24	Winston Stanley (1994–2003)
3	18	James Pritchard (2003–15)
=	18	Taylor Paris (2010–18)
5	15	Aaron Carpenter (2005–17)

CANADA'S SINGLE GAME RECORDS

The Canada record for the most tries in a match is four, by Kyle Nichols against Japan at Markham on 15 July 2000. The Canucks' record for the most points in a single match is 36, by James Pritchard (three tries, six conversions and three penalties) against the USA at St John's on 12 August 2006.

VAN DER MERWE SETS TRY-SCORING MARK

A powerful, speedy winger, D.T.H. van der Merwe is one of the most clinical finishers in world rugby. He made his first appearance for Canada against Barbados in Bridgetown on 24 June 2006 – and marked his debut by scoring twice in a crushing 69–0 victory. He has remained a regular source of tries for Canada ever since, and by 2018 had notched up a

BELOW: D.T.H. van der Merwe has scored a national record 32 tries in 51 appearances for his country.

UNITED STATES

Rugby was introduced to the United States as far back as the mid-nineteenth century, but it has always struggled to compete against American football, baseball, basketball and ice hockey and is considered a minority sport in the country. The national team, known as the Eagles, played its first international match in 1912, has appeared in seven of the eight Rugby World Cups contested and is currently placed 15th in the world rankings.

GOLDEN MOMENTS FOR UNCLE SAM

One has to go back many years to find the United States' greatest moments on a rugby pitch. They were one of only two teams to enter the rugby tournament at the 1920 Olympic Games in Antwerp and they beat France 8–0 in the 'final' to take gold. Four years later, in Paris, they beat Romania (37–0) and France (17–3) in the three-team tournament to defend their title. Rugby has not featured at the Games since and the United States remain the only country in history to win two gold medals for rugby at the Olympics.

OVERALL TEAM RECORD

Span	Mat	Won	Lost	Draw	%	For	Aga	Diff	Tries	Conv	Pens	Drop	GfM
1912–2018	248	84	155	4	35.39	4988	6538	-1550	580	388	443	20	1

RUGBY FIRSTS FOR UNCLE SAM

The United States played their first international match against Australia at Berkeley on 16 November 1912, but the day ended in disappointment when they slipped to a narrow 12–8 defeat. Their first victory came in their third match, when they beat Romania 21–0 in a warm-up match at Colombes, France, prior to the 1920 Olympic Games.

UNITED STATES' RECORD VICTORY

Of the United States' 84 wins in international rugby, all bar two of them – both against France (on 5 September 1920 and 18 May 1924) – have come against the rugby world's second- or third-tier nations. The biggest of those victories came against Barbados in a Rugby World Cup qualifying match at Santa Clara on 1 July 2006. Leading 49–0 at half-time, the USA romped to a 13-try, 91–0 victory.

TROUNCED AT TWICKENHAM

The United States have lost 58 of the 60 matches they have played against world rugby's top-tier nations (Argentina, Australia, England, France, Ireland, New Zealand, Scotland, South Africa and Wales) and lost 21 of those fixtures by a margin of 30 points or more. The heaviest defeat in their history came against England at Twickenham on 21 August 1999, when they crashed to a 106–8 reverse – it is the only time the Eagles have ever conceded more than 100 points in a match.

RECORD WINNING AND LOSING STREAKS

The United States have always struggled to put together consistent runs of good performances. It took them until 1991 (having played 79 years of international rugby) before they won three consecutive matches and until 2003 before they won four matches in a row for the first time in their history (between 12 April and 18 June). Losing, on the other hand, has come altogether more easily to the Eagles: they have recorded one six-game losing streak, one of seven games and twice they have lost eight in a row, but their longest run of consecutive losses is ten, between 18 May 2007 and 21 June 2008.

RUGBY WORLD CUP RECORD

The Eagles have appeared in seven of the eight Rugby World Cups (they failed to qualify for the 1995 tournament), but have never progressed beyond the group stages. Of the 25 matches they have played, they have only recorded three wins, two against Japan – 21–18 at Brisbane in 1987 and 39–26 at Gosford in 2003 – and one against Russia, 13–6 at New Plymouth in 2011.

HERCUS HEADS ALL-TIME POINTS LIST

Born in the USA (in Virginia on 6 June 1979) but brought up and educated in Sydney, Mike Hercus progressed through the junior ranks of Australian rugby (appearing for their Schoolboy and Under-21 sides) before answering the call from the country of his birth. He made his debut for the Eagles (at fly-half) in a 65–23 defeat to Scotland in San Francisco on 22 June 2002 and went on to be his country's key playmaker for the next seven years. He appeared at both the 2003 and 2007 Rugby World Cups, and made the last of his 48 international appearances against Uruguay in November 2009. Hercus bowed out of international rugby as the United States' all-time leading points-scorer with 465.

LEFT: The United States team took the Antwerp 1920 Olympic Games by storm when they beat France 8–0 in the final to claim the gold medal. They defended their title four years later, also against France, winning 17–3 in Paris.

SUCCESSFUL IMPORT

Born in Tonga on 20 September 1970, Vaea Anitoni moved to California as a 21-year-old student in 1991 and made his debut for the Eagles the following year, coming on as a replacement against Canada and scoring his first international try. A short but powerful winger, he did not become a regular in the side until 1994, but when he did he soon proved himself as the best finisher in USA rugby history. When he retired from international rugby in 2000, he had scored an impressive 26 tries in 46 matches – no other American player has ever scored more than 10 tries.

RIGHT: Vaea Anitoni is the best finisher in American rugby history, scoring a national record 26 tries in 46 matches between 1992 and 2000.

MOST TRIES: TOP FIVE

Pos	Tries	Player (Span)
1	26	Vaea Anitoni (1992–2000)
2	17	Paul Emerick (2003–12)
3	16	Chris Wyles (2007–15)
=	16	Todd Clever (2003–17)
5	13	Taku Ngwenya (2007–16)

LEFT: Prop Mike MacDonald was a loyal servant to the Eagles' cause, winning a USA record 67 caps between 2000 and 2012.

RIGHT: Todd Clever has led the United States a record 51 times.

MACDONALD MAKES HIS MARK FOR THE EAGLES

Prop Mike MacDonald made his international debut as a replacement in the Eagles' 37–21 defeat to Fiji at Apia on 30 June 2000. He made his first start against Canada in 2001 and has been a cornerstone of the USA pack ever since. A veteran of three Rugby World Cups (2003, 2007 and 2011), he went on to win 67 caps – a national record since broken by Todd Clever.

CAPTAIN CLEVER

All-action flanker Todd Clever made his international debut for the United States against Argentina in August 2004 and has gone on to amass a national record 73 caps. He was appointed national captain in 2008 and has gone on to lead his side on a record 51 occasions.

MOST POINTS IN A MATCH

The USA record for the most points scored by a player in a match is 26, achieved three times by two players. Chris O'Brien did it against Uruguay at Montevideo on 5 November 1989, and Mike Hercus did it twice, against Ru at Tokyo on 30 May 2004 and against Barbados at Santa on 1 July 2006.

MOST POINTS: TOP FIVE

Pos	Points	Player (Span)
1	465	Mike Hercus (2002–09)
2	286	Matt Alexander (1995–98)
3	222	Chris Wyles (2007–15)
4	185	A.J. MacGinty (2015–17)
5	144	Chris O'Brien (1988–94)

URUGUAY

Rugby has been growing steadily in popularity in Uruguay since the country contested its first international match in August 1948, against Chile. Now considered the second best team in South America, after Argentina, Los Teros (the Lapwings) won the South American Championship for the first and only time in their history in 1981 and appeared at the 1999, 2003 and 2015 Rugby World Cups. They are currently 18th in the world rankings.

CONTINENTAL CHAMPIONS

Argentina's decision not to enter the 1981 South American Championship – the only occasion the 32-time champions have not taken part in the tournament (which has been staged on 33 occasions) – provided the continent's other rugby-playing nations with a golden opportunity to lay their hands on the trophy for the first time. And, despite suffering a defeat to Chile (33–3), Uruguay took full advantage of the Pumas' absence, recovering to beat both Paraguay (54–14) and Brazil (77–0) to win the title for the first time in their history. The competition was split into divisions in 2013 and Uruguay, taking advantage of Argentina's absence (as they were ...ving in the Rugby ...ionship), took the ... 2014 and 2016.

OVERALL TEAM RECORD

Span	Mat	Won	Lost	Draw	%	For	Aga	Diff	Tries	Conv	Pens	Drop
1951–2018	271	126	141	4	47.23	6105	6864	-759	742	482	485	35

URUGUAY'S RUGBY WORLD CUP MATCH WINS

Uruguay have qualified for three Rugby World Cups – 1999, 2003 and 2015 – and have recorded two victories: 27–15 against Spain at Galashiels on 2 October 1999 (in their first-ever match in the tournament); and 24–12 against Georgia at Sydney on 28 October 2003.

RECORD WINNING AND LOSING STREAKS

Uruguay's longest-ever winning streak is five matches: it started with a surprise 25–23 victory over Canada in Montevideo on 24 August 2002 (arguably the greatest victory in the country's history) and continued with home wins over the USA (10–9), Chile twice (34–23 and 20–13) and Paraguay (53–7) and came to an end on 3 May 2003 following a 32–0 defeat to Argentina in Buenos Aires. Their worst-ever losing streak is seven matches, recorded between 18 November 2000 and 1 September 2001.

LAPWINGS BATTERED BY THE SPRINGBOKS

Matches against the world's top-ranked rugby nations have always proved at least one step too far for Uruguay: they have lost all 43 contests against Argentina, Australia, England, France, Ireland, New Zealand, Scotland, South Africa and Wales, and 13 of these defeats hae been by more than 50 points. The worst of those reversals – and the heaviest in Uruguay's history – came against South Africa at East London on 11 June 2005, when Los Teros capitulated to a 134–3 defeat, which was also South Africa's biggest victory. The 131-point losing margin is the ninth heaviest in international rugby history.

FIRSTS FOR URUGUAY

Uruguay contested their first international fixture against Chile in Buenos Aires, Argentina, on 5 August 1948, although it did not turn out to be a day to remember for Los Teros: they lost the match 21–3. Their first victory came in their third match, when they beat the same opponents 8–3 on 13 September 1951.

RUGBY WORLD CUP HEARTACHE

Uruguay's dreams of making a third successive appearance at the Rugby World Cup in 2007 ended in heartbreaking fashion. They faced off against Portugal in the final repechage round, with the aggregate winner of the two-legged tie earning a Rugby World Cup spot. They lost the first leg 12–5 in Lisbon on 10 March and, despite winning the second leg 18–12 two weeks later, lost out 24–23 on aggregate.

LOS TEROS PUT PARAGUAY TO THE SWORD

Every one of Uruguay's 11 50-points-plus victories has come against opponents from South American and seven of those have been in matches against Paraguay. The largest was in the South American Championship contest at Cataratas on 14 May 2011, when Los Teros ran out comprehensive 102–6 winners.

MOST TRIES: TOP FIVE

Pos	Tries	Player (Span)
1	33	Diego Ormaechea (1979–99)
2	23	Leandro Leivas (2008–18)
3	13	Alfonso Cardoso (1996–2003)
=	13	Gaston Mieres Valente (2010–18)
=	13	Rodrigo Silva Pisano (2012–18)

RIGHT: Federico Sciarra scored a record 261 points for Uruguay in 39 matches between 1990 and 1999.

SUPER SCIARRA SETS ALL-TIME RECORD POINTS MARK

A diminutive 5ft 8in scrum-half, Federico Sciarra enjoyed a spectacular debut for Uruguay, scoring a try, a conversion and two penalties during the Lapwings' 15–9 victory over Chile in Santiago on 3 November 1990. He was an ever-present in Uruguay's No.9 jersey for the next decade. He scored 20-plus points in a match on three occasions (against Argentina in 1995 and against Paraguay and Chile in 1998) and played in two of their matches at the 1999 IRB Rugby World Cup – the Lapwings' first-ever appearance (of three) in the tournament. It proved to be Sciarra's swansong: he retired at the end of the tournament but did so with his head held high. His career haul of 261 points is still an all-time record for a Uruguay player.

LEFT: When the biggest name in Uruguay's rugby history, Diego Ormaechea bowed out of international rugby in 1999, after his country's first appearance at the Rugby World Cup, he held a host of national records, including most tries (33).

URUGUAY LEGEND

Considered the greatest player ever to emerge from Uruguay, Diego Ormaechea was a stalwart for his country for 20 years between 1979 and 1999. A powerful No.8, he won 54 caps and has the distinction of being Uruguay's longest-serving captain (he led Los Teros on 36 occasions, including during their first-ever appearance at the Rugby World Cup in 1999 – aged 40, he is the oldest player to have played at the tournament). He is also his country's all-time leading try-scorer (with 33 tries).

MOST POINTS: TOP FIVE

Pos	Points	Player (Span)
1	261	Federico Sciarra (1991–99)
2	254	Juan Menchaca (1999–2007)
3	217	Felipe Berchesi Pisano (2011–18)
4	213	Jeronimo Cavanna (2008–16)
5	204	Matias Arocena (2005–14)

Argentina, Canada, the United States and Uruguay may well be the only countries from the Americas to have qualified for the Rugby World Cup, with their presence in the continent's other competitions casting a giant shadow over the rest of the teams, but rugby is alive and well in the region. Nations compete in Rugby World Cup qualifying rounds on a four-yearly basis and in domestic competitions (both in the North and South) on an annual basis.

CHILE: BEST OF THE REST

Chile, 31st in the world rankings, are the fourth best team in South America, the sixth best team in the Americas and the best team from either North or South never to have qualified for the Rugby World Cup. They have finished as runners-up in the South American Championship (a tournament dominated by Argentina) on eight occasions and third on 24 occasions. They have also scored more points in Rugby World Cup qualifying matches (756) than any other team in the region.

FIRING ON BLANKS

St Vincent and the Grenadines are one of only six teams to hold an unusual and unenviable record in rugby history. They have never won a Rugby World Cup qualifying match.

BRIGHT MOMENTS FOR BRAZIL ON THE RUGBY PITCH

Brazil's national rugby team, who have contested international matches since November 1951, have had to compete under the giant shadow cast by their successful national football team, but they have still found cause to celebrate: in 1964, they finished as runners-up in the South American Championship (losing out, predictably, to Argentina) and, despite never having qualified for the Rugby World Cup, have won more qualifying matches (18) than any other team in the Americas that has not qualified for the tournament proper. They are currently ranked 26th in the world.

ABOVE: Brazil (yellow shirts) beat Paraguay 36–21 in a RWC qualifier in Montevideo in May 2009, but they were unable to advance to the 2011 Rugby World Cup.

BELOW: Sergio Valdes of Chile is about to kick downfield during a 2003 Rugby World Cup qualifying match against United States of America in Salt Lake City. Chile, the best team in the Americas never to have qualified for main tournament of the Rugby World Cup, lost this match 35-22.

Best of the rest: world rankings

...il (26); Chile (31);
...uay (40); Colombia
...yana (47); Trinidad
...(51); Cayman
...Mexico (53);
...); Jamaica
...76); Peru
...The
...rbados
...Costa

18

PARAGUAY HIT AN ALL-TIME LOW

Paraguay hold the unfortunate distinction of having suffered the joint highest margin of defeat in international rugby history. Unlike Chinese Taipei, however, who lost 155–3 to Japan on 7 July 2002, Paraguay failed to score a single point during their history-making 152–0 capitulation to Argentina in Mendoza on 1 May 2002.

CARIBBEAN'S BEST RUGBY WORLD CUP QUALIFYING PERFORMERS

Trinidad and Tobago have played in more Rugby World Cup qualifying matches (20) and have notched up more victories in the tournaments (10) than any other of the Caribbean nations. They progressed the furthest of the Caribbean section of qualifying in 1999, 2003 and for 2011, although they have yet to qualify for the tournament proper.

MORE THAN 100 POINTS CONCEDED

Team	Opponent	Result	Venue	Date
Paraguay	Argentina	0–152	Mendoza	1 May 2002
Paraguay	Argentina	0–144	Montevideo	27 Apr 2003
Venezuela	Argentina	7–147	Santiago	1 May 2004
Brazil	Argentina	3–114	Sao Paulo	2 Oct 1993
Brazil	Argentina	0–111	Santiago	23 May 2012
Brazil	Argentina	3–109	Santiago	9 Oct 1979
Paraguay	France XV	12–106	Asuncion	27 June 1998
Paraguay	Chile	0–102	Montevideo	3 May 2003
Paraguay	Argentina	3–102	Asuncion	21 Sept 1985
Paraguay	Uruguay	6–102	Cataratas	14 May 2011
Brazil	Argentina	9–103	Montevideo	3 Oct 1989
Paraguay	Argentina	9–103	Asuncion	24 Sept 1995

CARIBBEAN'S LEADING POINTS-SCORERS

Bermuda have scored more points in international matches than any other of the Caribbean rugby-playing nations: 1,465 points in 60 matches since 1975.

BOTTOM OF THE PILE

Costa Rica hold the unenviable honour of being the lowest ranked team in the Americas – 93rd in the world rankings out of 105 teams.

WAITING TO GET OFF THE MARK

Two teams in the Americas region are still waiting for their first-ever victory in international rugby: Guadeloupe (no wins in three matches); and the Turks and Caicos Islands, who have yet to win in the eight international matches they have played between 2002 and 2015.

ABOVE: Trinidad & Tobago celebrate after beating their hosts, Cayman Islands, in the opening match of their 2011 Rugby World Cup qualifying campaign.

RIGHT: A line-out contested between the most prolific points-scorers in Caribbean rugby, Bermuda (blue shirts), and the lowest ranked Americas team, Bahamas. The match, a RWC qualifier in the Cayman Islands in 2008, went the way of Bermuda, 29–13 the final score.

80 AND OVER POINTS SCORED IN A MATCH

Team	Opponent	Result	Venue	Date
Chile	Paraguay	102–0	Montevideo	3 May 2003
Guyana	St Lucia	97–0	Port-of-Spain	10 Aug 2005
Mexico	Turks & C	96–0	Mexico City	28 Jun 2014
Brazil	Costa Rica	95–0	Caracas	16 Oct 2006
Chile	Venezuela	95–3	Santiago	28 Apr 2004
Paraguay	Venezuela	94–7	Asuncion	28 Sep 2005
Costa Rica	Panama	91–5	Tres Rios	27 Aug 2017
Barbados	St Lucia	87–0	Port-of-Spain	13 Aug 2005
Trinidad & Tobago	St Lucia	82–0	Port-of-Spain	7 Aug 2005
Paraguay	Colombia	82–8	Asuncion	23 Sep 2005

PART II
BRITISH AND IRISH LIONS

A team from Britain has been touring the southern hemisphere since 1888, although the first tour to New Zealand and Australia was an unofficial affair and, as such, does not form part of the team's official records. Three years later, a British representative team toured South Africa with official backing and a further five tours took place before 1910, when, for the first time, the touring party was selected by a committee represented by England, Ireland, Scotland and Wales.

The British Lions – the name was coined by British and South African journalists during the

side's 1924 tour there – came of age in the 1950s, with a 2–2 series draw against South Africa in 1955, but the golden era came in the 1970s, when the Lions recorded their one, and to date only, series victory over New Zealand (2–1 in 1971) and then beat a powerful South Africa side 3–0 three years later. Interest waned in the early 1980s, but a revival followed their memorable come-from-behind 2–1 series victory over Australia in 1989, and any fears that the onset of professionalism in the mid-1990s would threaten this most amateur of traditions were blasted away by a compelling 2–1 series win over reigning world champions South Africa in 1997. The Lions were here to stay and their last three tours – to South Africa (2009), Australia (2013) and New Zealand (2017) – have attracted massive attention, with Lions fans outnumbering their New Zealand counterparts for the third Test in 2017.

Today, British Lions tours are the stuff of legend, the highlight of a player's career and onw the most eagerly anticipated fixtures on the rugby calendar.

BELOW: The British Lions won the second Test against New Zealand in 2017 on the way to a 1–1 draw in the series.

TEAM RECORDS

OVERALL RECORD

Country (Span)	Mat	Won	Lost	Draw	%	For	Aga	Diff	Tries	Conv	Pens	Drop	GfM
South Africa (1891–2009)	46	17	23	6	43.47	516	600	-84	68	30	59	13	1
Australia (1899–2013)	23	17	6	0	73.91	414	248	+166	57	35	39	7	1
New Zealand (1904–2017)	41	7	30	4	21.95	399	700	-301	45	20	61	6	0
Argentina (2005)	1	0	0	1	50.00	25	25	0	1	1	6	0	0

SPREADING THE RUGBY GOSPEL

If the first tour by a British representative team to the southern hemisphere – to New Zealand in 1888 – had principally been an ad hoc affair (brought together by Alfred Shaw and Arthur Shrewsbury, the tourists played both rugby and Aussie Rules football), then the first official tour, to South Africa three years later, was largely a promotional one. Financially underwritten by Cecil Rhodes, then governor of Cape Colony Province, its main purpose was to promote the game in the colony. The 22-man touring party (featuring 18 Englishmen and four Scotsmen, including captain Bill MacLagan) played a total of 20 matches – including three Tests – and won every one of them, scoring 224 points and conceding just one.

RIGHT: British Lions captain Mike Campbell-Lamerton (with ball) leads from the front during his side's 11–0 opening Test triumph over Australia in Sydney in 1966.

RECORD AS BRITAIN AND IRELAND (FROM 1891 TO 1938)

Prior to 1950, the Home Nations touring side was known as Britain and Ireland. They made 12 official tours to the southern hemisphere between 1891 and 1938, winning four series – including the first three (two against South Africa and one against Australia). Their overall record in that time was: played 36, won 15, lost 17, drew 4 (a winning percentage of 41.67).

LIONS ROMP TO VICTORY IN BRISBANE

The British Lions ended their two-match tour to Australia in 1966 on a record-breaking high. Having edged the first Test 11–8 in Sydney on 28 May, they put their hosts to the sword in Brisbane a week later, scoring five unanswered tries – two of them from centre Ken Jones – on the way to recording a 31–0 victory. It is the biggest margin of victory for a British Lions team.

ABOVE: The British and Irish Lions class of 2017 line up before the start of the third Test against New Zealand in Auckland on 8 July 2017. The match ended in a 15–15 draw, as the Lions drew a series (1–1) for only the second time in their history.

CHANGING COLOURS OF THE LIONS

The Lions may have become synonymous with their famous red jerseys, but that has not always been the case. Between 1891 and 1896, the team wore red and white hooped jerseys with dark blue shorts; in 1899 and 1904 they wore blue hooped jerseys with thin red and white bands; 1908 saw the reintroduction of red and white hooped jerseys; and from 1910 to 1938 the team took to the field wearing dark blue jerseys. The Lions wore the red shirt, white shorts and green and blue socks – the four colours of the Home Nations – for the first time in 1950 and have continued to do so ever since.

SERIES

Year	Opponent	Result
TOURS AS GREAT BRITAIN		
1891	South Africa	3–0
1896	South Africa	3–1
1899	Australia	3–1
1903	South Africa	0–1
1904	Australia	3–0
1904	New Zealand	0–1
1908	New Zealand	0–2
1910	South Africa	1–2
1924	South Africa	0–3
1930	New Zealand	1–3
1930	Australia	0–1
1938	South Africa	1–2
TOURS AS THE BRITISH LIONS		
1950	New Zealand	0–3
1950	Australia	2–0
1955	South Africa	2–2
1959	Australia	2–0
1959	New Zealand	1–3
1962	South Africa	0–3
1966	Australia	2–0
1966	New Zealand	0–4
1968	South Africa	0–3
1971	New Zealand	2–1
1974	South Africa	3–0
1977	New Zealand	1–3
1980	South Africa	1–3
1983	New Zealand	0–4
1989	Australia	2–1
1993	New Zealand	1–2
1997	South Africa	2–1
2001	Australia	1–2
2005	Argentina	0–0*
2005	New Zealand	0–3
2009	South Africa	1–2
2013	Australia	2–1
2017	New Zealand	1–1

* One-off match, played in Cardiff, prior to the tour of New Zealand

HONOURS EVEN

Britain and Ireland's 1955 tour to South Africa – the 15th in their history and their second as the British Lions – was a record-breaking one and did much to foster the team's legendary status in the years to come. In what turned out to be a yo-yo series, the Lions won the first Test in Johannesburg on 6 August (23–22), lost the second in Cape Town two weeks later (25–9), edged out the Springboks 9–6 in the third Test in Pretoria on 3 September, but lost the final match of the series (22–8) in Port Elizabeth on 24 September. It was the first time the Lions had drawn a Test series– the second came in New Zealand in 2017 (1–1).

BIRTH OF THE BRITISH LIONS

The term British Lions was first used by journalists on the 1924 tour to South Africa (because of the emblem the tourists wore on their ties and jackets); and the name was used officially for the first time on the 1950 tour to Australia and New Zealand. This tour also saw the players wear the now-famous red jerseys for the first time.

LIONS' FIRST SERIES DEFEAT

The British Isles' first three official tours had all ended with a series victory – 3–0 against South Africa in 1891, 3–1 against the same opponents five years later and 3–1 against Australia in 1899 – but the tourists' series-winning ways came to an end during their 1903 tour to South Africa. The first two Tests were drawn – 10–10 in Johannesburg and 0–0 in Kimberley – before the Springboks won the deciding Test 8–0 in Cape Town to become the first nation in history to win a series against a British touring side.

LEFT: Jamie Roberts outpaces the Australian defence to score in the Lions series-deciding 41–16 victory at Sydney on 6 July 2013.

LAMENTABLE LIONS CRASH TO RECORD-BREAKING DEFEAT

The Lions endured a miserable tour to New Zealand in 1983, suffering narrow defeats in the first three Tests – 16–12 in Christchurch, 9–0 in Wellington and 15–8 in Dunedin – before capitulating 38–6 in the fourth and final Test in Auckland. Not only had they suffered a series whitewash for only the second time in their history (bar one-off Tests, that is), but the 32-point losing margin was the largest in their history.

RECORD AS THE BRITISH LIONS (FROM 1950)

The British Lions have undertaken 22 tours to the southern hemisphere (and played in a one-off Test against Argentina prior to their 2005 tour to New Zealand) and won only eight of them, with two series drawn. Their overall playing record is played 75, won 26, lost 42 and drawn 7 – a winning percentage of 34.67.

BIGGEST VICTORIES: TOP FIVE

Score	Opponent	Venue	Date
31–0	Australia	Brisbane	4 Jun 1966
41–16	Australia	Sydney	6 Jul 2013
24–3	Australia	Sydney	26 Aug 1950
24–3	Australia	Sydney	13 Jun 1959
28–9	South Africa	Pretoria	22 Jun 1974
28–9	South Africa	Johannesburg	4 Jul 2009

LEFT: Jeremy Guscott (right) celebrates hi last-gasp drop-goal which saw the Lions snatch an 18–15 second Test victory over South Africa in Durban in 1997. It laid the foundations for the tourists' last series win over the Springboks.

RECORD AGAINST SOUTH AFRICA

The British Lions provided South Africa with their first international opposition and, not surprisingly, the tourists eased to victory in the first two series played (winning 3–0 in 1891 and 3–1 five years later), but the British tourists' early supremacy over the Springboks did not last long. South Africa won the next four series (in 1903, 1910, 1924 and 1938), drew in 1955 (2–2) and have lost only two of the six series played since then – in 1974 and 1997. The Lions' overall record against South Africa reads: played 46, won 17, lost 23 and drawn 6.

WINNING WAYS AGAINST THE WALLABIES

Ever since their 13–3 victory at Sydney on 24 June 1899 – the first match played between the two sides – the Lions have enjoyed the upper hand in contests against Australia. Of the eight series played, the Lions have won six of them (most recently a 2–1 series win in 2013), losing only in 1930 (1–0) and in 2001. The Lions' overall record against Australia is a pretty impressive one and reads: played 23, won 17 and lost six.

THE LIONS' STRUGGLES AGAINST THE ALL BLACKS

Matches against New Zealand have always been a tough proposition for the British Lions. In the 12 series contested between the two sides (the first in 1904), the All Blacks have won ten of them, with the Lions' only series success coming in 1971 (2–1) and the 2017 series ending in a 1–1 draw. The tourists' overall record against New Zealand reads: played 41, won 7, lost 30 and drawn 4. The two sides' most recent encounters, in 2017, ended in a pulsating draw. The All Blacks romped to a 30–15 victory in the first Test, the Lions fought back to edge the second (24–21) before the third Test ended in a nail-biting 15–15 draw.

BIGGEST DEFEATS: TOP FIVE

Score	Opponent	Venue	Date
6–38	New Zealand	Auckland	16 Jul 1983
18–48	New Zealand	Wellington	2 Jul 2005
0–29	New Zealand	Auckland	25 Jul 1908
5–32	New Zealand	Dunedin	6 Jun 1908
14–35	Australia	Melbourne	7 Jul 2001

WILKINSON SAVES LIONS' BLUSHES

What was expected to be a comfortable victory against an under-strength Argentina side, as well as a gentle warm-up for the upcoming challenging tour to New Zealand in 2005, almost turned into a major embarrassment for the Lions and it took the unerring boot of Jonny Wilkinson to save their blushes. With the Lions trailing 25–22 going into the final moments of the one-off match at Cardiff on 23 May 2005, Wilkinson nailed a last-gasp penalty from the left touchline to secure a face-saving 25–25 draw. It is the only fixture contested between the two sides.

LEFT: Australia celebrates a 2–1 series victory over the British and Irish Lions in 2001 – only the second the Wallabies have recorded in eight attempts.

MOST DEFEATS AT A SINGLE GROUND

The Lions have suffered a record eight defeats at two separate venues: at Lancaster Park, Christchurch, New Zealand (where they have lost eight of the nine matches played – the only victory coming on 9 July 1977); and at Newlands Stadium, Cape Town, South Africa (where they have lost eight of the 12 matches played). Ironically, the Lions have scored more points at Newlands (116) than at any other venue.

MAKING HISTORY IN SOUTH AFRICA

The British Lions' 1974 tour to South Africa is considered by many to be the most famous of their illustrious history – and with good reason. They won the first Test in Cape Town (12–3) and eased to victory in both the second (28–9 in Pretoria) and third (26–9 in Port Elizabeth) before drawing the fourth and final Test (13–13 in Johannesburg). Their 3–0 series victory meant they had become the first touring team in the twentieth century to win a four-Test series in South Africa, and the 79 points they scored in the process is still an all-time Lions record.

WHITEWASHES – FOR

Of the 32 series the Lions have contested since 1891, four of them have ended in a series whitewash: against South Africa in 1891 (3–0) and against Australia in 1904 (3–0), 1950 (2–0) and 1959 (2–0).

WHITEWASHES – AGAINST

The British Lions have been on the receiving end of a series whitewash on only two occasions, both times against New Zealand – in 1983 (0–4) and 2005 (0–3). They also lost a one-off Test against the All Blacks in 1904 and against Australia in 1930.

MOST SUCCESSFUL VENUE FOR THE LIONS

The Lions have enjoyed more success at the Sydney Cricket Ground in Australia than at any other venue. They have played there on eight occasions between 1899 and 1966 and recorded six victories, scoring 100 points and conceding 40.

BELOW: Winger J.J. Williams (right) impressed with four tries when the British Lions secured a memorable 3–0 series triumph over South Africa in 1974.

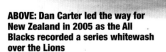

ABOVE: Dan Carter led the way for New Zealand in 2005 as the All Blacks recorded a series whitewash over the Lions

WON OPENING GAME AND GONE ON TO LOSE THE SERIES

The Lions have won the opening game but then gone on to lose the series on two occasions: against New Zealand in 1930, when they won 6–3 in Christchurch but went on to lose the next three Tests; and against Australia in 2001, when they won the opening game in Brisbane (29–13), but then lost in Melbourne (35–14) and Sydney (29–23) to lose the series 2–1.

LOST OPENING GAME AND COME BACK TO WIN THE SERIES

As a general rule of thumb, if the Lions lose the first Test, the chances are they will go on to lose the series. Only once have they disproved that theory: during their 1989 tour to Australia they lost the opening game 30–12 in Sydney, but then, remarkably, went on to win in Melbourne (35–14) and Sydney (29–23) to take the series 2–1.

BATTERED BY THE ALL BLACKS

The British Lions travelled to New Zealand in 2005 on a wave of optimism: their squad contained 15 members of England's 2003 Rugby World Cup-winning squad; Sir Clive Woodward, the only coach from the northern hemisphere to lift the Webb Ellis trophy, was head coach; and they had the support of an estimated 30,000 fans. The tour, however, was an unmitigated disaster: the Lions slipped to a 21–3 defeat in the opening Test in Christchurch; crashed 48–18 in the second Test in Wellington; and lost 38–19 in the final match in Auckland to suffer their first series whitewash since 1983. What's more, the 107 points they conceded in the three Tests was the most in their history.

LEFT: The 1989 British and Irish Lions made history when they became the first team to lose the opening Test (against Australia) and then gone on to win the series.

O'REILLY DISPLAYS LETHAL TRY-SCORING TOUCH

Before achieving success in the business world – he went on to become Ireland's first billionaire – Tony O'Reilly made his name on the rugby pitch. On 6 August 1955, aged 19 years 91 days, the Irish winger made a try-scoring debut for the British Lions during their narrow 23–22 victory over South Africa at Johannesburg. He was not only the youngest British Lion of all time, but also the side's youngest-ever try-scorer. He played in all four matches during the drawn series, scoring a try in the lost final Test at Port Elizabeth. He was back in a Lions shirt four years later for their tour to Australia and New Zealand and scored two tries during their 2–0 series win over the Wallabies and a further two during their 3–1 series defeat to the All Blacks. His six tries for the Lions is an all-time record.

MOST TRIES IN A MATCH (TEAM)

The British Lions team record for the most tries scored in a match is five, achieved on five occasions: against Australia at Sydney on 26 August 1950; against South Africa at Johannesburg on 6 August 1955; against Australia at Sydney on 13 June 1959; against Australia at Brisbane on 4 June 1966; and against South Africa at Pretoria on 22 June 1974.

MOST TRIES IN A MATCH (PLAYER)

Only two players have scored two tries in a match for the British Lions on two occasions: Malcolm Price (against Australia at Sydney on 13 June 1959 and against New Zealand at Dunedin on 18 July 1959); and J.J. Williams (against South Africa at Pretoria on 22 June 1974 and against the same opponents at Port Elizabeth on 13 July 1974).

MOST TRIES BY A PLAYER AT A SINGLE GROUND

Two players, hold the British Lions record for the most tries scored by a player at a single ground: Alfred Bucher (in 1899) and Willie Llewellyn (in 1904) both scored three tries at the Sydney Cricket Ground.

ABOVE: Willie Llewellyn's four tries for Britain and Ireland in the 1904 series has been equalled but never bettered.

MOST TRIES IN A SERIES (PLAYER)

The British Lions record for the most tries by a single player in a series is four, a feat achieved by four players: Willie Llewellyn (on the 1904 tour to Australia and New Zealand); Tony O'Reilly (on the 1959 tour to Australia and New Zealand); Malcolm Price (on the 1959 tour to Australia and New Zealand); and, most recently, J.J. Williams (on the 1974 tour to South Africa).

MOST TRIES IN A SERIES (TEAM)

The British Lions record for the most tries in a series is ten, a feat achieved on three occasions: against Australia in 1904 (they won the series 3–0); and twice against South Africa – in 1955 (the series ended in a 2–2 draw) and in 1974 (when the Lions won the four-match series 3–0).

ABOVE: Gerald Davies is one of six players to have scored three tries in his British Lions career.

LEFT: No player has scored more tries for the British Lions than Tony O'Reilly, with six on his two tours, in 1955 and 1959.

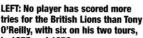

MOST TRIES: TOP TEN

Pos	Tries	Player (Span)
1	6	Tony O'Reilly (1955–59)
2	5	J.J. Williams (1974–77)
3	4	Willie Llewellyn (1904)
=	4	Malcolm Price (1959)
5	3	Carl Aarvold (1930)
=	3	Alfred Bucher (1899)
=	3	Jeff Butterfield (1955)
=	3	Gerald Davies (1968–71)
=	3	Ken Jones (1962–66)
=	3	Jack Spoors (1910)

FIRST TRY

Randolph Aston holds the distinction of scoring the first-ever try by an official touring team from Britain – he scored the opening try in his side's 4–0 victory over South Africa at Port Elizabeth on 30 July 1891.

FIRST TRY SCORED AS BRITISH LIONS

Ken Jones holds the honour of scoring the first try in a British Lions Test (post-1950): he scored his side's opening try in their 9–9 draw against New Zealand at Dunedin on 27 May 1950.

TRYLESS JEEPS SETS ALL-TIME MARK FOR THE BRITISH LIONS

One of an elite group of players to have made their international debut for the Lions before making a first appearance for their country, scrum-half Dickie Jeeps forged a memorable half-back partnership with Welsh fly-half Cliff Morgan during the Lions' 1955 tour to South Africa (which ended in a 2–2 draw). He was back in a Lions shirt for their 1959 tour to Australia and New Zealand (playing in five of the six matches) and again in 1962, when he appeared in all four Tests during the Lions' 3–0 series defeat. His final match for the Lions – in the fourth Test of the 1962 tour against South Africa – was also his final international appearance and he retired from the game's big stage with an unwanted landmark: he holds the Lions all-time record for having made the most appearances (13) without scoring a single try.

MOST TRIES SCORED AS CAPTAIN

Only six (of 38) British Lions captains have scored tries in Tests: Bill MacLagan (against South Africa at Cape Town on 5 September 1891); Teddy Morgan (against Australia at Sydney on 30 July 1904); Carl Aarvold (against New Zealand at Auckland on 26 July 1930); Bleddyn Williams (against Australia at Brisbane on 19 August 1950). Ronnie Dawson (against Australia at Sydney on 13 June 1959); and Gareth Thomas (against New Zealand at Wellington on 2 July 2005).

MOST TRIES IN A LOSING CAUSE

The British Lions record for the most tries scored by a player in a match the team went on to lose is two, a feat achieved by four players: Carl Aarvold (against New Zealand at Christchurch on 5 July 1930); Malcolm Price (against New Zealand at Dunedin on 18 July 1959); Gerald Davies (against New Zealand at Christchurch on 10 July 1971); and, most recently, Tom Croft (against South Africa at Durban on 20 June 2009).

OLDEST TRY-SCORER

Bill MacLagan set two new records when he scored Great Britain's second try during their 4–0 victory over South Africa at Cape Town on 5 September 1891: he was the first-ever Lions captain to score a try and, at 32 years 330 days, became the oldest try-scorer for the Lions of all time.

LIONS TRY-SCORERS: BY NATIONALITY	
England	38
Ireland	26
Scotland	18
Wales	42

ONE-OFF WARD A RECORD-BREAKER

Despite the huge controversy surrounding it (given the growing momentum of the anti-apartheid movement), the Lions tour to South Africa in 1980 got under way at Newlands Stadium, Cape Town, on 31 May. It was a cracking game, which South Africa edged 26–22. Despite the defeat, it had been a good day for Lions fly-half Tony Ward. The Irishman slotted five penalties and a drop-goal, a haul of 18 points, to set the record for the most points ever scored by a player making their first-ever appearance for the Lions. Remarkably, that was Ward's only appearance for the Lions.

THE LIONS LEAN ON HALFPENNY

It would have been hard to find a single pundit questionining the selection of Leigh Halfpenny at full-back for the Lions tour to Australia in 2013. The Swansea-born full-back had been in scintillating form for Wales during the previous two Six Nations, scoring 66 points in 1012 and 74 in 2013. And his magical touch with the boot continued in Australia: Halfpenny scored 13 points in the first Test at Brisbane, 15 in the second at Melbourne and 21 in the famous third Test win at Sydney to help the Lions secure their first series victory since 1997. His series haul of 49 points is an all-time record.

BELOW: Leigh Halfpenny amassed a record haul of 49 points during the British Lions 2–1 series victory over Australia in 2013.

BELOW: Neil Jenkins's record series haul against the Springboks did much to help the Lions to an unexpected 2–1 series victory against South Africa in 1997.

LEADING ALL-TIME POINTS-SCORERS AGAINST EACH OPPONENT

Opponent	Points	Player
Argentina	20	Jonny Wilkinson
Australia	49	Leigh Halfpenny
New Zealand	38	Gavin Hastings
South Africa	41	Neil Jenkins

ALL-TIME LEADING POINTS-SCORERS: BY POSITION

Position	Player (Span)	Points
Full-back	Gavin Hastings (1989–93)	66
Winger	J.J. Williams (1974–77)	20
Centre	Owen Farrell (2013–17)	26
Fly-half	Jonny Wilkinson (2001–05)	64
Scrum-half	Matt Dawson (1997–2001)	10
No.8	John Faull (1959)	5
	Scott Quinnell (2001)	5
	Toby Faletau (2013–17)	5
Flanker	Tom Croft (2009)	10
Lock	Gordon Brown (1971–77)	8
Prop	John Robins (1950)	10
Hooker	Ronnie Dawson (1959)	3
	Ken Kennedy (1966)	3
	Bryn Meredith (1955–62)	3
	Dai Parker (1930)	3

THE BRITISH LIONS' ALL-TIME LEADING POINTS-SCORER

Jonny Wilkinson made a barnstorming debut for the British Lions, notching up three conversions and a penalty during the tourists' impressive 29–13 win in the first Test of the 2001 series against Australia at Brisbane. However, despite the mercurial fly-half's best efforts (he contributed 27 points in the next two Tests, including one try), the Wallabies rallied to claim the series 2–1. Sidelined for 18 months after his Rugby World Cup-winning exploits for England in 2003, Wilkinson returned to the international rugby fold in a British Lions shirt and showed he had lost none of his formidable kicking prowess – contributing 20 points to save the Lions' blushes during their 25–25 draw against Argentina on 23 May 2005. His performance earned him a place on the Lions tour to New Zealand a month later and, though not at his best, contributed 11 points in two Tests before a shoulder injury prematurely ended his tour. He has not appeared for the Lions since, although he remains their all-time leading points-scorer, with 67 points.

THE LIONS' SERIAL RECORD-BREAKER

A stalwart of two British and Irish Lions tours (to Australia in 1989 and New Zealand in 1993, the latter as captain), Gavin Hastings set several all-time records for the British Lions: he has kicked the most penalties (20); he shares the record with Jonny Wilkinson for the most penalties in a match – six, against New Zealand at Christchurch on 12 June 1993 (Wilkinson kicked six penalties against Argentina at Cardiff on 23 May 2005); his haul of 18 points in the match against New Zealand at Christchurch is a record for a Lions captain and the most by a Lions player in a match against the All Blacks; and he has scored the most points by a British and Irish Lions player at a single ground (21 in two matches at the Sydney Football Stadium in 1989).

BELOW: England's all-time leading points-scorer, fly-half Jonny Wilkinson found points-scoring form in a Lions shirt too, scoring a record 67 points in six matches between 2001 and 2005.

UNUSED WEAPON

It may be that British Lions sides have decided on a more attacking, ball-in-hand game plan over the years, but surprisingly, given their considerable points value (they have been worth three points since 1891) and their frequency in the modern game (England's Jonny Wilkinson has scored 33 in 86 internationals – 2.6 per game), drop goals have been a rarity in Lions matches. The record for the most drop goals in a Lions career is two, achieved by five players: Percy Bush, David Watkins, Barry John, Phil Bennett and Rob Andrew. John and Bennett did it in the same game, against South Africa at Port Elizabeth on 13 July 1974.

ABOVE: Scotland's Gavin Hastings was an outstanding performer on the two tours for the British Lions (in 1989 and 1993) and he broke host of records along the way.

WILSON'S RECORD-BREAKING DEBUT

Former Oxford Blue Stewart Wilson made a record-breaking contribution in his Test debut for the British and Irish Lions. During the comprehensive 31–0 second Test victory over Australia at Lang Park, Brisbane, on 4 June 1966, the Scotland full-back nailed five conversions (out of five) – the most conversions by any Lions player in a single match.

MOST POINTS IN A MATCH AGAINST EACH OPPONENT

Opponent	Points	Player	Venue	Date
Argentina	20	Jonny Wilkinson	Cardiff	23 May 2005
Australia	21	Leigh Halfpenny	Sydney	6 July 2013
New Zealand	18	Gavin Hastings	Christchurch	12 Jun 1993
South Africa	20	Stephen Jones	Pretoria	27 Jun 2009

MOST POINTS: TOP TEN

Pos	Points	Player (Span)
1	67	Jonny Wilkinson (2001–05)
2	66	Gavin Hastings (1989–93)
3	53	Stephen Jones (2005–09)
4	49	Leigh Halfpenny (2013–17)
5	44	Phil Bennett (1974–77)
6	41	Neil Jenkins (1997–2001)
7	35	Tom Kiernan (1962–68)
8	31	Owen Farrell (2013–17)
9	30	Barry John (1968–71)
=	30	Stewart Wilson (1966)

SCANT CONSOLATION FOR JONES AGAINST SOUTH AFRICA

The Lions' series-deciding 28–25 defeat to South Africa at Pretoria on 27 June 2009 may have come as a crushing disappointment to both the players and their loyal legion of followers, but at least there was a small crumb of comfort for Stephen Jones. The Wales fly-half scored 20 points in the match: an all-time record for a Lions player who has ended up on the losing side.

WILLIE-JOHN MCBRIDE: THE ULTIMATE LION

A latecomer to the game – he did not pick up a rugby ball until well into his teens – Willie-John McBride made his international debut (at lock) during Ireland's second match of the 1962 Five Nations – against England at Twickenham – kept his place in the side and performed well enough in his country's final two matches of the campaign to earn selection for that year's British Lions tour to South Africa, making his first appearances for the tourists in the final two matches of the series. For McBride, it was the start of an enduring love affair with the Lions: he was back in a red shirt for the 1966 tour to Australia and New Zealand and was a key member of the tourists' series-winning performances against New Zealand in 1971 (as pack leader) and against South Africa in 1974 (as captain in his final tour). With 17 caps – gathered over five tours – he is the most capped British Lion of all time.

THE BRITISH LIONS' OLDEST PLAYER

Supreme fitness allied to a tireless work rate made Neil Back a stand-out performer in international rugby – but not before he had silenced his critics. He made his debut for England in 1994, but struggled to shake off the widely held notion that, at 5ft 10in (1.78m), he was too small for an international flanker, and made only four more appearances for his country over the next two years. It was during the Lions' 1997 tour to South Africa, however, that the rugby world started to appreciate his true worth: he made a decisive contribution when he came on as a replacement during the series-clinching win in the second Test and was an ever-present in international rugby from that moment on: touring Australia with the Lions in 2001; helping England to the Rugby World Cup in 2003; and bowing out of international rugby after the Lions' 2005 tour to New Zealand, during which – in the third Test at Christchurch – he became, aged 36 years 160 days, their oldest-ever player.

BELOW: No one has embodied the British and Irish Lions' spirit better than Willie-John McBride, who made a record-breaking 17 Test appearances in the famous red shirt.

ABOVE: Still in the thick of it (lying on the ground, bottom right) in his 37th year, Neil Back has the distinction of being the British Lions' oldest player.

LIONS PLAYERS: BY COUNTRY	
England	203
Ireland	114
Scotland	79
Wales	153
TOTAL	**549**

MOST APPEARANCES IN A WINNING SIDE

The British Lions all-time record for the most appearances in a winning side is six, held by two players: Froude Hancock (in seven matches between 1891 and 1896) and Blair Swannell (in seven matches between 1899 and 1904). Of the 26 players who have played in eight or more matches for the Lions, all of them have tasted defeat at least once.

MOST LIONS TOURS

5	Willie-John McBride (Ireland)
4	Brian O'Driscoll (Ireland)
3	Neil Back (England)
3	Gordon Brown (Scotland)
3	Matt Dawson (England)
3	Gareth Edwards (Wales)
3	Ieuan Evans (Wales)
3	Mike Gibson (Ireland)
3	Jeremy Guscott (England)
3	Richard Hill (England)
3	Andy Irvine (Scotland)
3	Dickie Jeeps (England)
3	Martin Johnson (England)
3	Alun-Wyn Jones (Wales)
3	Jason Leonard (England)
3	Syd Millar (Ireland)
3	Paul O'Connell (Ireland)
3	Graham Price (Wales)
3	Derek Quinnell (Wales)
3	Jeff Squire (Wales)
3	Phil Vickery (England)

MOST APPEARANCES: TOP TEN

Pos	Caps	Player (Span)
1	17	Willie-John McBride (1962–74)
2	13	Dickie Jeeps (1955–62)
3	12	Mike Gibson (1966–71)
=	12	Graham Price (1977–83)
5	10	Gareth Edwards (1968–74)
=	10	Tony O'Reilly (1955–59)
=	10	Rhys Williams (1955–59)
8	9	Andy Irvine (1974–80)
=	9	Syd Millar (1959–68)
=	9	Alun-Wyn Jones (2009–17)

PRICE ENDURES THE BITTER TASTE OF DEFEAT

A legend in Welsh rugby and one of the most celebrated prop forwards in international rugby history, Pontypool's Graham Price suffered more than anyone in a British Lions shirt. A stalwart of three tours (1977, 1980 and 1983) and a veteran of 12 appearances (only Willie-John McBride and Dickie Jeeps have made more), he tasted victory only twice – against New Zealand at Christchurch on 9 July 1977 and against South Africa at Pretoria on 12 July 1980. His ten appearances on a losing Lions side are an all-time record.

ABOVE: Graham Price has suffered the misery of defeat more often than any other Lions player, being on the losing side in ten Test matches.

ALL-TIME LEADING APPEARANCES: BY POSITION

Position	Player (Span)	Appearances
Full-back	J.P.R. Williams (1971–74)	8
Winger	Tony O'Reilly (1955–59)	9
Centre	Mike Gibson (1966–71)	8
	Jeremy Guscott (1989–97)	8
	Brian O'Driscoll (2001–13)	8
Fly-half	Phil Bennett (1974–79)	8
Scrum-half	Dickie Jeeps (1955–62)	13
No.8	Mervyn Davies (1971–74)	8
Flanker	Noel Murphy (1959–66)	8
Lock	Willie-John McBride (1962–74)	17
Prop	Graham Price (1977–83)	12
Hooker	Bryn Meredith (1955–62)	8

MOST APPEARANCES: BY OPPONENT

Opponent	Player	Appearances
Australia	Blair Swannell	6
New Zealand	Mike Gibson	8
South Africa	Willie-John McBride	10

LEFT: Ronnie Dawson (left, carrying the Lion mascot) shares the honour (with Martin Johnson) of having the captained the British Lions on the most occasions (six).

MOST APPEARANCES AS CAPTAIN

The all-time British Lions record for the most appearances as captain is six, held by two players: Ronnie Dawson (in 1959) and Martin Johnson (between 1997 and 2001). Johnson and Sam Warburton are the only two players to have led the Lions on two separare tours.

ONE-CAP WONDERS

Of the 549 players to have represented the British Isles (and then the British Lions) over the years, 123 of them have made only one appearance – a surprising 22.4 per cent. Of those one-cap wonders, six have the distinction of scoring a try in their one and only Lions appearance: Bill Cunningham (v South Africa on 13 September 1924); John Young (v New Zealand on 15 August 1959); Ron Cowan (v South Africa on 25 August 1962); John Rutherford (v New Zealand on 2 July 1983); Ollie Smith (v Argentina on 23 May 2005); and Alex Cuthbert (v Australia on 22 June 2013).

RIGHT: Alex Cuthbert is one of only six players who have scored a try in their one and only appearance for the British Lions.

IAN McGEECHAN: A LIONS LEGEND

Ian McGeechan would have possessed a distinguished rugby resumé even without his exploits as coach of the British Lions. He was good enough as a player to win 32 caps for Scotland (at centre between 1972 and 1979) and eight caps for the Lions (on the 1974 and 1977 tours), and as Scotland coach he led his side to a historic grand slam in 1990 and to the Rugby World Cup semi-finals a year later. But it is his role as Lions coach that propelled him to legendary status: he has coached them on an unprecedented four tours: to a 2–1 series win over Australia in 1989; to a 1–2 series reverse against New Zealand in 1993; to a 2–1 series win over reigning world champions South Africa in 1997; and to South Africa again in 2009 (the Lions lost the gripping series 2–1).

ABOVE: Ian McGeechan's legend in the game was enhanced by his exploits with the British Lions.

RIGHT: Graham Henry is one of only three non-British or Irish coaches to have led the Lions.

FAR RIGHT: England Rugby World Cup-winning coach Sir Clive Woodward could not find the winning formula with the British Lions in 2005; his side crashed to a 3–0 series defeat against New Zealand.

COACHES AND CAPTAINS

Year	Opponent	Head coach	Captain
1891	South Africa	Edwin Ash	Bill MacLagan
1896	South Africa	Roger Walker	Johnny Hammond
1899	Australia	Matthew Mullineux	Matthew Mullineux (1)/ Frank Stout (3)
1903	South Africa	Johnny Hammond	Mark Morrison
1904	Australia	Arthur O'Brien	David Bedell-Sivright
1904	New Zealand	George Harnett	Arthur Harding
1908	New Zealand/Australia	W. Cail/Walter Rees	Tommy Smyth
1910	South Africa	R.V. Stanley	John Raphael
1924	South Africa	Harry Packer	Ronald Cove-Smith
1930	New Zealand	James Baxter	David MacMyn
1930	New Zealand/Australia	James Baxter	Doug Prentice
1938	South Africa	B.C. Hartley	Sam Walker
1950	New Zealand/Australia	L.B. Osborne	Karl Mullen
1955	South Africa	Jack Siggins	Robin Thompson
1959	Australia/New Zealand	O.B. Glasgow	Ronnie Dawson
1962	South Africa	Harry McKibbin	Arthur Smith
1966	Australia/New Zealand	John Robins	Mike Campbell-Lamerton (4)/ David Watkins (2)
1968	South Africa	Ronnie Dawson	Tom Kiernan
1971	New Zealand	Carwyn James	John Dawes
1974	South Africa	Syd Millar	Willie-John McBride
1977	New Zealand	John Dawes	Phil Bennett
1980	South Africa	Noel Murphy	Bill Beaumont
1983	New Zealand	Jim Telfer	Ciaran Fitzgerald
1989	Australia	Ian McGeechan	Finlay Calder
1993	New Zealand	Ian McGeechan	Gavin Hastings
1997	South Africa	Ian McGeechan/Jim Telfer	Martin Johnson
2001	Australia	Graham Henry	Martin Johnson
2005	New Zealand	Clive Woodward	Brian O'Driscoll (1)/ Martin Corry (1)/ Gareth Thomas (1)
2009	South Africa	Ian McGeechan	Paul O'Connell
2013	Australia	Warren Gatland	Sam Warburton
2017	New Zealand	Warren Gatland	Sam Warburton (2)/Peter O'Mahoney (1)

GUIDED BY A FOREIGN HAND

Of the 25 men to coach the British Lions since their first official tour (to South Africa in 1891), only three of them have not come from Britain or Ireland: New Zealand's Arthur O'Brien (to Australia and New Zealand in 1904); and fellow Kiwis Graham Henry (to Australia in 2001 and Warren Gatland (to Australia in 2013 and New Zealand in 2017).

BELOW: Martin Johnson established his reputation as a fearsome leader on the 1997 British Lions tour to South Africa.

CAPTAIN FANTASTIC

Martin Johnson may have been an unexpected choice as captain for the British Lions' 1997 tour to South Africa (he had, after all, not yet captained his country – that would come in 1999), but it was an inspirational one. He led the Lions to a memorable 2–1 series victory over the reigning world champions. His appointment to lead the Lions to Australia in 2001 was the complete reverse – it was completely expected and the tour ended in a 2–1 series defeat – but it was, nonetheless, a history-making moment: Johnson became the first player to lead the Lions on two tours.

CAPTAINS BY NATIONALITY

England	12
Ireland	11
Scotland	8
Wales	6

LIONS SEEING YELLOW OR RED

No British Lion has ever received a red card, but five have received a yellow card: Martin Corry and Phil Vickery (against Australia on 30 June 2001); Paul O'Connell (against New Zealand on 25 June 2005); Simon Shaw (against South Africa on 4 July 2009); and Mako Vunipola (against New Zealand on 1 July 2017).

COACHES BY NATIONALITY

England	12
Ireland	6
Scotland	2
Wales	6
Other	3

THE LIONS AT HOME

The British and Irish Lions have made only three official appearances on British soil: against the Barbarians at Twickenham in 1977 (a charity fundraiser held as part of the Queen's Silver Jubilee celebrations, which they won 23–14); against a Rest of the World XV at Cardiff in 1986 (to celebrate the IRB's centenary – they won the match 15–7); and against Argentina at Cardiff in May 2005 (which ended in a surprising 25–25 draw). Only the last of these three matches was given international status.

NATURAL-BORN LEADER

Sydney John Dawes has a special place in the British Lions' roll of honour. In 1971, he marshalled perhaps the greatest backline ever assembled – Gareth Edwards, Barry John, David Duckham, Mike Gibson, Dawes, Gerald Davies and J.P.R. Williams – to a 2–1 series win over New Zealand. It is still the Lions' only series success in the Land of the Long White Cloud. Dawes retired as a player after the series, but wasn't out of international rugby for long. In 1974, he became Wales coach; and three years later he was handed the Lions' coaching reins for their tour to New Zealand. This series may have ended in defeat (3–1), but Dawes became, and remains, the only person to captain the Lions on one tour and be coach on another tour.

CHANGING SIDES

Only two players have appeared in matches playing both for and against the British Lions: Tom Reid, who played for the tourists on their 1955 tour to South Africa and against the 1959 Lions for East Canada; and Riki Flutey, who played against the 2005 Lions for Wellington and, having qualified for England through residency, was selected and played for the Lions during their 2009 tour to South Africa.

ABOVE: John Dawes is the only man in history to have been both captain and coach of the British Lions.

THE LIONS' ONLY PLAYER-COACH

An ordained deacon off the rugby pitch and a scrum-half on it (he played with distinction for Cambridge University), Matthew Mullineux was selected for the British Isles' 1896 tour to South Africa and made his international debut in the first Test at Port Elizabeth. Three years later, for the Lions' first-ever tour to Australia, he was captain and coach – the only man to fill both roles on the same tour – though he played in only the first Test. The tourists won the series 3–1.

MIDWEEK SIDE

The midweek side, made up of those selected for the touring party but who have failed to make it into the test team, are charged with the honour of representing the Lions against state or regional sides. It has become an increasingly important part of British Lions tours. Only three times in history has it recorded a 100 per cent record during a tour: in 1959 (to Australia/New Zealand), 1971 (New Zealand) and 2005 (New Zealand).

LEFT: Rikki Flutey is one of only two men in history to have played for and against the British Lions.

OVERSEAS-BORN LIONS

Player (Span)	Place of birth	Appearances
Cuthbert Mullins (1896)	South Africa	2
Pat McEvedy (1904–08)	New Zealand	5
Arthur O'Brien (1904)	New Zealand	4
Tom Richards (1910)	Australia	2
Brian Black (1930)	New Zealand	5
Mike Catt (1997)	South Africa	1
Ronan O'Gara (2005–09)	United States	2
Riki Flutey (2009)	New Zealand	1
Jamie Heaslip (2009)	Israel	3
Simon Shaw (2009)	Kenya	2
Taulupe Faletau (2013–17)	Tonga	4
Manu Tuilagi (2013)	Samoa	1
Alex Corbisiero (2013)	United States	2
Mako Vunipola (2013–17)	New Zealand	6
Ben Te'o (2017)	New Zealand	3
CJ Stander (2017)	South Africa	1

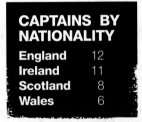

PART III

RUGBY WORLD CUP

If one day in 1823, when William Webb Ellis picked up a ball and ran with it during a football match on a playing field at Rugby School, provided the game of rugby with its most apocryphal moment, then a meeting of the IRB committee at Paris in 1985 provided it with its most pivotal one.

On 21 March 1985, votes were cast to decide whether a Rugby World Cup should take place: Australia, New Zealand and France were in favour of the idea; the Home Nations – keen to preserve the game's amateur ideals – were against it and the inevitable commercialism that would come with

such a tournament; but South Africa still had to vote. Whether or not the prospect of facing years in the international sporting wilderness – as a result of its government's oppressive apartheid policy – had any influence on its decision will never be known, but South Africa voted in favour of the idea, and the votes were locked at 4–4. It was a stalemate and the process started all over again. First England rescinded, Wales soon followed, and the die had been cast. The Rugby World Cup was born, with the first tournament, hosted by Australia and New Zealand, to be staged in 1987.

The inaugural Rugby World Cup was an invitation-only, 16-team affair that saw New Zealand stroll to victory over France in the final. Australia took the spoils in 1991, beating England in a closely contested final at Twickenham. The third edition of the event, 1995, was the year the tournament came to life: hosts South Africa, competing for the game's biggest prize for the first time, prompted a previously disharmonious nation to dance in the streets in united celebration when they beat New Zealand in the final. In 1999, Australia became the first team to win the trophy for the second time; it was another first in 2003, when England became the first team from the northern hemisphere to be crowned world champions. South Africa took the top prize in 2007 and, in 2011 in and 2015, New Zealand proved their status as world rugby's No.1 nation by winning back-to-back titles.

BELOW: New Zealand beat Australia 34–17 in the 2015 Rugby World Cup final to become the first team in the tournament's history to make a successful defence of the trophy.

RUGBY WORLD CUP 2015

The Rugby World Cup returned to the northern hemisphere in 2015, with England as tournament hosts. It turned out to be a southern hemisphere affair as, for the first time in the competition's history, no northern hemisphere team made it beyond the quarter-finals. In the end, the world's two best teams, Australia and New Zealand contested the final, with the All Blacks powering their way to a third title.

BACK-TO BACK JOY FOR THE ALL BLACKS

In 2015, not for the first time in their history, New Zealand arrived at a Rugby World Cup as the firm favourites to lift the trophy. They had been the standout team in world rugby since winning the 2011 edition of the tournament, and they would live up to the favourites tag with aplomb. They edged past Argentina (26–16) in their opening match, before brushing aside the challenges of Namibia (58–14), Georgia (43–10) and Tonga (47–9) to win their group. They took their game to another level against France in the quarter-finals, crushing Les Bleus 62–13. They may not have been at their best as they saw off a stubborn South Africa (20–18) in the semi-finals, but produced a performance to remember in the final, thumping Australia (34–17) to become the first team in the tournament's history to make a successful defence of their title.

MOST POINTS: TOP TEN

Pos	Points	Player (Country)
1	97	Nicolas Sanchez (Argentina)
2	93	Handre Pollard (South Africa)
3	82	Dan Carter (New Zealand)
4	82	Bernard Foley (Australia)
5	79	Greig Laidlaw (Scot)
6	58	Ayumu Goromaru (Japan)
7	56	Dan Biggar (Wales)
8	44	Tommaso Allan (Italy)
9	43	OA Farrell (England)
10	40	Julian Savea (New Zealand)

VICTORIES BY A SINGLE POINT

There were two victories by a single-point margin at the 2015 Rugby World Cup: when Georgia beat Namibia 17–16 at Exeter on 7 October 2015 in their Pool C encounter; and when Australia controversially beat Scotland 35–34 at Twickenham on 18 October 2015 in the quarter-finals.

FABULOUS FOLEY PUTS ENGLAND TO THE SWORD

Australia were presented with a perfect opportunity in their third pool match of the 2015 Rugby World Cup. Victory would see them eliminate England, the tournament hosts, in their own backyard. And they did just that, with Bernard Foley providing the star turn. The fly-half produced a blistering performance, kicking four penalties and three conversions as well as scoring two tries as Australia romped to a 33–13 victory. Foley's haul of 28 points was a record at the 2015 Rugby World Cup.

SPRINGBOKS BATTER THE EAGLES

South Africa did not get off to the best of starts at the 2015 Rugby World Cup, losing their opening match (34–32) to Japan in what has been dubbed as the tournament's biggest-ever shock. But the Springboks rallied superbly in the remainder of their pool matches, beating Samoa (46–6), Scotland (34–16) and, finally, the United States (64–0), also known as the Eagles – the latter was the biggest margin of victory at the 2015 Rugby World Cup.

ABOVE: New Zealand's Richie McCaw lifts the Webb Ellis Cup – the only captain in Rugby World Cup history to lift the trophy twice.

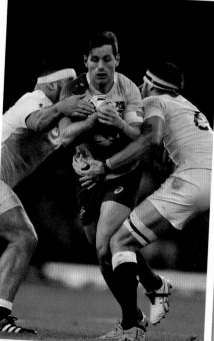

RIGHT: Bernard Foley scored 28 points for Australia to end England's involvement in the tournament.

ORMAECHEA SEES RED

It was a tough night all round for Uruguay when they played Fiji at Milton Keynes in their penultimate pool match at the 2015 Rugby World Cup. They conceded seven tries (albeit scoring two), to lose the match (47–15) and, in the 65th minute, saw their scrum-half Agustin Ormaechea given his marching orders for a second yellow-card offence. It was the only red card produced during the tournament.

TOUGH GOING FOR URUGUAY

Although they won their first-ever match at a Rugby World Cup, beating Spain 27–15 at Galashiels at the 1999 edition of the tournament, Uruguay have always struggled at the event. And the 2015 Rugby World Cup was no different: the South Americans lost all four of their matches, conceding 226 points and scoring just 30 – the lowest points-haul of any of the 20 teams.

MOST TRIES IN A MATCH

The record for the most tries scored by a single player in a match was three, a feat achieved by seven players: Cory Allen (Wales) against Uruguay; JP Pietersen (South Africa) against Samoa; Julian Savea (New Zealand, twice) against Georgia and against France; Bryan Habana (South Africa) against USA; Nick Easter (England) against Uruguay; Jack Nowell (England) against Uruguay; and Adam Ashley-Cooper (Australia) against Argentina.

RIGHT: New Zealand's Julian Savea was the tournament's leading try-scorer, with eight – and was the only player to score three tries in a match twice.

ABOVE: Argentina's Nicolas Sanchez ended up as the leading points-scorer at the 2015 Rugby World Cup, with 97 points.

MOST TRIES: TOP TEN

Pos	Tries	Player (Country)
1	8	**Julian Savea** (New Zealand)
2	6	Nehe Milner-Skudder (New Zealand)
3	5	Gareth Davies (Wales)
=	5	Bryan Habana (South Africa)
=	5	Juan Imhoff (Argentina)
=	5	JP Pietersen (South Africa)
7	4	Adam Ashley-Cooper (Australia)
=	4	Drew Mitchell (Australia)
=	4	Tommy Seymour (Scotland)
=	4	DTH van der Merwe (Canada)

NO BRIGHTON BLUES FOR THE CHERRY BLOSSOMS

Perhaps only Japan thought they had any chance of upsetting South Africa when the two sides met in their opening Pool B match at Brighton at the 2015 Rugby World Cup. The bottom line was that the Cherry Blossoms had not won a match at the tournament since 1991; while two-time champions South Africa were seeking to

become the first team in the tournament's history to collect a hat-trick of titles. But history meant nothing that day: Japan matched South Africa stride for stride and proved why they are considered one of the most improved teams in world rugby by powering their way, thanks to a last-minute Karne Hesketh try, to an improbable 34–32 victory. The result ranks as the greatest upset in the tournament's history.

BELOW: Japan celebrate their shock 34–32 victory over South Africa at the 2015 Rugby World Cup.

Dan Carter produced a Man of the Match-winning performance in the 2015 Rugby World Cup final, scoring 19 points, including this opportunistic, 70th-minute drop-goal as New Zealand beat Australia 34–17.

RUGBY WORLD CUP ALL-TIME RECORDS

Since the first tournament was staged in 1987, 25 countries have contested 329 matches in eight separate Rugby World Cups – and there have been numerous ground-breaking moments along the way. This section takes a comprehensive look at the tournament's all-time records (both team and individual), from points scored and penalties kicked to the most matches played and the stadiums that have been host to the most games.

BELOW: Ellis Park, Johannesburg, hosted the 1995 Rugby World Cup final, the last time the hosts had been triumphant until New Zealand in 2011. Before the match, fans saw a South African Airways jet flying overhead, bearing the message, "Good Luck Bokkie".

OVERALL RECORD

Country (Span)	Mat	Won	Lost	Draw	%	For	Aga	Diff	Tries	Conv	Pens	Drop
Australia (1987–2015)	48	39	9	0	81.25	1645	646	+999	209	149	107	8
Argentina (1987–2015)	37	19	18	0	51.35	992	748	+244	101	72	106	11
Canada (1987–2015)	29	7	20	2	27.58	527	838	-311	56	33	57	8
England (1987–2015)	44	31	13	0	70.45	1379	708	+671	147	107	131	21
Fiji (1987–2015)	28	10	18	0	35.71	622	863	-241	69	53	54	6
France (1987–2015)	48	33	14	1	69.79	1487	895	+592	171	122	135	10
Georgia (2003–15)	16	4	12	0	25.00	197	524	-327	14	14	32	1
Ireland (1987–2015)	35	21	14	0	60.00	973	662	+311	114	87	76	9
Italy (1987–2015)	28	11	17	0	39.28	529	899	-370	54	38	62	3
Ivory Coast (1995)	3	0	3	0	0.00	29	172	-143	3	1	4	0
Japan (1987–2015)	28	4	22	2	17.85	526	1259	-733	60	36	55	3
Namibia (1999–2015)	19	0	19	0	0.00	214	1148	-934	24	17	16	4
New Zealand (1987–2015)	50	44	6	0	88.00	2302	681	+1621	311	226	109	10
Portugal (2007)	4	0	4	0	0.00	38	209	-171	4	3	3	1
Romania (1987–2015)	28	6	22	0	21.42	365	1068	-703	40	19	45	1
Russia (2011)	4	0	4	0	0.00	57	196	-139	8	4	2	1
Samoa (1991–2015)	28	12	16	0	42.85	654	732	-78	75	49	61	2
Scotland (1987–2015)	38	22	15	1	59.21	1142	748	+394	130	96	104	10
South Africa (1995–2015)	36	30	6	0	83.33	1250	486	+764	141	103	98	15
Spain (1999)	3	0	3	0	0.00	18	122	-104	0	0	6	0
Tonga (1987–2015)	25	7	18	0	28.00	405	861	-456	44	28	43	1
United States (1987–2015)	25	3	22	0	12.00	350	892	-542	37	26	38	2
Uruguay (1999–2015)	11	2	9	0	18.18	128	578	-450	12	7	18	0
Wales (1987–2015)	37	21	16	0	56.75	1049	718	+331	127	94	76	7
Zimbabwe (1987–91)	6	0	6	0	0.00	84	309	-225	11	5	10	0

ENGLAND AND FRANCE RECOVER FROM SETBACKS

England were the first team to lose a Rugby World Cup pool match and recover to reach the final. In 1991, they lost to New Zealand (18–12), but rallied to reach the final (in which they lost 12–6 to Australia). In 2007, South Africa crushed them 36–0, but England went to play in the final, only to lose to the Springboks for a second time (15–6). In 2011, France lost two pool games (37–17 to New Zealand and 19–14 to Tonga), but still got to the final, where the All Blacks again beat them 8–7.

1987: ALL BLACKS REVEL IN HOME COMFORTS

New Zealand rugby was in turmoil as they entered the inaugural Rugby World Cup in 1987. An unsanctioned rebel tour to South Africa the previous year had left many of their star players facing a ban and the New Zealand rugby public was becoming disillusioned with its team. Their performances in the World Cup changed that: they easily won all three pool matches against Italy (70–6), Fiji (74–13) and Argentina (46–15) to top the group; cruised past Scotland in the quarter-finals (30–3); found their try form to crush Wales 49–6 in the semi-finals and went on to face France in the final. It was a no-contest: the All Blacks – in front of a now passionate home crowd – cantered to a much-deserved 29–9 victory to become rugby's first world champions.

ABOVE: David Kirk was the first New Zealand captain to have lift the Rugby World Cup.

TOURNAMENT WINNERS

1987	New Zealand
1991	Australia
1995	South Africa
1999	Australia
2003	England
2007	South Africa
2011	New Zealand

1991: WALLABIES BATTLE TO WORLD CROWN

Having entered the 1987 Rugby World Cup among the favourites to win the tournament, only to see France dash their hopes in the semi-finals, Australia went to Europe for the 1991 competition with a point to prove ... and, despite a few wobbles along the way, how they proved it. They battled to victory in their pool, beating Argentina (32–19), Western Samoa (9–3) and Wales (38–3); needed a last-gasp try to see off a dogged Ireland side in the quarter-finals (19–18); and found form in the semi-finals to defeat New Zealand (16–6). In the final, against England at Twickenham, a Tony Daly try ultimately proved the difference as the Wallabies edged a closely fought contest 12–6. Australia were on top of the world.

1995: SPRINGBOKS LIVE THE DREAM

South Africa's fairytale began with a confidence-boosting 27–18 opening victory over defending champions Australia in Cape Town and simply carried on from there. They beat Romania (21–8) and Canada (20–0) to win their pool; beat Western Samoa (42–14) in the quarter-finals and dug deep to see off France (19–15) in a rain-soaked semi-final in Durban. Few, however, thought they could beat New Zealand in the final, but some things, it seems, are simply meant to be. The Springboks were resolute in defence; their fly-half, Joel Stransky, was deadly with the boot; and the whole of South Africa danced in the streets following a 15–12 victory.

MOST RUNNERS-UP FINISHES

The record for the most runners-up finishes in the Rugby World Cup is three, by France. In 1987, they lost 29–9 to New Zealand, in 1999 it was a 35–12 defeat to Australia), and in 2011, New Zealand broke French hearts by the narrowest of margins, 8–7.

ABOVE: Martin Johnson becomes the first and, to date, only captain from the northern hemisphere to lift the Webb Ellis trophy after England beat Australia in the 2003 final in Sydney.

1999: THE WALLABIES' SECOND RUGBY WORLD CUP WIN

A 28–7 home victory over New Zealand in their final match of the 1999 Tri-Nations (in which they finished second) meant that Australia travelled to the Home Nations and France for that year's Rugby World Cup with a huge amount of belief. Their good form continued in the group stages, with comfortable victories over Romania (57–9), Ireland (23–3) and the United States (55–19). They cruised past Wales in the quarter-finals (24–9); and then needed extra time – and the boot of Matthew Burke (eight penalties) – to end South Africa's reign as world champions with a 27–21 victory in the semi-finals. Their final opponents were France, who had produced arguably the best performance in Rugby World Cup history to beat New Zealand in the semi-finals (43–31). But the French could not repeat the performance in tthe final and Australia dominated, scoring two unanswered tries during a comfortable 35–12 victory that saw them become the first team in history to lift the Rugby World Cup for a second time.

2003: ENGLAND LIVE UP TO PRE-TOURNAMENT BILLING

England travelled to the 2003 Rugby World Cup off the back of a Six Nations grand slam, away victories over New Zealand (15–13) and Australia (25–14), and ranked as the best team in the world – and they duly lived up to their pre-tournament billing. Blessed with a mighty pack and the unerring boot of Jonny Wilkinson, they won their pool – beating Georgia (84–6), South Africa (25–6), Samoa (35–22) and Uruguay (111–13) – beat Wales in the quarter-finals (28–17), France in the semi-finals (24–7) and defending champions and hosts Australia in the final (20–17) to become the first team from the northern hemisphere to lift the Rugby World Cup.

2007: SPRINGBOKS DOWN ENGLAND TO CLAIM SECOND TITLE

South Africa started their 2007 Rugby World Cup campaign with a 36–0 demolition of defending champions England in their second. It set the tone for the rest of the tournament. Victories over Tonga (30–25) and the United States (64–15) saw them win their pool; they beat Fiji in the quarter-finals (37–20) and Argentina in the semi-finals (37–13) to face England in the final. It was a much closer affair this time round, but South Africa won the battle of the boot 15–6 to win the Rugby World Cup for the second time in their history.

2011: MISSION ACCOMPLISHED FOR NEW ZEALAND

If ever New Zealand were to break what had become the most talked-about hoodoo in the game – their 24-year Rugby World Cup jinx – then 2011 seemed the perfect time to do it. The All Blacks would be hosting the event for the first

time since 1987, the only time they had lifted the trophy. And home comforts, coupled with passionate support, seemed to do the trick: they romped through the pool stage – beating Tonga (41–10), Japan (83–7), France (37–17) and Canada (79–15), beat Argentina in the quarter-finals (33–10) and trans-Tasman rivals Australia in the semi-finals (20–6) to reach the final for the first time since 1995. And although they did not have it all their own way in the final showdown – France surpassed them in many of the match's statistical categories, including metres run with the ball (309 to 238), defenders beaten (13 to 7) and offloads (12 to 2), New Zealand won the only battle that mattered, the one on the scoreboard, to win 8–7 and become world champions for the second time in their history.

2015: ALL BLACKS STILL NO.1

Twenty teams arrived to fight for the 2015 Rugby World Cup in England – although, disappointing, this was the first not to feature a tournament newcomer. The action got off to a sensational start when Japan shocked two-time champions South Africa 34–32 in the opening round of matches. With three games gone, England had crashed out of their own tournament after failing to qualify from the so-called group of death, including Australia and Wales. But that proved the last of the surprises. In the quarter-finals, South Africa were too strong for Wales (23–19), New Zealand hammered France (62–13), Argentina beat reigning Six Nations champions Ireland (43–20) and Australia edged past Scotland (35–34). The last-four encounters ran to form: New Zealand saw off South Africa (20–18) and Australia ended Argentina's dream (29–15). New Zealand saved their best for the final, romping to a 34–17 victory to become the first team in history to make a successful defence of their Rugby World Cup crown.

LEFT: Chris Latham was the star of the show for Australia during their ecord-breaking 142–0 victory over Namibia in 2003. The full-back ran in five tries.

TOP FIVE: BIGGEST VICTORIES

Pos	Score	Team	Opponent	Venue	Date
1	142–0	Australia	Namibia	Adelaide	25 Oct 2003
2	145–17	New Zealand	Japan	Bloemfontein	4 Jun 1995
3	101–3	New Zealand	Italy	Huddersfield	14 Oct 1999
=	111–13	England	Uruguay	Brisbane	2 Nov 2003
5	108–13	New Zealand	Portugal	Lyon	15 Sep 2007

ALL BLACKS FAIL TO MAKE THEIR DOMINANCE PAY

Before 2011, New Zealand had the tag of being the Rugby World Cup's great chokers and statistics alone highlight how the All Blacks have failed to convert world dominance into tournament success. In 2003, for example, they scored 361 points and 52 tries (both records for a team in one tournament), but lost to Australia in the semi-finals. New Zealand also hold the all-time records for the most victories (44), the most tries scored (311) and the most points scored (2.302). The All Blacks have won rugby's greatest prize three times (in 1987, 2011 and 2015), but suffered many low points over the years.

RIGHT: Dejected England players reflect on their 36–0 pool match defeat to South Africa at the 2007 Rugby World Cup.

WALES VALIANT IN DEFEAT

By dint of winning their opening three matches both New Zealand and Wales had already qualified for the knockout stages of the 2003 Rugby World Cup, so, on paper, the final Group D match between the two sides at Sydney on 2 November was a simple showdown to decide which team would top the group. The match turned out to be both an entertaining and record-breaking one: New Zealand won as expected (53–37), but the 37 points scored by Wales are an all-time Rugby World Cup record for a team that has gone on to lose the match.

FAILING TO SHINE ON THE BIG STAGE

Qualifying for the Rugby World Cup has become a matter of course for Namibia in recent years: they have secured qualification for the last five tournaments (in 1999, 2003, 2007, 2011 and 2015). Once on the game's biggest stage, however, they appear to freeze in the limelight: they have not won a single game in 19 attempts and in 2003 conceded a demoralizing 310 points – a record for a team in a single tournament.

TOUGH GOING FOR NEW BOYS SPAIN

A hard-fought 21–17 victory over Portugal at Murrayfield on 2 December 1998 represented the greatest moment in Spain's rugby history: it meant that they had secured qualification for the following year's Rugby World Cup. However, they were drawn in a tough group, lost all three matches (27–15 to Uruguay, 47–3 to South Africa and 48–0 to Scotland) and remain the only team ever to have played in the Rugby World Cup and not scored a single try.

FAILING TO SCORE A SINGLE POINT

Team	Opponent	Score	Venue	Date
Ivory Coast	Scotland	0–89	Rustenberg	26 May 1995
Canada	South Africa	0–20	Port Elizabeth	3 Jun 1995
Spain	Scotland	0–48	Murrayfield	16 Oct 1999
Namibia	Australia	0–142	Adelaide	25 Oct 2003
England	South Africa	0–36	Paris	14 Sep 2007
Romania	Scotland	0–42	Murrayfield	18 Sep 2007
Scotland	New Zealand	0–40	Murrayfield	23 Sep 2007
Namibia	Georgia	0–30	Lens	26 Sep 2007
Namibia	South Africa	0–87	North Shore City	22 Sep 2011
Fiji	Wales	0–66	Hamilton	2 Oct 2011
United States	South Africa	0–64	London	7 Oct 2015

GAMES DECIDED BY A SINGLE POINT

Score	Winner	Opponent	Venue	Date
22–21	Wales	Australia	Rotorua	18 Jun 1987
19–18	Australia	Ireland	Dublin	20 Oct 1991
24–23	Ireland	Wales	Johannesburg	4 Jun 1995
19–18	Fiji	USA	Brisbane	15 Oct 2003
16–15	Ireland	Argentina	Adelaide	26 Oct 2003
17–16	Australia	Ireland	Melbourne	1 Nov 2003
17–16	South Africa	Wales	Wellington	11 Sep 2011
13–12	Argentina	Scotland	Wellington	25 Sep 2011
9–8	France	Wales	Auckland	15 Oct 2011
8–7	New Zealand	France	Auckland	23 Oct 2011
17–16	Georgia	Namibia	Exeter	7 Oct 2015
35–34	Australia	Scotland	Twickenham	18 Oct 2015

RIGHT: Dan Parks (third left) watches his drop goal miss the posts, condemning Scotland to a 13–12 loss to Argentina.

STRUGGLING TO MAKE AN IMPACT

Japan may have experienced ecstasy during the 2015 Rugby Cup when they beat two-time champions South Africa 34–32 in the opening round of matches, but the Cherry Blossoms have also experienced plenty of Rugby World Cup lows. They are one of three teams (including Romania and the United States) to have suffered a record number of defeats (20) and they also hold the ignominious record for having conceded the most points in the tournament's history (1,259).

WALES SLUMP TO LAST-GASP DEFEAT

It was one of the most memorable matches in Rugby World Cup history. Shortly before half-time in the final Pool B match at Nantes on 29 September 2007 (with the winner guaranteed a place in the quarter-finals), Fiji led Wales 25–3 and the Welsh needed to dig deep to keep their tournament dreams alive. They rallied in spectacular fashion, scoring five unanswered tries to edge into a 34–31 lead with just six minutes remaining. But, three minutes from time, disaster struck when Fiji's Graham Dewes crashed over the line and Nicky Little slotted the conversion to secure a 38–34 victory and send Wales crashing out of the competition. The fact that they had scored the most tries by a team in a losing cause in Rugby World Cup history would have come as little consolation to the Welsh – it was the third time in six attempts that they had failed to progress beyond the group stages at a Rugby World Cup.

SORRY ROMANIA HIT RECORD-BREAKING LOW

Romania hold the distinction of being one of only 12 teams to have appeared in all seven Rugby World Cups, and have recorded one victory in every tournament bar two – 1995 and 2011. But 1995, in particular, was forgettable for Romania: paired with hosts South Africa, Canada and Australia, they lost all three matches and scored only 14 points – the lowest in a Rugby World Cup tournament.

BELOW: Fiji's players celebrate after Graham Dewes's last-gasp try secured a famous 38–34 victory over Wales at the 2007 Rugby World Cup.

HONOURS EVEN

There have been three draws in the Rugby World Cup. First France drew 20–20 with Scotland at Christchurch in 1987. And Japan and Canada have drawn twice, at Bordeaux in 2007 (12–12), and at Napier in 2011 (23–23).

WAITING TO GET OFF THE MARK

Six countries are still waiting to record their first Rugby World Cup victory: Namibia (in five tournament appearances), Zimbabwe in two and Portugal, Russia, Spain, and the Ivory Coast in one.

WINNING MARGINS BREAKDOWN

Margin (points)	No. of matches
1–10	99
11–20	58
21–30	59
31–40	35
41–50	29
51 plus	39

TRY-SCORING RECORDS

RECORDS TUMBLE AS THE ALL BLACKS RUN RIOT

With their progression to the quarter-finals all but assured following comfortable opening wins over Ireland (43–19) and Wales (34–9), New Zealand opted to give their second-string XV a run-out for their final pool match of the 1995 Rugby World Cup against Japan in Bloemfontein. It was one-way traffic: the All Blacks won the match 145–17 (the most points ever scored by a team in a Rugby World Cup match), notching up 21 tries – six of them were scored by Marc Ellis, an all-time Rugby World Cup record for a player in one match.

MOST TRIES: TOP TEN

Pos	Tries	Player (Country, Span)
1	15	Jonah Lomu (New Zealand, 1995–99)
=	15	Bryan Habana (South Africa, 2007–15)
3	14	Drew Mitchell (Australia, 2007–15)
4	13	Doug Howlett (New Zealand, 2003–07)
5	11	Rory Underwood (England, 1987–95)
=	11	Chris Latham (Australia, 1999–2007)
=	11	Joe Rokocoko (New Zealand, 2003–07)
=	11	Vincent Clerc (France, 2007–11)
=	11	Adam Ashley-Cooper (Australia, 2007–15)
10	10	David Campese (Australia, 1987–95)
=	10	Brian Lima (Samoa, 1991–2007)
=	10	Shane Williams (Wales, 2003–11)

THE YOUNGEST TRY-SCORER

Wales winger George North is the Rugby World Cup's youngest try-scorer. He was aged 19 years 166 days when he touched down against Namibia at New Plymouth on 26 September 2011.

BELOW: Explosive winger George North starred for Wales during the 2011 Rugby World Cup and earned a place for himself in the record books.

THE MOST DESTRUCTIVE PLAYER IN RUGBY HISTORY

Jonah Lomu made his international debut for New Zealand against France in Christchurch on 26 June 1994 (becoming the youngest-ever All Black), but it wasn't until the following year's Rugby World Cup in South Africa in 1995 that the world got its first glimpse of the most destructive player ever to appear on a rugby pitch. The 6ft 5in (1.96m) winger may have scored two tries against Ireland in the All Blacks' opening match and once against Scotland in the quarter-finals, but it was his single-handed, bulldozing, four-try destruction of England in the semi-finals – a performance that left defeated England captain Will Carling labelling him a 'freak' – that made an indelible impression on the game of rugby and led to Lomu becoming the sport's first true icon. That South Africa managed to find a way of shackling him in the final was the principal reason they won the competition. Ironically, that was the best the world would see of Lomu. Health problems struck in 1996; he missed all of 1997, and struggled back to form and near total fitness for the 1999 Rugby World Cup. Once again he provided the All Blacks with a formidable attacking option, scoring seven tries in the tournament, including two in the semi-final defeat to France. His tally of 15 tries is a record, shared with South Africa's flying winger Bryan Habana.

ABOVE: Marc Ellis scored a Rugby World Cup record six of New Zealand's 21 tries against Japan at Bloemfontein in 1995.

LEFT: Jonah Lomu was at his destructive best against England in New Zealand's 45–29 semi-final victory at Cape Town in 1995.

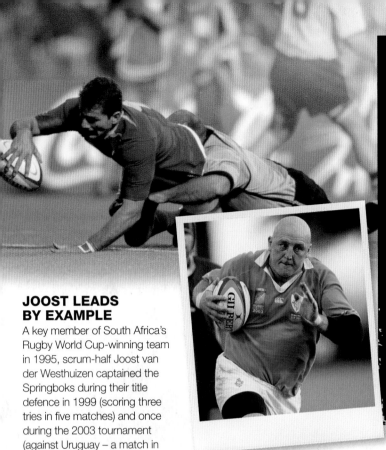

ALL-TIME LEADING TRY-SCORERS: BY POSITION

Position	Player (Country, Span)	Tries
Full-back	Chris Latham (Aus, 1999–2007)	11
Winger	Jonah Lomu (NZ, 1995–99)	15
Centre	Jaque Fourie (SA, 2003–11)	9
Fly-half	Michael Lynagh (Aus, 1987–95)	4
	Carlos Spencer (NZ, 2003)	4
	Matt Giteau (Aus, 2003)	4
Scrum-half	Joost van der Westhuizen (SA, 1995–2003)	6
No.8	Pablo Bouza (Arg, 2003)	4
	Adriaan Richter (SA, 1995)	4
	Brian Robinson (Ire, 1991)	4
	Laurent Rodriguez (Fr, 1987)	4
Flanker	John Jeffrey (Sco, 1987–91)	6
	Jerome Kaino (NZ, 2011-15)	6
Lock	Lionel Nallet (Fr, 2007–11)	4
Prop	Nigel Popplewell (Ire, 1991–95)	3
	Rod Snow (Can, 1995–2007)	3
Hooker	Keith Wood (Ire, 1995–2003)	5

JOOST LEADS BY EXAMPLE

A key member of South Africa's Rugby World Cup-winning team in 1995, scrum-half Joost van der Westhuizen captained the Springboks during their title defence in 1999 (scoring three tries in five matches) and once during the 2003 tournament (against Uruguay – a match in which he scored three tries). His total of six tries is an all-time record for a captain in Rugby World Cup matches.

TOP: South Africa's captain and scrum-half Joost van der Westhuizen scores against Uruguay in 2003

ABOVE: No hooker has scored more tries the Rugby World Cup than Ireland's Keith Wood (with five).

LEONARD DRAWS A RECORD-BREAKING TRY-SCORING BLANK

A veteran of four Rugby World Cups (1991–2003) and one of 29 players to appear in two finals (in 1991 and when he collected a winners' medal in 2003), England prop Jason Leonard holds the tournament record for having made the most appearances (22) without scoring a try.

MOST TRIES IN A SINGLE TOURNAMENT

The record for the most tries in a single tournament is eight, achieved by three players: New Zealand's Jonah Lomu (in 1995) and South Africa's Bryan Habana (in 2007); and New Zealand's Julian Savea (in 2015).

MOST TRIES BY A PLAYER IN A MATCH IN A LOSING CAUSE

The most tries by a player in a single match for a team that has gone on to lose is two, a feat achieved by 22 players.

OLDEST TRY-SCORER

Uruguay's Diego Ormaechea holds the distinction of being the oldest try-scorer in Rugby World Cup history. The veteran No.8 was 40 years 13 days old when he touched down against Spain at Galashiels on 2 October 1999.

BELOW: Bryan Habana's eight tries in the 2007 Rugby World Cup did much to guide South Africa to victory in the tournament.

RUGBY WORLD CUP TRY-SCORING FIRSTS

One of the stranger footnotes to New Zealand's 70–6 victory over Italy in the first-ever Rugby World Cup match, at Eden Park, Auckland, on 22 May 1987, was that the first-ever try in the tournament's history was a penalty try. Flanker Michael Jones added New Zealand's second try, and so holds the distinction of being the first individual try-scorer in Rugby World Cup history. Jones was also the first-ever try-scorer in a Rugby World Cup final, registering the first of the All Blacks' three tries (David Kirk and John Kirwan added the others) during the co-hosts' 29–9 victory over France.

LEADING TRY-SCORERS: BY TOURNAMENT

Year	Player (Country)	Tries
1987	Craig Green (New Zealand)	6
	John Kirwan (New Zealand)	
1991	David Campese (Australia)	6
	Jean-Baptiste Lafond (France)	
1995	Marc Ellis (New Zealand)	7
	Jonah Lomu (New Zealand)	
1999	Jonah Lomu (New Zealand)	8
2003	Doug Howlett (New Zealand)	7
	Mils Muliaina (New Zealand)	
2007	Bryan Habana (South Africa)	8
2011	Chris Ashton (England)	6
	Vincent Clerc (France)	
2015	Julian Savea (New Zealand)	8

POINTS-SCORING RECORDS

FANTASTIC MR FOX SPOT ON FOR NEW ZEALAND

Grant Fox may not have been the greatest of fly-halves when he had the ball in his hands, but he was a true master of the art of goal-kicking and few could question the major contribution he made to New Zealand's Rugby World Cup-winning cause in 1987. The New Plymouth-born No.10 nailed a tournament record 30 conversions and scored 126 points (42.3 per cent of the All Blacks' overall points total) during the tournament – another record.

ABOVE: Grant Fox made an enormous contribution to New Zealand's Rugby World Cup triumph in 1987.

BELOW: Argentina's Gonzalo Quesada holds the record for the most penalties kicked at a single Rugby World Cup, with 31 in 1999.

MOST POINTS: TOP TEN

Pos	Points	Player (Country, Span)
1	277	Jonny Wilkinson (England, 1999–2011)
2	227	Gavin Hastings (Scotland, 1987–95)
3	195	Michael Lynagh (Australia, 1987–95)
4	191	Dan Carter (New Zealand, 2003–15)
5	170	Grant Fox (New Zealand, 1987–91)
6	163	Andrew Mehrtens (New Zealand, 1995–99)
7	140	Chris Paterson (Scotland, 1999–2011)
8	136	Frederic Michalak (France, 2003–15)
9	135	Gonzalo Quesada (Argentina, 1999–2003)
10	125	Matt Burke (Australia, 1995–2003)
=	125	Nicky Little (Fiji, 1999–2011)
=	125	Felipe Contepomi (Argentina, 1999–2011)

CULHANE SHINES IN RARE STARTING ROLE

As New Zealand ran in try after try (21 of them) during their record-breaking 145–17 rout of Japan at Bloemfontein during the 1995 Rugby World Cup, debutant Simon Culhane, the All Blacks' understudy fly-half (who would only win a total of six caps for his country), had a day to remember as he kicked his way into the record books: as well as scoring a try, he slotted 20 conversions (out of 21) and contributed 45 points to his team's cause – both are all-time Rugby World Cup records for a player in a single match.

MOST POINTS BY A REPLACEMENT

Veteran fly-half Nicky Little, his country's most capped player, embarked on a 70-minute journey that would end up with him earning an obscure place in the record books when he replaced Waisale Serevi in the tenth minute of Fiji's 2003 Rugby World Cup Pool B match against Japan at Townsville. He ended up scoring 13 points (three penalties and two conversions) during Fiji's 41–13 win – not a substantial amount, but, remarkably, the most points ever scored by a replacement in a Rugby World Cup match.

SPEEDY GONZALO HAS THE LAST LAUGH

The often-cutting English press may have dubbed him 'Speedy Gonzalo' because of it, but Gonzalo Quesada's meticulous at best – spectacularly slow at worst – preparation before attempting a kick at goal paid dividends during the 1999 Rugby World Cup. The Argentina fly-half nailed a record 31 penalties during the course of the tournament.

MOST POINTS: BY POSITION

Position	Player (Span)	Points
Full-back	Gavin Hastings (Sco, 1987–95)	227
Winger	Chris Paterson (Sco, 2003–07)	83
Centre	Thierry Lacroix (Fra, 1991–95)	112
Fly-half	Jonny Wilkinson (Eng, 1999–2011)	277
Scrum-half	Greig Laidlaw (Sco, 2015)	79
No.8	Pablo Bouza (Arg, 2003)	20
	Ariaan Richter (SA, 1995)	20
Flanker	Jerome Kaino (NZ, 2011–15)	30
Lock	Lionel Nallet (Fra, 2007–11)	20
Prop	Rod Snow (Can, 1995–2007)	15
Hooker	Keith Wood (Ire, 1995–2003)	25

HASTINGS MAKES HIS MARK

Gavin Hastings will always be remembered for, and almost certainly haunted by, his glaring, in-front-of-the-posts miss in the final moments of Scotland's 1991 Rugby World Cup semi-final match against England (a brutal encounter the Auld Enemy went on to win 9–6), but, that lapse apart, the full-back proved a reliably consistent goal-kicker over the years. In 13 Rugby World Cup matches between 1987 and 1995 – he scored 227 points – an all-time tournament record for a full-back. He is also one of four players to have kicked eight penalties in a Rugby World Cup match – a feat he achieved against Tonga at Pretoria on 30 May 1995. The others to have equalled Hastings' feat are: Thierry Lacroix (France) against Ireland at Durban on 10 June 1995; Gonzalo Quesada (Argentina) against Samoa at Llanelli on 10 October 1999; and Matt Burke (Australia) against South Africa at Twickenham on 30 October 1999.

BELOW: Gavin Hastings enjoyed spectacular highs and lows in a Scotland shirt in Rugby World Cup matches.

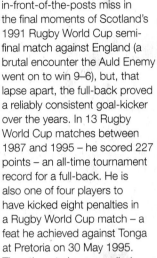

DE BEER STRIKES DROP-GOAL GOLD

Jannie de Beer produced a performance that neither his country nor opponents England would forget during South Africa's 44–21 1999 Rugby World Cup quarter-final at the Stade de France, Paris. The occasional fly-half became a national hero when he kicked a remarkable – and tournament record – five drop goals during the match.

ABOVE: South Africa's Jannie de Beer was in inspired form against England in the 1999 Rugby World Cup quarter-final, dropping five goals.

BELOW: England's Jonny Wilkinson has enjoyed some magical moments at the Rugby World Cup and he has set all-time numerous records.

HUMPHREYS GOES DOWN FIGHTING

Thankfully used only once, the 1999 Rugby World Cup's ill-conceived and much criticized format saw Ireland (the runners-up in Pool 5) having to appear in a play-off match for one of the three remaining quarter-final places against Argentina (the third-placed team in Pool 4). And although the match at Lansdowne Road proved a calamity for the men in green – they lost 28–24 to crash out of the tournament – no one could have pointed the finger of blame in the direction of David Humphreys. The Ulster fly-half scored all 24 of Ireland's points – seven penalties and a drop goal – the most by any player to end up on the losing side in Rugby World Cup history.

ENGLAND'S NO.10 KICKS HIS WAY INTO THE RECORD BOOKS

Jonny Wilkinson was only 20 years 130 days old when he made his Rugby World Cup debut in England's opening pool match against Italy at the 1999 tournament and scored a try, 11 conversions and a penalty (a haul of 32 points) during their comfortable 67–7 victory. He was dropped following England's 30–16 defeat to New Zealand in their next match and sat out the remainder of the pool matches, but returned for their quarter-final play-off victory over Fiji, scoring 23 points. He was controversially left out of England's starting XV for their quarter-final defeat against South Africa, and many cite his absence as a big factor in England's loss. By 2003, however, and now established as the best fly-half in world rugby, no one would have dreamt of leaving Wilkinson out of a starting line-up. He contributed 113 points in five matches during the tournament – including a last-gasp, match-winning drop goal in the final – to help England to the world crown. He returned from an injury nightmare in time for the 2007 Rugby World Cup and his 67 points in five matches did much to help England reach a second successive final (in the process he became the only player in history to have scored in two finals). The mercurial fly-half also played at the 2011 tournament and holds the all-time Rugby World Cup records for: the most points (277), the most penalties (58), the most drop goals in a tournament (8 in 2003) and the most drop goals overall (14).

LEADING POINTS-SCORERS: BY TOURNAMENT

Year	Player (Country)	Points
1987	Grant Fox (New Zealand)	126
1991	Ralph Keyes (Ireland)	68
1995	Thierry Lacroix (France)	112
1999	Gonzalo Quesada (Argentina)	102
2003	Jonny Wilkinson (England)	113
2007	Percy Montgomery (South Africa)	105
2011	Morne Steyn (South Africa)	62
2015	Nicolas Sanchez (Argentina)	97

THE RUGBY WORLD CUP'S OLDEST PLAYER

Having battled for Uruguay's cause for a decade and one day, Diego Ormaechea chose to bow out of international rugby after his country's greatest hour – their first appearance at the Rugby World Cup, for which Ormaechea was captain. He did so not only with his status as his country's greatest-ever rugby player assured, but also as a record-breaker: when he made his final appearance, against South Africa in Uruguay's last Pool A match in 1999, he was 40 years 26 days old – the oldest player ever to appear in the tournament.

PALAMO IS THE RUGBY WORLD CUP'S YOUNGEST PLAYER

A junior international for Samoa, powerful winger Thretton Palamo chose to play for the country of his birth, the United States, and made history when he came off the bench to make his international debut for the Eagles during their Pool A match against South Africa at Montpellier during the 2007 Rugby World Cup. Aged just 19 years 8 days, he became the youngest player in Rugby World Cup history.

LOMU BREAKS RECORD IN DEFEAT

Having made such an enormous impact on both the tournament, and the game of rugby itself, during the 1995 Rugby World Cup, Jonah Lomu would have wanted to end the tournament with a winners' medal around his neck, which was no less than his barnstorming performances deserved. It wasn't to be: South Africa found a way to shackle his explosive power and the match ended in defeat for the All Blacks. At 20 years 43 days, however, Lomu remains the youngest-ever player to have appeared in a Rugby World Cup final.

HISTORY-MAKING WORLD CUP FINAL

There were plenty of records at stake when England faced off against South Africa in the 2007 Rugby World Cup final: England were looking to become the first team in history to make a successful defence of their title; their veteran back Mike Catt (at 36 years 33 days) was seeking to usurp Jason Leonard (35 years 100 days) as the oldest-ever Rugby World Cup winner; and the Springboks' young tyro Francois Steyn (at 20 years 159 days) was attempting to become the youngest Rugby World Cup winner in history. As it was, Steyn and South Africa took the spoils following a hard-fought 15–6 victory, although Catt did have the consolation of becoming the oldest player ever to appear in a Rugby World Cup final – a record broken by New Zealand's Brad Thorne (36 years 262 days) in the 2011 final.

ABOVE: South Africa's 15–6 victory over England in the 2007 final at the Stade de France in Paris saw Francois Steyn become the youngest-ever winner of the Rugby World Cup.

BELOW: When he faced South Africa aged 40 years and 26 days old in 1999, Uruguay's Diego Ormaechea became the oldest player to appear in the Rugby World Cup match

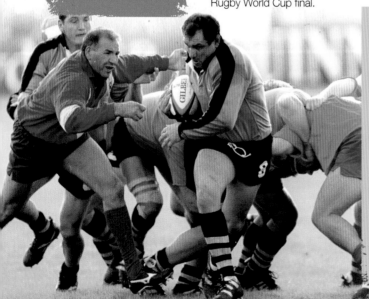

MOST APPEARANCES: TOP TEN

Pos	Apps	Player (Country, span)
1	22	Jason Leonard (England, 1991–2003)
=	22	Richie McCaw (New Zealand, 2003–15)
3	20	Schalk Burger (South Africa, 2003–15)
=	20	George Gregan (Australia, 1995–2007)
=	20	Keven Mealamu (New Zealand, 2003–15)
6	19	Mike Catt (England, 1995–2007)
=	19	Jonny Wilkinson (England, 1999–2011)
8	18	Bryan Habana (South Africa, 2007–15)
=	18	Raphael Ibanez (France, 1999–2007)
=	18	Gethin Jenkins (Wales, 2003–15)
=	18	Martin Johnson (England, 1995–2003)
=	18	Mario Ledesma Arocena (Argentina, 1999–2011)
=	18	Brian Lima (Samoa, 1991–2007)
=	18	Victor Matfield (South Africa, 2003–15)
=	18	Lewis Moody (England, 2003–11)

LEONARD IN FOR THE LONG HAUL

Just 17 days short of his 22nd birthday when he packed down at prop for England for the first time in an international match, against Argentina in Buenos Aires on 28 July 1990, Jason Leonard appeared in his first Rugby World Cup match just over a year later, during England's 18–12 opening-game defeat to New Zealand. He remained the cornerstone of the impressive pack that inspired their rally to the final, which they lost 12–6 to Australia after inexplicably abandoning their forward-oriented approach. Leonard recovered from a serious neck injury to earn selection for England's squad at the 1995 Rugby World Cup and played in four matches as they reached the semi-finals. He was first choice in 1999 (making five appearances) and, three months after his 35th birthday and by now the most capped player in the game's history, appeared in all seven of England's games at the 2003 Rugby World Cup, ending his fourth tournament with a winners' medal around his neck. He has appeared in 22 Rugby World Cup matches – a record shared with New Zealand's two-time Rugby World Cup-winning captain, Richie McCaw.

MOST RUGBY WORLD CUP FINAL APPEARANCES

Twenty-nine players have appeared in two Rugby World Cup finals, but only 14 of them have ended up on the winning side on both occasions: Dan Crowley, John Eales, Tim Horan, Phil Kearns and Jason Little (for Australia in 1991 and 1999); Os du Randt (for South Africa in 1995 and 2007); and Owen Franks, Keven Mealamu, Ma'a Nonu, Kieran Read, Sam Whitelock, Richie McCaw and Sonny Bill Williams (for New Zealand in 2011 and 2015.

MOST APPEARANCES AS A REPLACEMENT

Australia's Jeremy Paul has made the most Rugby World Cup appearances as a replacement. Of his 11 appearances in the tournament between 1999 and 2003, ten of them came off the replacements' bench.

ONE MATCH ONLY

Of the 2,823 players to have played in a Rugby World Cup match, 428 of them appeared in one match only – a surprising 15.16 per cent.

BELOW: A winner in 2003, England's Jason Leonard has appeared in 22 Rugby World Cup matches – a tournament record shared with New Zealand's Richie McCaw.

NO RUGBY WORLD CUP LOVE FOR ROMEO

A regular presence at centre for Romania in four Rugby World Cups (1995, 1999, 2003 and 2007), Romeo Gontineac holds the record for having appeared on the losing side in the tournament on more occasions than other player in history (11). It has not all been bad news for Gontineac, however: he tasted victory on three occasions – against the United States in 1999 (27–25), against Namibia in 2003 (37–7) and against Portugal in 2007 (14–10).

ABOVE: Centre Romeo Gontineac experienced defeat in 11 of his 14 Rugby World Cup matches for Romania – an all-time tournament record.

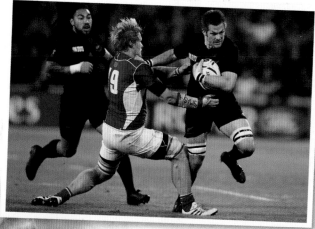

ABOVE: Richie McCaw led New Zealand in 13 Rugby World Cup matches – a record for a captain.

CAPTAIN FANTASTIC

It would be safe to say that the finest moments of Richie McCaw's glittering career have been reserved for the Rugby World Cup. The All Black great is the only player in the tournament's history to have lifted the Webb Ellis Cup on two occasions (in 2011 and 2015) and he also holds the tournament record for captaining a team on the most occasions – 13 between 2007 and 2015.

MOST ILL-DISCIPLINED TEAM

As is the custom with teams from that part of the world, Tonga engage in a war dance before the start of a match. Their dance – known as the 'kailao' – calls for players 'to maul and loose forwards shall I know and crunch any fierce hearts I know'. The players, it appears, take the words literally: the Sea Eagles are the most ill-disciplined team in Rugby World Cup history, having received three red cards and 11 yellow cards in 25 matches in the tournament between 1987 and 2015.

RED CARDS: BY COUNTRY

3 Canada, Tonga
2 Samoa South Africa, Wales
1 Argentina, Australia, Fiji, Namibia, Uruguay

THE FIRST MAN TO REFEREE A RUGBY WORLD CUP MATCH

Australia's Bob Fordham has the distinction of refereeing the first-ever Rugby World Cup match. He was in charge when New Zealand played Italy at Eden Park, Auckland, on 22 May 1987. The All Blacks won 70–6.

CONTEPOMI THE FIRST TO SEE RUGBY WORLD CUP YELLOW

Sixty-five yellow cards have been issued in Rugby World Cup matches since they were introduced in 2003. The first of them was shown to Argentina's Manuel Contepomi (for an illegal tackle on the Wallabies' Mat Rogers) in the Pumas' match against Australia at Sydney on 10 October 2003.

MOST YELLOW CARDS

The record for the most yellow cards received by a player in Rugby World Cup matches is three, a fate suffered by Italy's Fabio Ongaro. The hooker was sent to the sin-bin twice during the 2007 tournament and once more in 2011.

LEFT: Argentina's Manuel Contepomi made history against Australia in 2003 when he became the first player in the Rugby World Cup to receive a yellow card.

RICHARDS GETS THE RUGBY WORLD CUP'S FIRST RED CARD

Wales's Huw Richards infamously became the first player to be given his marching orders in a Rugby World Cup match as a result of throwing a punch at New Zealand's Guy Whetton in the 1987 semi-final. In the subsequent melee, the All Blacks' Buck Shelford flattened Richards, but only the Welshman, after he had recovered his senses, was shown the red card. There have been a further 15 instances of a player being shown a red card in the Rugby World Cup.

LEFT: Wales's Huw Richards holds the unfortunate distinction of being the first player in the Rugby World Cup to be sent off.

BELOW: Jonathan Kaplan is the Rugby World Cup's most experienced referee, having taken charge of 13 matches.

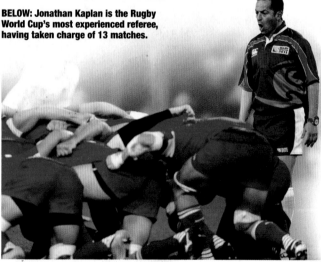

RUGBY WORLD CUP FINAL REFEREES

Year	Name (country)
1987	Kerry Fitzgerald (Australia)
1991	Derek Bevan (Wales)
1995	Ed Morrison (England)
1999	Andre Watson (South Africa)
2003	Andre Watson (South Africa)
2007	Alain Rolland (Ireland)
2011	Craig Joubert (South Africa)
2015	Nigel Owens (Wales)

MOST MATCHES AS REFEREE

Jonathan Kaplan has refereed more matches than any other official in Rugby World Cup history. The South African took charge of 13 matches between 1999 and 2011.

MOST YELLOW CARDS FOR A TEAM THAT HAS GONE ON TO WIN THE MATCH

The most yellow cards received by a team that has gone on to win a Rugby World Cup match is two, and it has happened seven times: to Wales (Colin Charvis and Sonny Parker), during their 41–10 victory over Canada in 2003; Australia (Drew Mitchell and Nathan Sharpe), during their 32–20 triumph against Wales in 2007; South Africa (Bryan Habana and Francois Steyn), in their 30–25 win against Tonga in 2007; Argentina (Rimas Alvarez Kairelis and Juan Manuel Leguizamon), during their 34–10 third-place play-off win over France in 2007; Tonga (Halani Aulika and Lua Lokotui) in their 31–18 defeat of Japan at Whangarei in 2011; New Zealand (Richie McCaw and Conrad Smith) in their 26–16 victory over Argentina in 2015; and Australia (Dean Mumm and Will Genia) in their 15–6 victory over Wales in 2015.

ONLY MAN TO REFEREE TWO RUGBY WORLD CUP FINALS

An engineer by trade who left his profession to become a full-time referee, South Africa's Andre Watson went on to become the most capped referee of all time (taking charge of 27 internationals) and is the only man in history to have officiated at two Rugby World Cup finals: in 1999 (Australia against France at Cardiff) and in 2003 (England against Australia in Sydney).

THE FAMOUS WHISTLE

The opening game of every Rugby World Cup has been started by a shrill blast from the same whistle. The chosen whistle is more than a century old and was used for the first time by referee Gil Evans in the international between New Zealand and England at Dunedin in December 1905 (the All Blacks won 15–0). A true piece of rugby history, the whistle was also used, it is believed, during the 1924 Olympic final (when the USA beat hosts France 17–13) and in January 1925 for England's match against New Zealand at Twickenham (during which England's Cyril Brownlie became the first person in international rugby history to be sent off).

BELOW: South Africa's Andre Watson is the only official in history to referee two Rugby World Cup finals – in 1999 and 2003.

RIGHT: The fiery match between South Africa and Canada at Port Elizabeth in 1995 culminated in three players being sent off.

YELLOW CARD FEVER AT EXETER

Namibia had lost their opening two matches at the 2015 Rugby World Cup – against New Zealand (58–14) and Tonga (35–21) – and facing the prospect of another mismatch in their fourth pool match (against Argentina), would have seen their penultimate pool match against Georgia at Exeter on 7 October as their one chance of victory. Perhaps the intensity of the situation got to them, as three of their players received yellow cards (Renaldo Bothma, Aranos Coetzee and Raoul Larson) compared to just one yellow card for Georgia (Jaba Bregvadze). The Africans suffered as a result: Georgia, taking advantage of the extra men, edged to a 17–16 victory. The four yellow cards in the match is a tournament record.

THE BATTLE OF BOET ERASMUS

It was the most inglorious moment of South Africa's fairytale march to glory at the 1995 Rugby World Cup. An ill-disciplined, often brutal, Pool A match between the Springboks and Canada at the Boet Erasmus Stadium in Port Elizabeth degenerated into a mass brawl ten minutes from time. When the dust settled, Canada's Gareth Rees and Rod Snow and South Africa's John Dalton were given their marching orders. It is the only time in history that three players have been shown a red card in a single Rugby World Cup match. For the record, South Africa went on to win 20–0.

ALL BLACK BLOOD IN HIS VEINS

One of the best No.8s the All Blacks have ever produced and one of his country's finest captains, Brian Lochore won 20 caps for New Zealand between 1964 and 1971. He switched to coaching at the end of his playing career and achieved considerable success at club level before being appointed a national selector in 1983 and then coach of the national team in 1985. In 1987, he achieved the finest moment of his career, leading the All Blacks – known as the 'Baby Blacks' at the time – to Rugby World Cup glory. He will be remembered as the first coach in the tournament's history to lay his hands on the game's greatest prize.

ABOVE: A great All Black as a player, Brian Lochore added to his legacy as New Zealand's victorious coach in the inaugural Rugby World Cup in 1987.

ABOVE: Alex Wyllie was coach of the New Zealand in 1991 and led Argentina to the Rugby World Cup quarter-finals eight years later.

FIRST TO COACH TWO TEAMS AT A RUGBY WORLD CUP

A Canterbury legend (he made 210 appearances for the province over 15 years between 1964 and 1979, then became their coach in 1982 and achieved instant success), Alex Wyllie was assistant coach to Brian Lochore as New Zealand won the Rugby World Cup in 1987. He succeeded Lochore as coach of the national team in 1988 and enjoyed enormous success, losing only two games in 23 – both defeats to Australia. With a Rugby World Cup looming, back-to-back defeats to the Wallabies made the New Zealand Rugby Union nervous and they appointed Wyllie's Auckland rival, John Hart, as joint coach for the 1991 tournament. It was an uncomfortable pairing: the All Blacks lost to Australia in the semi-finals and Laurie Mains took over the coaching reins. That was not the last the competition saw of Wyllie, however. In 1999 he became the first person in history to coach two sides at a Rugby World Cup, leading the Pumas to the quarter-finals. Others to have achieved the feat are: Pierre Berbizier (France and Italy), Graham Henry (Wales and New Zealand) and John Kirwan (Italy and Japan).

CAPTAIN FANTASTIC AS WELL AS A FIERY COACH

Daniel Dubroca, a hard-nosed hooker, was appointed France captain for the 1986 Five Nations, led Les Bleus to the final of the 1987 Rugby World Cup and retired as a player the following year. But his nous and passion for the game were not lost to French rugby and in 1990, following the resignation of Jacques Fouroux, he was appointed coach of the national team, leading them at the 1991 Rugby World Cup (and becoming the first person in history to have played in one Rugby World Cup and then coached a team in the next). His final act in a Rugby World Cup match will linger long in the memory: having seen his side crash out to England (19–10) in a brutal clash in Paris in the quarter-finals, he manhandled referee David Bishop in the tunnel shortly after the final whistle and resigned soon afterwards.

RIGHT: Rod Macqueen was coach of Australia during a golden run that started with victory at the 1999 Rugby World Cup.

MACQUEEN LEADS WALLABIES ON GOLDEN RUN

Rod Macqueen was appointed coach of Australia's national team in September 1997 and, although he did not get off to the most blistering of starts (the Wallabies lost 18–16 to Argentina in Buenos Aires in his second match in charge), he would ultimately lead them on one of the greatest runs in their history. It all started at the 1999 Rugby World Cup when he led Australia to their second tournament triumph (thus becoming the first nation to win the cup twice); in 2000 they won the Tri-Nations for the first time in their history; and in 2001 they secured a memorable 2–1 series win over the British Lions.

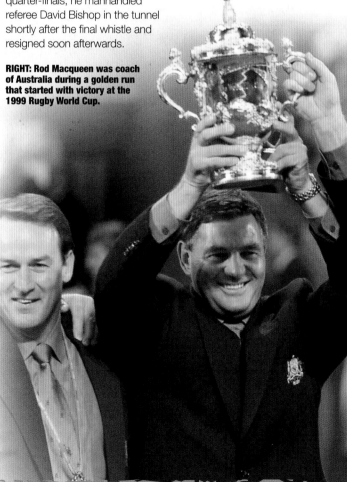

RIGHT: A Rugby World Cup winner as a player with New Zealand in 1987, John Kirwan returned to the tournament as a coach with Italy and Japan.

RUGBY WORLD CUP-WINNING COACHES

Year	Coach (country)
1987	Brian Lochore (New Zealand)
1991	Bob Dwyer (Australia)
1995	Kitch Christie (South Africa)
1999	Rod Macqueen (Australia)
2003	Clive Woodward (England)
2007	Jake White (South Africa))
2011	Graham Henry (New Zealand)
2015	Steve Hansen (New Zealand)

WHITE NURSES WOUNDED SPRINGBOKS BACK TO HEALTH

A former schoolteacher who made a name for himself when he coached South Africa U21 to Rugby World Cup glory in 2002, Jake White was appointed coach of the senior Springbok side in early 2004, at a time when South African rugby was in turmoil: they had endured a disappointing 2003 Rugby World Cup campaign, had slipped to sixth in the world rankings and were having to fend off damaging revelations about their controversial preparations for the tournament. Renowned throughout the game for his technical acumen, White set about revitalizing the Springboks: he led them to Tri-Nations glory in 2004, and by 2007 had assembled a squad capable of challenging for that year's Rugby World Cup. They were the best team in the tournament and beat England 15–6 in the final to regain the world title and claim the no.1 spot in the rankings for the first time. His job done, White duly stepped down.

ALL BLACKS STILL SHINE BRIGHT UNDER HANSEN

Steve Hansen had been assistant coach under Graham Henry when, in 2011, New Zealand finally ended a 24-year wait to lift the Rugby World Cup, and he was the natural choice to succeed Henry as coach when the latter decided to step down from the role following the tournament. But, in many ways, promotion to the job created a no-win situation for Hansen: in the past, New Zealand Rugby World Cup frailty had almost become an accepted part of rugby legend; now they had won the trophy,

the team considered to be best in the world, by some stretch, were expected to win every tournament they entered – and anything other than victory would be seen as a colossal failure. So it is to Hansen's great credit that he took the impossibly team he inherited and moulded them into an even better one. Under his charge, the All Blacks romped to three successive Rugby Championship titles between 2012 and 2014, losing only one of the 18 matches they contested (27–25 to South Africa in Johannesburg on 4 October 2014). They may have lost out to Australia in the curtailed 2015 edition of the competition, but still travelled to the 2015 Rugby World Cup, held three months later, as firm favourites to retain the Webb Ellis Cup. They survived a few scares along the way, notably against South Africa in the semi-finals, but they did just that, producing a scintillating performance against Australia in the final (34–17) to become the Rugby World Cup's first back-to-back champions. Hansen could not have achieved more.

COACHING THE DEFENDING CHAMPIONS

Steve Hansen is the only coach in Rugby World Cup history to have led the defending champions to a successful defence of their trophy. New Zealand, had won the title in 2011 under Graham Henry and won again in 2015. The worst performance is to reach the quarter-finals: first by Bob Dwyer (with Australia in 1995) and then by Peter de Villiers (with South Africa in 2011).

MOST TOURNAMENTS AS COACH

Two coaches hold the record for overseeing the most Rugby World Cup matches as coach: Jim Telfer (for Scotland in 1991, 1995 and 1999); and Bryan Williams (for Samoa, also in 1991, 1995 and 1999).

HENRY ENDS NEW ZEALAND'S RUGBY WORLD CUP HOODOO

New Zealand enjoyed success after appointing Graham Henry as coach in 2004, winning five Tri-Nations titles and spending years at the top of the IRB world rankings, but one entry was missing from the Auckland coach's CV: a Rugby World Cup triumph. When the All Blacks lost sensationally to France in a 2007 quarter-final, the 2011 tournament represented Henry's final chance to secure a permanent place in his country's rugby history. His players responded magnificently, winning all four pool matches, before beating Argentina in the quarter-finals (33–10), Australia in the semi-finals (20–6) and France in the final (8–7) to bring the impatient wait for rugby's most passionate nation to an end.

ABOVE: Graham Henry ended his tenure as coach of the All Blacks with the 2011 Rugby World Cup in his hands.

LEFT: Steve Hansen guided New Zealand to the title in 2015, four years after serving as assistant coach to Graham Henry.

STADIUMS, HOSTS AND ATTENDANCES

JOINT EFFORT RESULTS IN FIRST RUGBY WORLD CUP

The idea of staging a World Cup-style tournament for rugby had first been mooted in the 1950s, but was rejected on the grounds that it would threaten the amateur spirit of the game, and so lay dormant for the next three decades. By the 1980s, however, things were about to change: in the early years of the decade two companies approached the IRB with proposals for a World Cup – both were rejected. In 1983, Gideon Lloyd International and London-based sports promoter Neil Durden-Smith put forward another proposal – again it was rejected. Later that year, the rugby unions of Australia and New Zealand lodged separate bids to stage the tournament – both were rejected, but this time with a caveat: the IRB suggested the two countries pool their resources and come up with a tournament feasibility study. In March 1985, in a hotel in Paris, the results of that study were put to the IRB vote: the outcome was that, in 1987, Australia and New Zealand would co-host rugby's first World Cup.

HIGHEST ATTENDANCES (MATCH): TOP FIVE

Pos	Attendance	Match	Venue	Date
1	89,267	Ireland v Romania	Wembley, London	27 Sep 2015
2	89,019	Argentina v New Zealand	Wembley, London	20 Sep 2015
3	82,957	Australia v England	Telstra Stadium, Sydney	22 Nov 2003
4	82,444	Australia v New Zealand	Telstra Stadium, Sydney	15 Nov 2003
5	82,346	England v France	Telstra Stadium, Sydney	16 Nov 2003

A RUGBY WORLD CUP OF FIRSTS AND LASTS

The 1995 Rugby World Cup in South Africa (which would mark the country's debut appearance in the tournament) was a ground-breaking one: it was the first major sporting event ever to take place on African soil; it was the first time the tournament was staged within the boundaries of one country; and was the last Rugby World Cup of the game's amateur era.

FUTURE HOSTS

On 28 July 2009, the IRB announced that England had beaten off bids from Italy, Japan and South Africa for the right to host the Rugby World Cup in 2015. At the same time, the IRB declared that Japan, who many had expected to be given the tournament in 2011 (rather than New Zealand), would host the 2019 tournament. It will mark the first time that rugby's biggest tournament will have been staged in Asia.

LOWEST-EVER CROWD FOR A RUGBY WORLD CUP FINAL

The least attended Rugby World Cup in history – just 448,318 spectators attended the 32 matches of the 1987 tournament – culminated in the lowest-ever attendance for a Rugby World Cup final: 48,035 spectators gathered at Eden Park, Auckland, on 20 June 1987 to watch New Zealand beat France 29–9 and become the competition's inaugural winners.

BELOW: Total spectator numbers at the 2007 Rugby World Cup in France topped two million for the first time in the tournament's history.

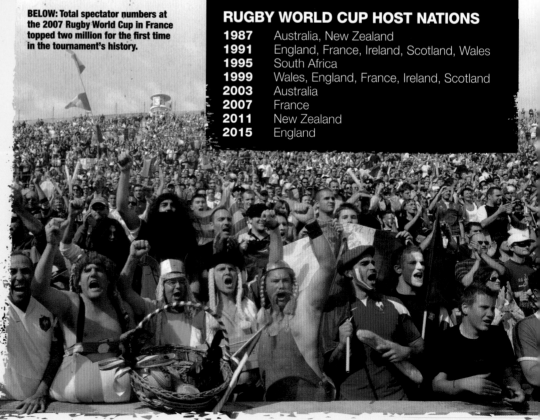

RUGBY WORLD CUP HOST NATIONS

1987	Australia, New Zealand
1991	England, France, Ireland, Scotland, Wales
1995	South Africa
1999	Wales, England, France, Ireland, Scotland
2003	Australia
2007	France
2011	New Zealand
2015	England

RUGGBY WORLD CUP: AVERAGE ATTENDANCES

Year	Match average	Spectators total	Matches total
1987	14,010	448,318	32
1991	33,127	1,060,065	32
1995	29,281	936,990	32
1999	37,965	1,556,572	41
2003	38,263	1,836,607	48
2007	46,786	2,245,731	48
2011	30,711	1,474,126	48
2015	51,621	2,477,805	48

BELOW: Huge crowds turned up at River Plate's stadium in Buenos Aires to watch Argentina's unexpected progress to the semi-finals of the 2007 Rugby World Cup.

CLUB ATLÉTICO RIVER PLATE

EL MAS GRANDE. LEJOS.

BELOW: A crowd of 82,267 flocked to Sydney's Telstra Stadium to watch the 2003 Rugby World Cup final between Australia and England.

INCREASING APPEAL

It didn't take long for the Rugby World Cup to find both its public appeal and its commercial bite: by 1991, the number of spectators reached over one million for the first time (the figure would rise to two million-plus in 2007); by 1999, the tournament had grossed over £70 million; and by 2015, a year when the final attracted an estimated television audience of over 120 million, ticket sales alone generated over £250 million.

CROWDS FLOCK TO WATCH THE RUGBY WORLD CUP SHOW

If any proof were needed to show just how far the Rugby World Cup has grown in stature, look no further than Australia. In 1987, as co-hosts of the inaugural tournament, the country hosted nine matches at two stadiums – the Concord Oval in Sydney (with a capacity of 20,000) and Ballymore Stadium in Brisbane (24,000 capacity) – with an average attendance of just 9,501 spectators per match. Sixteen years later, this time as sole tournament hosts, the country staged 48 matches in 11 state-of-the-art stadiums and attracted an average crowd of 38,263 (a dramatic 402.7 percent increase from 1987) – including the highest-ever attendance for a Rugby World Cup final, when England triumphed 20–17 against Australia at the Telstra Stadium in Sydney on 22 November 2003 in front of 82,957 spectators.

LOWEST ATTENDANCES (MATCH): TOP FIVE

Pos	Attendance	Match	Venue	Date
1	3,000	Tonga v Ireland	Ballymore, Brisbane	3 Jun 1987
=	3,000	USA v Romania	Lansdowne Road, Dublin	9 Oct 1999
=	3,000	Uruguay v South Africa	Hampden Park, Glasgow	15 Oct 1999
4	3,761	Spain v Uruguay	Netherdale, Galashiels	2 Oct 1999
5	4,000	Zimbabwe v France	Eden Park, Auckland	2 June 1987

THE LONG AND THE SHORT OF IT

The longest Rugby World Cup was the 2011 tournament, which covered 44 days (from 9 September to 23 October). The shortest tournament was the first, in 1987. It lasted a mere 29 days (between 22 May and 20 June 1987).

RIGHT: The deserted Hampden Park stands in the background attest to the fact that South Africa's game against Uruguay at the 1999 Rugby World Cup shares the record as the least attended match in the tournament history

A VENUE FOR EVERY STAGE OF THE RUGBY WORLD CUP

Only one stadium in history has hosted a match at every stage of a Rugby World Cup: the Stade de France in Paris (which was built for the FIFA World Cup in 1998) hosted pool matches (in 2007), England's quarter-final against South Africa in 1999, the two semi-finals and the final won by South Africa against England in 2007.

BELOW: Murrayfield in Edinburgh was the first stadium to have been used at three Rugby World Cups (in 1991, 1999 and 2007); Twickenham and the Millennium Stadium have since followed.

MOST SEMI-FINAL MATCHES STAGED

London's Twickenham stadium, the home of rugby, has staged more Rugby World Cup matches than any other venue – four. It staged both last-four matches in 1999 – Australia v South Africa (27–21, after extra-time) and France v New Zealand (43–31); and both semi-finals in the 2015 edition of the tournament – New Zealand v South Africa (20–18) and Australia v Argentina (29–15).

ABOVE: The Stade de France in Paris is the only stadium in Rugby World Cup history to have hosted a match at every stage of one tournament.

MOST MATCHES HOSTED (BY STADIUM): TOP TEN

Pos	Matches	Stadium (Years)
1	20	Twickenham, London (1991, 1999, 2015)
2	19	Millennium Stadium, Cardiff (1999, 2007, 2015)
3	16	Eden Park, Auckland (1987, 2011)
4	13	Murrayfield, Edinburgh (1991, 1999, 2007)
5	9	Lansdowne Road, Dublin (1991, 1999)
=	9	Suncorp Stadium, Brisbane (2003)
7	8	Stade de France, Paris (1999, 2007)
=	8	Westpac Stadium, Wellington (2011)
9	7	Telstra Stadium, Sydney (2003)
=	7	Telstra Dome, Melbourne (2003)

LARGEST STADIUM

Wembley Stadium, the home of football, entered the Rugby World Cup record books on 27 September 2015 when it hosted the Pool D match between Ireland and Romania. A massive 89,267 spectators (a record) flocked in to see the match, which Ireland won 44–10. (A week earlier, a crowd of 89019 at the same venue had seen New Zealand beat Argentina 26–16.)

POPULAR VENUE

A multi-sport stadium in every sense – it is the home of the All Blacks, has hosted a Rugby League World Cup final (in 1988) and has been a Test venue for New Zealand's national cricket team since 1930 – the 61,079-capacity Eden Park in Auckland is a Rugby World Cup record-breaking stadium. It is the only ground in the tournament's history: to have hosted three quarter-finals (France v. Fiji in 1987 and France v. England and New Zealand v. Argentina in 2011), to have been the venue for two Rugby World Cup finals (in 1987 and 2011)

ABOVE: London's Wembley Stadium, the home of football, proved an inspired choice of venue at the 2015 Rugby World Cup, and attracted record-breaking crowds.

MOST STADIUMS USED

The most stadiums used in a single Rugby World Cup tournament is 19, in 1991; the fewest stadiums used in a single tournament is nine, in 1995, when the tournament was staged inside one country (South Africa) for the first time.

SMALLEST STADIUM

Once the venue for a famous victory by the North of England against the mighty All Blacks (21–9 on 17 November 1979), Otley RUFC's rustic ground, Cross Green, in West Yorkshire, England, is the smallest-ever ground to host a Rugby World Cup match. Not that this deterred the fans because, when Italy played the United States in a pool match there at the 1991 Rugby World Cup – a fixture the Azzurri won 30–9, the match was a complete sell-out.

MULTIPLE RUGBY WORLD CUP FINAL HOST STADIUMS

Two stadiums used in Rugby World Cup matches have hosted World Cup finals in different sports. The Stade de France in Paris, hosted the 1998 FIFA World Cup (France 3 Brazil 0) and 2007 Rugby World Cup (South Africa 15 England 6), and Eden Park, Auckland, which hosted the 1987 and 2011 Rugby World Cup finals and 1988 Rugby League World Cup final (Australia 25 New Zealand 12).

BELOW: Eden Park has played host to 16 matches at the Rugby World Cup, in 1987 and 2011.

RUGBY WORLD CUP FINAL VENUES

1987	Eden Park, Auckland
1991	Twickenham, London
1995	Ellis Park, Johannesburg
1999	Millennium Stadium, Cardiff
2003	Telstra Stadium, Sydney
2007	Stade de France, Paris
2011	Eden Park, Auckland
2015	Twickenham, London

MATCHES STAGED BY COUNTY

1	70	New Zealand (1987–2011)
2	58	Australia (1987–2003)
=	58	France (1991–2007)
4	56	England (1991–2015)
5	32	South Africa (1995)
6	28	Wales (1991–2015)
7	15	Scotland (1991–2007)
8	12	Ireland (1991–99)

QUALIFYING TOURNAMENT RECORDS

Regional qualifying tournaments for the Rugby World Cup were staged for the first time for the 1991 tournament and are now not only an integral and much-anticipated part of the sporting calendar for rugby's lower-ranked nations, but also an invaluable means of assisting the game's growth throughout the world. And how it has grown: in 1991, 25 teams battled it out for eight available spots; for the 2015 Rugby World Cup, 102 teams participated in the regional qualifying tournaments.

RIGHT: Will Greenwood in action for England against Italy in a qualifying match for the 1999 Rugby World Cup – the only time England have been forced to qualify.

MOST AVAILABLE QUALIFYING SPOTS

It is the only time in Rugby World Cup history that such a qualifying tournament has been used, but only four teams were granted automatic entry into the 1999 competition, the three top-placed teams from the 1995 event (South Africa, New Zealand and France) and tournament hosts Wales. For the rest, they would have to participate in an elongated – and as it turned out entirely unnecessary – qualification process. As a result, 16 places were up for grabs for the 1999 Rugby World Cup – the most in history. Thankfully, this particular format was abandoned for the 2003 tournament and has not been used since.

GULF IN CLASS

The vast difference between the game's haves and have-nots is not restricted to the Rugby World Cup finals but it is also evident in the regional qualifying tournaments. There have been 16 instances of teams scoring more than 100 points in a match in Rugby World Cup qualifying matches (but only six in the tournament itself). The biggest victory (155–3 – the joint-highest winning margin in international rugby history) recorded by Japan against Chinese Taipei in Tokyo on 7 July 2002.

SPAIN SET ALL-TIME MARK FOR MOST MATCHES AND MOST VICTORIES

Although they have earned entry into the tournament on only one occasion (in 1999, courtesy of a 21–17 victory over Portugal in the final stages of qualifying at Murrayfield on 2 December 1998), Spain have played in and won more Rugby World Cup qualifying matches than any other nation – 30 in 60 matches between 1989 and 2014 (with 27 defeats and one draw).

RIGHT: Romania's Madalin Lemnaru surges through Uruguay's defence in the 21–21 draw in the 2011 Rugby World Cup final repechage round in Montevideo.

OVERALL POINTS FOR AND AGAINST

The all-time Rugby World Cup qualifying record for the fewest points scored in all matches played is 17, set by Pakistan (in four matches between 2008 and 2012). The record for the fewest points conceded by a team in all Rugby World Cup qualifying matches is eight, set by Cyprus in the only qualifying match in 2012.

FINAL REPECHAGE RESULTS (PIC)

Year	Qualifier	Opponent	Home	Away	Aggregate
1999	Tonga	Korea	58–26	82–15	140–41
	Uruguay	Morocco	18–3	18–21	36–24
2003	United States	Spain	58–13	62–13	120–26
	Tonga	Korea	119–0	75–0	194–0
2007	Portugal	Uruguay	12–5	12–18	24–23
	Tonga	Korea	–	–	85–3*
2011	Romania	Uruguay	39–12	21–21	60–33
2015	Uruguay	Russia	36–27	21–22	57–49

* one-off match played in Auckland, New Zealand

Note: repechage matches were first introduced for the 1999 tournament.

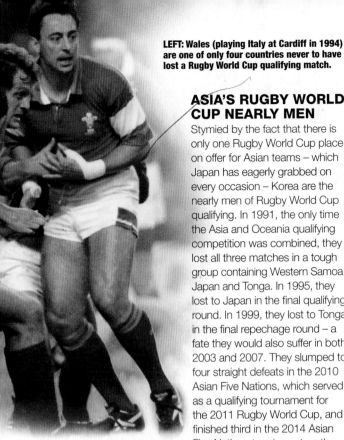

LEFT: Wales (playing Italy at Cardiff in 1994) are one of only four countries never to have lost a Rugby World Cup qualifying match.

ASIA'S RUGBY WORLD CUP NEARLY MEN

Stymied by the fact that there is only one Rugby World Cup place on offer for Asian teams – which Japan has eagerly grabbed on every occasion – Korea are the nearly men of Rugby World Cup qualifying. In 1991, the only time the Asia and Oceania qualifying competition was combined, they lost all three matches in a tough group containing Western Samoa, Japan and Tonga. In 1995, they lost to Japan in the final qualifying round. In 1999, they lost to Tonga in the final repechage round – a fate they would also suffer in both 2003 and 2007. They slumped to four straight defeats in the 2010 Asian Five Nations, which served as a qualifying tournament for the 2011 Rugby World Cup, and finished third in the 2014 Asian Five Nations to miss out on the chance of a repechage match for the 2015 tournament. They hold two unwanted records: they have lost the most matches (27 – shared with Spain) and have conceded more points (1,1,710) than any other team in Rugby World Cup qualifying history.

FEWEST DEFEATS

Four sides have never lost a Rugby World Cup qualifying match: Australia (three matches in 1998); England (two matches in 1998); Ireland (four matches between 1998 and 2002); and Wales (four matches in 1994).

RIGHT: Fernando Diez drives Spain forward during their 21–17 Rugby World Cup qualifying victory over Portugal at Murrayfield in December 1998.

BELOW: Georgia's David Zirakishvili (with ball) in action during his country's 17–9 victory over Spain in a 2011 Rugby World Cup qualifyng match in Tbilisi.

WAITING TO GET OFF THE MARK

The following sides have never won a Rugby World Cup qualifying match: Nigeria (played five, lost five between 2004 and 2012); Pakistan (played four, lost four between 2008 and 2012); St Vincent and Grenadines (played four, lost four between 2005 and 2012); the UAE, played four, lost four in 2013; and Vanuatu (played five, lost five between 2001 and 2009).

FEWEST AVAILABLE QUALIFYING SPOTS

The eight quarter-finalists from the 1991 Rugby World Cup, plus tournament hosts South Africa, all received automatic entry into the 1995 edition of the tournament. Consequently, as this was the last of the 16-team Rugby World Cups (tournament entry was increased to 20 for 1999), it meant that only seven qualifying places were up for grabs – the fewest in history.

RECORD FOR BIGGEST HALF-TIME LEAD

Hong Kong did not take long to show their supremacy over Singapore in the Asian section Rugby World Cup qualification match at Kuala Lumpur on 27 October 1994: they raced into an 83–3 lead by half-time (the biggest interval lead in international rugby history) and went on to win the match 164–13 (the most points ever scored by an international team in a single match).

CHERRY BLOSSOMS ARE THE WORLD CUP QUALIFYING KINGS

Along with Romania, Japan are the only side in history to have qualified for every Rugby World Cup, and they have set records along their trailblazing way: no side in history has scored more points (2,398) or more tries (360 in 35 matches – a staggering 10.29 tries per match) in Rugby World Cup qualifying history.

QUALIFIERS BY YEAR

Year	Qualifiers (Continent)
1987	None – entry to the tournament was by invitation only
1991	Zimbabwe (Africa); Western Samoa, Japan (Asia and Oceania); Italy, Romania (Europe); Argentina, Canada, United States (Americas)
1995	Ivory Coast (Africa); Argentina (Americas); Japan (Asia); Wales, Italy, Romania (Europe); Tonga (Oceania)
1999	Namibia (Africa); Argentina, Canada, United States, Uruguay (Americas); Japan (Asia); England, Ireland, Italy, Romania, Scotland, Spain (Europe); Australia, Fiji, Tonga, Western Samoa (Oceania)
2003	Namibia (Africa); Ireland, Italy, Romania, Georgia (Europe); Japan (Asia); Canada, Uruguay, United States (Americas); Fiji, Samoa, Tonga (Oceania)
2007	Namibia (Africa); Italy, Romania, Portugal, Georgia (Europe); Japan (Asia); Argentina, Canada, United States (Americas); Fiji, Samoa, Tonga (Oceania)
2011	Namibia (Africa); Georgia, Romania, Russia (Europe); Japan (Asia); Canada, United States (Americas); Samoa (Oceania)
2015	Namibia (Africa); Georgia, Romania (Europe); Japan (Asia); Canada, United States, Uruguay (Americas); Fiji (Oceania)

MOST CONVERSIONS (IN A WORLD CUP QUALIFYING MATCH)

The record for the most conversions in a Rugby World Cup qualifying match is 17, held by two players: J. McKee, for Hong Kong against Singapore at Kuala Lumpur on 27 October 1994; and Pierre Hola, for Tonga against Korea at Nuku A'lofa on 22 March 2003.

MOST QUALIFYING ROUND APPEARANCES

Nobody has played in more Rugby World Cup qualifying matches that Spain's Pablo Feijoo Ugalde. The versatile back has appeared in 32 Rugby World Cup qualifiers between 2002 and 2014, and has scored ten tries.

MOST POINTS (INDIVIDUAL): TOP TEN

Pos	Points	Player (Country, Span)
1	212	Merab Kvirikashvili (Georgia, 2009–14)
2	207	Florin Vlaicu (Romania, 2006–14)
3	206	Esteban Roque Segovia (Spain, 2004–06)
4	201	Yurij Kushnarev (Russia, 2006–14)
5	196	Mike Hercus (USA, 2002–09)
6	174	Ayumu Goromaru (Japan, 2009–14)
7	170	Daisuke Ohata (Japan, 1998–2006)
8	154	Pierre Hola (Tonga, 1998–2006)
9	129	Toru Kurihara (Japan, 2002)
=	129	Federico Sciarra (Uruguay, 1993–99)

BELOW: International rugby's all-time leading try-scorer, Daisuke Ohata has prospered in Rugby World Cup qualifying matches, scoring a record 34 for Japan.

ABOVE: Toru Kurihara was the star of the show for Japan during the Cherry Blossoms' 120–3 2003 Rugby World Cup qualifying victory over Chinese Taipei, scoring an individual record 60 points in the match.

LETHAL FINISHER

Those who question the real value of Daisuke Ohata's status as the leading try-scorer in international rugby history (with 69 tries) will point to the fact that he played the majority of his games against lesser opponents (of those 69 tries only 14 of them came against teams that have appeared at the Rugby World Cup), but you can only play the cards you are dealt and there is no doubt that Ohata played them exceptionally well, particularly in qualifying matches: he holds the all-time qualifying records for the most tries scored (34) and for the most tries scored in a single qualifying tournament (17 in Japan's successful 2007 Rugby World Cup qualifying campaign).

CLINICAL KURIHARA PROSPERS AGAINST CHINESE TAIPEI

In the space of two weeks in July 2002, Japan played two matches against Chinese Taipei (at home and away) and scored 275 points to Chinese Taipei's six. In the first match, at Tokyo on 7 July, the Cherry Blossoms won 155–3 to record the joint-highest winning margin in international rugby history. The return match (a 120–3 victory at Tainan on 21 July) saw another record-breaking performance: winger, Toru Kurihara, contributed 60 points (six tries and 15 conversions) to his team's cause – an all-time record for a player in a single Rugby World Cup qualifying match.

MOST TRIES (INDIVIDUAL): TOP TEN

Pos	Tries	Player (country, span)
1	34	Daisuke Ohata (Japan, 1998–2006)
2	17	Cesar Sempere Padilla (Spain, 2004–14)
3	16	Hirotoki Onozawa (Japan, 2002–13)
4	14	Ashley Billington (Hong Kong, 1994–98)
=	14	Takashi Kikutani (Japan, 2006–14)
6	11	Yoshikazu Fujita (Japan, 2013–14)
7	10	Pablo Feijoo Ugalde (Spain, 2002–14)
=	10	Yuta Imamura (Japan, 2006–13)
=	10	Toru Kurihara (Japan, 2002)
10	9	*four players*

LEFT: Juan Menchaca of Uruguay celebrates victory his four drop goals helped his country to defeat Chile 34–23 in Montevideo in September 2002.

THE YOUNGEST TRY-SCORER

Robin Bredbury holds the distinction of being the youngest player to score a try in the history of the Rugby World Cup qualifying competition. The young fly-half, making his debut for Hong Kong aged 17 years and 145 days, scored the first of his team's 14 tries in their thumping 93–0 victory over Thailand in Kuala Lumpur on 25 October 1994. He made just five further appearances for his country.

SEGOVIA IS A SERIAL RECORD-BREAKER

It took time for diminutive fly-half Esteban Roque Segovia to get his chance to play for Spain – he was 30 years 188 days old when he made his debut against Hungary in Madrid on 20 November 2004 – but when he was finally handed his opportunity he grabbed it with both hands, particularly in Rugby World Cup qualifying matches. In 14 qualifying matches between 2004 and 2006, he set all-time records for: the most points scored (206); the most penalties (36); the most conversions (45); and the most points in a single qualifying tournament (206 during the qualification campaign for the 2007 Rugby World Cup).

AGE NO BARRIER FOR ORMAECHEA

A legend in Uruguay's rugby history, Diego Ormaechea became the oldest try-scorer in Rugby World Cup qualifying history when, on 3 April 1999, at the tender age of 39 years 195 days, he scored a try during his side's crucial 33–24 first-round repechage victory over Portugal in Lisbon. The veteran No.8 also holds the all-time record for the most appearances as captain in Rugby World Cup qualifying matches, having led Uruguay on 11 occasions between 1993 and 1999.

RECORD FOR MOST TRIES IN A MATCH BY A SINGLE PLAYER

The main beneficiary of Hong Kong's 164–13 demolition of Singapore in the Asian section Rugby World Cup qualifying match at Kuala Lumpur on 27 October 1994 was Ashley Billington. The full-back ran in ten tries during the match – a record in international rugby.

MOST DROP GOALS (OVERALL)

The record for the most drop goals in a single Rugby World Cup qualifying match is four, by Uruguay's Juan Menchaca during his side's 34–23 victory over Chile at Montevideo on 7 September 2002. Menchaca also holds the record for the most drop goals in all Rugby World Cup qualifying matches, with five in 13 matches between 1999 and 2007).

MOST PENALTIES (IN A MATCH)

The record for the most penalties in a Rugby World Cup qualifying match is eight, held by two players: Diego Dominguez, for Italy against Romania at Catania on 1 October 1994; and Roger Warren, for Samoa against Tonga at Apia on 29 May 2004.

RIGHT: Italy's Diego Dominguez (with ball against England in a Rugby World Cup qualifying match at the McAlpine Stadium, Huddersfield in 1994) is one of only two players to have slotted eight penalties in a qualifying match.

PART IV
INTERNATIONAL RUGBY

International rugby denotes any match played between any of the International Rugby Board's (IRB) 95 full member or 19 associate member countries. It all started on 27 March 1871 when Scotland beat England in the first-ever international rugby match played, at Raeburn Place in Edinburgh, and has grown steadily ever since. By the end of the nineteenth century, 130 international matches had been played; by 1950, that number had risen to 725; and, remarkably, by March 2018, more than 9,000 international fixtures had been contested in a variety of competitions.

In Europe, the elite playing nations contest the Six Nations Championship, while those in the second and third tiers take part in the European Nations Cup. The southern hemisphere giants (Argentina, Australia, New Zealand and South Africa) compete in the Rugby Championship on an annual basis. In the Americas, there is the South American Championship; in Africa, the Africa Cup and the CAR Development Trophy; and in Asia and Oceania, teams play in the various divisions of the Asian Rugby Championship and the Oceania Cup. Add to these the numerous continental Rugby World Cup qualifying competitions, the Rugby World Cup itself, as well as tours from representative teams and it does not take long to discover that the modern international fixture list has become a congested one – in 2015 alone, a Rugby World Cup year, over 300 international matches were contested around the globe.

This section deals with the all-time record holders in international rugby, from overall team records (such as the largest victories and the most matches won) to team records (with statistics for the leading try-scorers, points-scorers and appearance records), and includes records from the major annual competitions in both the northern and southern hemispheres – the Six Nations Championship (which has been contested in its many guises since 1883) and the Tri-Nations/Rugby Championship (which has been played since 1996).

BELOW: Australia's Israel Folau was international rugby's leading try-scorer in 2017 with 12 tries.

CHANGING POINTS SYSTEMS

The first 18 years of international rugby (covering 118 international matches) were played under a points system whereby a team scoring a try earned the chance to kick at goal, with the winning team being the one that kicked the most goals. The first international match to use a different points system (try = 1 point; conversion = 2; penalty = 2; drop goal = 3; goal from mark = 3) was England against the New Zealand Natives at Blackheath, London, on 16 February 1899 (the last match of the New Zealand Natives' tour – they had played Ireland and Wales in matches using the old points system). England scored five tries and one conversion to win the match 7–0. But that was only an experiment: the following year's Four Nations tournament reverted to the tried-and-tested points system of old, and the 'new' system was implemented only in 1890. Remarkably, it wasn't until 1971 that a try became the most rewarded source of points – and the modern points system (try = 5 points; penalty = 3; drop goal = 3; conversion = 2) was introduced for the first time in 1992.

ABOVE: Agony for Greig Laidlaw as Scotland suffer an agonizing one-point to Australia in the quarter-finals of the 2015 Rugby World Cup.

FEWEST MATCHES PLAYED BY A TEAM

Five countries have played only one international rugby match: Honduras (lost 7–25 against Guatemala in 2015); Macau (won 46–7 against Cambodia in 2005); Saudi Arabia (lost 13–43 v Jordan in 2016); Tokelau (lost 15–28 v Papua New Guinea in 1983); and the US Virgin Islands (lost 6–7 to the British Virgin Islands in 2013).

RIGHT: The sweet taste of victory as France celebrate grand-slam glory. Les Bleus have have played more matches (755) than any other team in international rugby history.

ENGLAND HAVE AN EYE FOR A DRAW

England have drawn more matches than any other team in international history. The first of their record-breaking 50 draws (in 697 matches) came against Scotland on 3 March 1873 (0–0); their most recent stalemate was against South Africa (14–14 at Port Elizabeth on 23 June 2012).

MIXED FORTUNES FOR THE MEN IN BLUE

They may now be fifth in the world rankings and considered among the strongest teams on the global rugby stage, but success in the international arena did not always come easily to Scotland. As their fortunes have risen and fallen over the years, they have lost 356 (out of 685) matches – an all-time record in international rugby.

MOST MATCHES AND MOST WINS

France hold the distinction of having played more international matches than any other rugby-playing nation. *Les Bleus* opened their international rugby account on 1 January 1906 (with a 38–6 defeat to New Zealand) and have gone on to play 755 matches. New Zealand hold the record for the most wins in international rugby (437).

LEFT: More success for New Zealand in 2010 as they celebrated their tenth Tri Nations championship – the All Blacks' all-time winning percentage in international rugby stands at an impressive 78.97.

LEOPARDS, LIONS AND OTHERS

A combined South America side played in eight internationals against South Africa between 1980 and 1984, winning one of the matches and losing seven. The African Leopards (a representative side made up of players from CAR development countries), played one match (for which they received international caps) against a South Africa Students XV in Johannesburg on 23 July 2005 and lost 30–15. Other representative sides to have played international rugby (featured elsewhere in the book) are the British Lions and the Pacific Islanders.

ESTABLISHING THE GAME'S GOVERNING BODY (WORLD RUGBY)

It was not long before the other Home Nations countries – Ireland, Scotland and Wales – began to challenge England's self-proclaimed role (as founders of the game) as rugby's rule-makers, and the situation came to a head in 1885. A year earlier, Scotland had questioned the legitimacy of a match-winning England try, only to be told, in no uncertain terms, that those were the rules. Understandably unhappy, the Scots refused to honour their 1886 Home Nations Championship match against England and, the following year, along with Ireland and Wales, formed the International Rugby Football Board (the IRFB) – a body tasked with governing the game and its rules. England, unwilling to relinquish their control over the game, refused to take part; the IRFB forbade its members to play against England until they joined; and the stand-off continued until 1890, when England became the IRFB's fourth member nation. A few angry words had been exchanged along the way, but the game's global governing body was born – and, by 2017, now known as World Rugby, it had 102 full members, 17 associate members and six regional associations.

HARD TO BEAT

Of all teams in international rugby to have played 50 matches or more, New Zealand have the highest winning percentage. The All Blacks have won 437 of 577 matches played – 78.97 per cent – between 1903 and 2017. There are, however, two countries with a 100 per cent record: Gibraltar and Macau. Gibraltar have won all four of the matches they have played, while Macau's record reads played one, one won.

FIRST MATCH IN THE SOUTHERN HEMISPHERE

Twenty long years passed between the first-ever international rugby match – Scotland's victory over England at Raeburn Place, Edinburgh, on 27 March 1871 – and the first international match to be played in the southern hemisphere. On 30 July 1891, a touring team from Great Britain beat South Africa 4–0.

RIGHT: Argentina's legendary fly-half Hugo Porta not only played for South America in a series of matches against South Africa, but also for the South African Barbarians when they played two matches against the touring British Lions in South Africa in 1980.

LOWEST WINNING PERCENTAGE

Winning rugby matches has not come easily to Azerbaijan: in 20 matches played since 2005, they have won only one of them. Their winning percentage of 5.00 is the lowest of any country to have played 20 internationals or more.

SIDES STILL AWAITING FIRST INTERNATIONAL VICTORY

Country (Span)	Matches
Guadeloupe (1977–2018)	4
Belarus (2014–16)	3
Libya (2010)	2
Honduras (2015)	2
Saudi Arabia (2016)	1
Tokelau (1983)	1
US Virgin Islands (2013)	1

ALL BLACKS PROVIDE TRUE MEASURE OF GREATNESS

New Zealand made a blistering entrance on to the international rugby scene, losing only once in their first 15 matches between 1903 and 1910 and, notwithstanding their many Rugby World Cup disappointments prior to 2011, have remained the standard against which other teams have been judged ever since. The All Blacks hold the all-time records for: the most points scored (15,425 in 577 matches between 1903 and 2018 – an average of 26.7 points per match); best points difference (+7,971 – the next best is Argentina with +3,840); most tries (2,010); most conversions (1,327); most matches won at an away venue (180 in 261 matches between 1906 and 2017); and best winning percentage in away matches of all teams to have played 20 internationals or more (72.28).

BELOW: New Zealand captain Richie McCaw with the Tri-Nations trophy and the Bledisloe Cup in 2007. The All Blacks have scored more points (15,425) than any other country in international history.

ABOVE: New Zealand enjoyed their biggest ever victory over South Africa, 57–0, at North Shore City in the 2017 Rugby Championship. Nehe Milner-Scudder, scoring one his two tries, has been on the winning side in 10 of his 11 Tests for the All Blacks.

STEADFAST SLOVENIA HOLD AN UNLIKELY ALL-TIME RECORD

Slovenia may be relative newcomers to the international rugby scene (they did not play their first international match until 1992 – a 21–19 victory over Austria) and are currently locked in the third tier of European rugby, but they hold a unique record: they have conceded the fewest points (2,001 in 101 matches) of any country to have played in 100 internationals or more.

ALL BLACKS ENJOY HOME COMFORTS

New Zealand are a formidable force wherever you happen to play them, but the All Blacks are all but impossible to beat on home soil (their last home defeat was to South Africa way back in 2009). Overall, they have won 226 of 279 home matches played between 1909 and 2017 and their win percentage, 84.68, is the highest of any country to have played 20 or more home international matches.

NEW BOYS ON THE RUGBY BLOCK

Qatar played their first international as recently as May 2011 (recording a 26–8 victory over Jordan), and have gone on to win ten of the 12 games they have played, losing only to Malaysia (31–22 in Doha on 23 May 2014). Of all the countries to have played ten internationals or more, the men from the Gulf have the best winning percentage (83.33 per cent).

UNWANTED RECORD FOR ITALY

They may now form part of Europe's elite rugby-playing nations, but life among rugby's big boys has come at a considerable price for Italy. They have won only 12 of 95 matches in the tournament and have suffered some thumping defeats along the way: 12 of them by 40 points or more. As a result, their points difference has plummeted to -2,764 – the worst of any international team on the world rugby circuit.

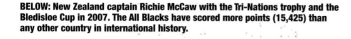

RUGBY GLORY EVADES LIBYA

Libya may be famous for many things – Leptis Magna (a notable Mediterranean archaeological sight), the splendours of Jebel Acacus in the Sahara Desert and the headline-grabbing part it played in the Arab Spring Uprising (which culminated in the downfall of its long-time leader Colonel Gadaffi) – but the country has still to prove its prowess on the rugby field. Their national team has played only two matches and lost them both: 50–0 against Algeria on 26 September 2010 and 10–5 against Mauritania three days later. Their haul of only five points scored is the fewest by any side in international rugby history.

THE KUALA LUMPUR TRY-FEST

If tries were the order of the day, there would have been no better place to be than at Hong Kong's Rugby World Cup qualifying match against Singapore in Kuala Lumpur on 27 October 1994. Hong Kong ran in a remarkable 26 tries – one every three minutes – during their thumping 164–13 victory. Their performance set new records for the most tries and the most points scored by a team in an international match.

A LONG LIST OF RECORDS FOR *LES BLEUS...*

As a consequence of having played more international matches than any other nation (755, as opposed to the All Blacks' 577), France hold numerous all-time records in international rugby. *Les Bleus* have kicked the most penalty goals (1,256) and drop goals (223), but they have also conceded more points than any other team in history (11,344) and, along with Wales (10,702), Italy (11,119) and Australia (10,790) are the only team in international rugby history to have conceded more than 10,000 points.

FAILING TO BREAK THE DEADLOCK

There have been 21 0–0 draws in international rugby, the most recent of which came between Togo and Nigeria on 3 July 2004.

RIGHT: Thomas Castaignede (10) celebrates his match-winning drop-goal against in England in 1998.

BELOW: Full-back Percy Montgomery scored 15 points for South Africa in their 134–3 demolition of Uruguay.

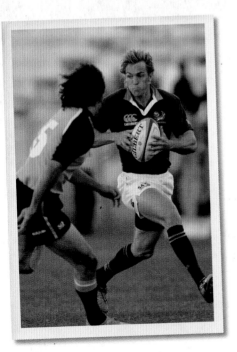

BIGGEST VICTORIES: TOP TEN

Pos	Winner	Score	Opponent	Venue	Date
1	Argentina	152–0	Paraguay	Mendoza	1 May 2002
=	Japan	155–3	Chinese Taipei	Tokyo	7 Jul 2002
3	Hong Kong	164–13	Singapore	Kuala Lumpur	27 Oct 1994
4	Argentina	144–0	Paraguay	Montevideo	27 Apr 2003
5	Australia	142–0	Namibia	Adelaide	25 Oct 2003
6	Argentina	147–7	Venezuela	Santiago	1 May 2004
7	England	134–0	Romania	Twickenham	17 Nov 2001
=	Mauritius	134–0	Swaziland	Gaberone	21 Jan 2014
9	Japan	134–6	Chinese Taipei	Singapore	27 Oct 1998
10	Korea	135–3	Malaysia	Hong Kong	20 Sep 1992

FIRST TRY IN INTERNATIONAL RUGBY HISTORY

Scotland's Angus Buchanan holds the distinction of scoring the first-ever try in international rugby. The Inverary-born forward touched down for a push-over try against England at Edinburgh on 18 March 1871, a try that William Cross converted to hand Scotland the first victory in international rugby history.

FEW AWAY-DAY BLUES FOR CAMPESE

Given his consistently incisive try-scoring performances over the years against the world's top rugby-playing nations, Australia's David Campese is viewed by many as the deadliest finisher ever to have played the international game. He made a typically bullish try-scoring debut against New Zealand in Christchurch on 14 August 1982 and continued to bewitch opposition defences for the next 14 years. He appeared in three Rugby World Cups, notably as a key member of the Wallabies' triumphant squad in 1991, and bowed out of international rugby in December 1996 having scored a then record 64 tries – a total since passed by Japan's Daisuke Ohata. Campese does, however, still have one all-time record to his name: he has scored more tries in away matches than any other player – 24 in 39 matches between 1982 and 1996.

RIGHT: Australian winger David Campese scored more tries in away matches (24) than any other player in international rugby history.

MOST TRIES BY A PLAYER IN A LOSING CAUSE

The record for the most tries in a match by a player whose team has gone on to lose is three, a feat achieved by 13 players: Robert Montgomery (Ireland v Wales on 12 March 1887); Howard Marshall (England v Wales on 7 January 1893); Roland Raymond (Australia v New Zealand Maori on 24 June 1922); Sevaro Walisoliso (Fiji v Wales on 26 September 1964); Vilikesa Mocelutu (Fiji v New Zealand Maori on 31 August 1974); Yuji Matsuo (Japan v England on 20 May 1979); Ray Mordt (South Africa v New Zealand on 12 September 1981); Emile Ntamack (France v Wales on 6 March 1999); Josh Taumalolo (Tonga v Georgia on 28 March 1999); Goncalo Malheiro (Portugal v Barbarians on 10 June 2004); Blaine Scully (USA v Japan, 14 June 2014; Kehoma Brenner (Germany v Russia, 14 February 2015); and Tomas Vergara (Chile v Korea, 19 November 2016).

BILLINGTON'S DAY

The stand-out performer during Hong Kong's 26-try, 164–13 demolition of Singapore at Kuala Lumpur on 27 October 1994 was Ashley Billington. The full-back ran in ten of his team's tries during the game – a record for a player in a single international match.

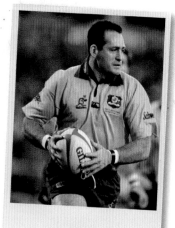

JAPAN'S TRY-SCORING GEM

Although he established a glowing reputation in the World Sevens Series as a player with both enormous natural ability and searing pace, few would have expected Daisuke Ohata to evolve into the most prolific try-scorer international rugby has ever seen. He made his debut for Japan against Korea on 9 November 1996, scoring a hat-trick of tries, and went on to become a constant presence in the Cherry Blossoms' line-up from that moment on. He appeared at the 1999 Rugby World Cup and caught the eye with a blistering try against Wales. On 7 July 2002, he scored a sensational eight tries during Japan's world-record-equalling 155–3 demolition of Chinese Taipei in Tokyo and ended the calendar year with 17 tries to his name (a record equalled by New Zealand's Joe Rokocoko in 2003). He made his second Rugby World Cup appearance in 2003, scoring against France and the USA. On 14 May 2006, he scored his 65th try (his second of three in the Cherry Blossoms' 32–7 victory over Georgia in Osaka) to break David Campese's all-time record for the most tries in international rugby. He made the last of his

ABOVE: Daisuke Ohata is the most prolific try-scorer in international rugby history with 69 tries in 58 appearances for Japan.

58 appearances for Japan in November 2006 and bowed out of the international game having scored 69 tries. He also holds the all-time records for: the most tries by a player in home matches (44) and shares the most tries by a player at a single ground (28, at Chichibunomiya in Tokyo) with Shane Williiams of Wales (at Cardiff's Millennium Stadium).

MOST TRIES: TOP TEN

Pos	Tries	Player (Country, span)
1	69	Daisuke Ohata (Japan, 1996–2006)
2	67	Bryan Habana (South Africa, 2004–16)
3	64	David Campese (Australia, 1982–96)
4	60	Shane Williams (Lions/Wales, 2000–11)
5	55	Hirotoki Onozawa (Japan, 2001–13)
6	50	Rory Underwood (Lions/England, 1984–96)
7	49	Doug Howlett (New Zealand, 2000–07)
=	47	Brian O'Driscoll (Lions/Ireland, 1999–2013)
9	46	Christian Cullen (New Zealand, 1996–2002)
=	46	Joe Rokocoko (New Zealand, 2003–10)
=	46	Julian Savea (New Zealand, 2012–17)

ABOVE: Former Uruguay captain Diego Ormaechea is the oldest-ever try-scorer in international rugby history.

MOST TRIES IN A CALENDAR YEAR: RECORD PROGRESSION (MORE THAN TWO TRIES)

Tries	Player (Country)	Year
17	Daisuke Ohata (Japan)	2002
17	Joe Rokocoko (New Zealand)	2003
14	Uriel O'Farrell (Argentina)	1951
8	Cyril Lowe (England)	1914
7	Reggie Gibbs (Wales)	1908
5	George Lindsay (Scotland)	1887
4	George Burton (England)	1881
4	Henry Taylor (England)	1881
3	Robert MacKenzie (Scotland)	1877

YOUNGEST AND OLDEST TRY-SCORERS

Diminutive 5ft 8in (1.73m) fly-half Robin Bredbury made rugby history on 25 October 1994 when he scored the first of his two tries (and his team's 14 tries) during Hong Kong's emphatic 93–0 victory over Thailand in Kuala Lumpur: aged 17 years 141 days, he had become the youngest try-scorer in international rugby history. The oldest try-scorer is Uruguay's Diego Ormaechea, who was 40 years 13 days old when he scored against Spain at Galashiels during the 1999 Rugby World Cup.

A WEEK TO REMEMBER

Uriel O'Farrell's international career was as brief as it was splendid. Remarkably, the Argentine winger scored 13 tries in two matches in the space of five days: seven during Argentina's 62–0 victory over Uruguay in Buenos Aires on 9 September 1951 and six during the Pumas' 72–0 victory over Brazil in Buenos Aires on 13 September 1951. He played in only one more match for his country – a try-scoring appearance during Argentina's 13–3 victory over Chile on 16 September 1951 – and ended the calendar year having scored 14 tries. It was a record which stood for 51 years (until Japan's Daisuke Ohata scored in 17 tries in 2002). .

MOST TRIES AGAINST A SINGLE OPPONENT

Daisuke Ohata is the most prolific try-scorer in international rugby history, with 69 tries in 58 appearances for Japan, and he particularly enjoyed playing against Korea. He scored 19 tries against them, including four in the Cherry Blossoms' 90–24 victory at Tokyo on 16 June 2002 and a pair of hat-tricks (in Japan's 41–25 victory at Taipei on 9 November 2006 and during their 54–0 win in Hong Kong on 25 November 2006). He only went scoreless against them twice.

CAPTAIN MANS LEADS BY EXAMPLE

Appointed captain of the Namibia national team for their first post-independence international, against Zimbabwe on 24 March 1990 in Windhoek, just 26 days short of his 38th birthday, speedy winger Gerhard Mans gave his all for the Welwitschias in his 25-match Test career (all of them as captain). By the time he lowered the curtain on his international career in August 1994, aged 42 years 127 days, he had scored 27 tries – the most by any captain in international rugby history.

TRYLESS FRANKS SETS ALL-TIME MARK

A mobile, powerful prop forward who made his debut for New Zealand against Italy at Christchurch on 27 June 2009, Owen Franks has been the cornerstone of a consistently impressive All Black pack for the last nine years. In 95 international appearances, however, he has never scored a try – an all-time record in international rugby.

BELOW: An impressive peformer for New Zealand since 2009, Owen Franks has played in 95 internationals without scoring a try.

ALL-TIME LEADING TRY-SCORERS: BY POSITION

Position	Player (Teams, Span)	Tries
Full-back	Christian Cullen (New Zealand, 1996–2002)	41
Winger	Bryan Habana (South Africa, 2004–16)	66
Centre	Brian O'Driscoll (Lions/Ireland, 1999–2014)	47
Fly-half	Dan Carter (New Zealand, 2004–15)	25
Scrum-half	Joost van der Westhuizen (South Africa, 1993–2003)	38
No.8	Diego Ormaechea (Uruguay, 1979–99)	29
Flanker	Richie McCaw (New Zealand, 2001–15)	26
Lock	Pedro Sporleder (Argentina, 1990–2003)	14
Prop	Martin Castrogiovanni (Italy, 2002–16)	12
Hooker	Keith Wood (Lions/Ireland, 1994–2003)	15

POINTS-SCORING RECORDS

THE MAN WITH THE GOLDEN BOOT

Wales's points-gatherer-in-chief for over a decade (between 1991 and 2002), Neil Jenkins divided opinion throughout his career. No one questioned the golden nature of his right boot, but did he have the attacking flair required for a No.10, the rugged defence of a centre or the pace of a full-back?

In short, his ability to garner points made him the first name on the teamsheet, but where to play him? Jenkins simply got on with his game while the debate raged around him and for a while in the late 1990s he was the most prolific scorer in world rugby.

In 1999, he smashed Gavin Hastings' record for the most points in a calendar year (263 to the Scot's 196, set in 1995) and when he retired in 2002, he did so as the only player in history to have scored more than 1,000 international points (1,090). Jonny Wilkinson and Dan Carter have since passed that mark, but Jenkins will go down in rugby history as the game's first true points-scoring machine.

LEFT: Wales's Neil Jenkins was the first player to score 1,000 points in international rugby.

WORLD-RECORD POINTS HAUL FOR KURIHARA

As Japan ran riot against Chinese Taipei in Tainan on 21 July 2002, winning the match by the colossal margin of 120–3, Turu Kurihara helped himself to a place in the record books. The winger contributed 60 points to his team's total (with six tries and 15 conversions) – an all-time record for a player in a single international match.

DEFEAT FOR TEIXEIRA WITH ALL GUNS BLAZING

Thierry Teixeira produced an almighty performance for Portugal against Georgia in Lisbon on 8 February 2000, scoring nine penalties and a drop goal, but the visitors still ended up winning the match 32–30. The fly-half's contribution of 30 points is the most ever by a player in international rugby who has ended up on the losing side.

ENGLAND'S MOST PROLIFIC POINTS-SCORER

English rugby has had no greater hero than Jonny Wilkinson and it was highly appropriate that the mercurial fly-half's magical boot nailed the match-winning points to secure the greatest moment in England's rugby history – victory over Australia in the 2003 Rugby World Cup final. Wilkinson burst on to the international scene in 1998 as an 18-year-old and, as a result of his relentless accuracy with the boot, his eye for a gap with ball in hand and his formidable defence – not to mention an almost obsessive training regimen – soon established himself as England's first-choice No.10. When free from injury – his catalogue of ailments has brought tears to the eyes of every England fan – he has been a consistent source of points and stands second on all-time points-scoring list (1,246 in 97 matches). He does hold the records for the most points at a single ground (650 in 42 matches at Twickenham) and for the most drop goals in a career (36).

MOST PENALTIES IN A MATCH

Four players have kicked nine penalties in a match, but only New Zealand's Andrew Mehrtens has done so twice, against Australia at Auckland on 24 July 1999 and against France at the Stade de France on 11 November 2000. The three other players to achieve the feat on one occasion are: Keiji Hirose (for Japan against Tonga at Tokyo on 8 May 1999); Neil Jenkins (for Wales against France at the Millennium Stadium on 28 August 1999); and Thierry Teixeira (for Portugal against Georgia at Lisbon on 8 February 2000).

BELOW: England's Jonny Wilkinson stands second on international rugby's all-time points-scoring list with 1,246.

MOST POINTS: TOP TEN

Pos	Points	Player (Country, span)
1	1,598	Dan Carter (New Zealand, 2003–15)
2	1,246	Jonny Wilkinson (Lions/England, 1998–2011)
3	1,090	Neil Jenkins (Lions/Wales, 1991–2002)
4	1,083	Ronan O'Gara (Lions/Ireland, 2000–13)
5	1,010	Diego Dominguez (Argentina/Italy, 1989–2003)
6	970	Stephen Jones (Lions/Wales, 1998–2011)
7	967	Andrew Mehrtens (New Zealand, 1995–2004)
8	911	Michael Lynagh (Australia, 1984–95)
9	893	Percy Montgomery (South Africa, 1997–2008)
10	886	Florin Vlaicu (Romania, 2006–18)

ABOVE: Dan Carter overtook Jonny Wilkinson during the 2011 Tri Nations Tournament to become the leading points-scorer in international rugby history and has gone on to amass 1,598 points.

MOST POINTS IN A CALENDAR YEAR: RECORD PROGRESSION (TEN POINTS PLUS)

Points	Player (Country)	Year
263	Neil Jenkins (Wales)	1999
196	Gavin Hastings (Scotland)	1995
181	Neil Jenkins (Wales)	1994
140	Grant Fox (New Zealand)	1987
132	Hugo Porta (Argentina)	1985
113	Eduardo Morgan (Argentina)	1973
89	Guy Camberabero (France)	1967
45	Michel Vannier (France)	1957
43	Lewis Jones (Lions/Wales)	1950
32	Bot Stanley (Australia)	1922
25	Dickie Lloyd (Ireland)	1913
24	Daniel Lambert (England)	1911
23	Reggie Gibbs (Wales)	1908
22	John Gillespie (Scotland)	1901
17	Charlie Adamson (England)	1899
17	Lonnie Spragg (Australia)	1899
16	Fred Byrne (England)	1896
12	Dicky Lockwood (England)	1894

THE KING OF MODERN FLY-HALVES

In recent times, Dan Carter has taken over the mantle from Jonny Wilkinson as the most lethal fly-half in world rugby. Blessed with a searing turn of pace, an ability to read the game in front of him at lightning speed and an unerringly accurate left boot, he is perhaps the main reason why New Zealand remain the team to beat in international rugby. Aided in no small part by Wilkinson's lengthy absences through injury, Carter heads the England fly-half on the all-time points-scoring list (1,598 to 1,246) and also holds the all-time records for: the most conversions (293 in 112 matches), the most penalties (281) and for scoring the most points against a single opponent (366 in 27 matches against Australia between 2003 and 2015).

MAKING AN IMPACT FROM THE BENCH

It was the one bright moment in what was otherwise a fairly ordinary eight-match career spread over six years. On 27 October 1998, Keisuke Sawaki came off the bench for Japan (to win only his second cap) during the Cherry Blossoms' comprehensive 134–6 mauling of Chinese Taipei and scored one try and seven conversions. His haul of 19 points in the match is an all-time record for a replacement in international rugby.

MOST POINTS ON DEBUT

Simon Kulhane had a debut to remember for New Zealand when the All Blacks played Japan at Bloemfontein at the 1995 Rugby World Cup. The fly-half scored 20 conversions and one try in the All Blacks' 145–17 massacre of the Cherry Blossoms – a haul of 45 points (a record on debut for an international player). Kulhane would go on to make five further appearances for his country.

MOST DROP GOALS IN A MATCH

Russia's Konstantin Rachkov may have endured the frustration of a stop-start international career, but the utility back had a day to remember against Spain at Mallorca on 16 February 2003. Winning only his 15th cap, six years after his debut, he posted 27 points during his country's commanding 52–19 victory, including six drop-goals – an all-time record for a player in a single match.

PUMAS POWERED BY CAPTAIN'S BOOT

Considered one of the finest fly-halves in history, Hugo Porta defined the Argentina national rugby team for more than two decades. It was clear the Pumas had unearthed a points-scoring diamond from the moment he made his debut, against Chile, in October 1971. Appointed captain in June 1977, he continued to lead by example, registering 496 points in 46 matches as skipper – an all-time record for a captain in international rugby.

BELOW: Simon Kulhane scored 45 points on his debut for New Zealand, against Japan at the 1995 Rugby World Cup – a record for a player on debut in international rugby.

UNWANTED RECORD FOR PARISSE

Sergio Parisse made his debut for Italy against New Zealand in Hamilton on 8 June 2002. An extraordinarily gifted No.8, he soon established himself as being among the game's pre-eminent players, and has been an ever-present for the Azzurri as they continue to establish themselves among the game's elite. There have been a number of highlights – including Six Nations victories over Scotland and Ireland, and a surprise home victory against South Africa in 2016 – but there have been plenty of lows too: he h as been on the losing side on 100 occasions in the 134 matches he has played – an all-time record in international rugby.

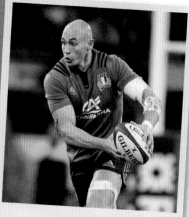

ABOVE: Italy's Sergio Parisse has been on the losing side more times than any other player in international rugby history – 100 times between 2002 and 2018.

ONLY PLAYER TO HAVE PLAYED FOR THREE COUNTRIES

Remarkably, 54 players have played international rugby for two countries, but only one player has represented three countries in international matches. Astonishingly Enrique Edgardo Rodriguez won 13 caps for Argentina between 1979 and 1983 and then went on to win 26 caps for Australia between 1984 and 1987. What's more, in 1981, he also made a one-off appearance for Tahiti in their match against France on 13 July.

THE WORLD'S MOST-CAPPED PLAYER

New Zealand's Richie McCaw will go down in history as one of the game's modern greats. He emerged onto the international scene as a 20-year-old against Ireland in November 2001, showing all the qualities that would come to define his career: effective at ball-carrying, strong in the offload, a powerful defender and an unbelievable asset at the breakdown. He was appointed New Zealand captain on a permanent basis from 2006 and, under his charge, the All Blacks became the No.1 side in world rugby, sweeping all before them – until they came to the Rugby World Cup, that is. Having fallen at the semi-final stage in 2003, they fell in the quarter-finals in 2007 (against France) – Rugby World Cup success was a must if this All Black tem were to be considered great. They had the perfect opportunity to deliver when they hosted the 2011 tournament, and, in McCaw, the perfect man to lead them: they edged France 8–7 in the final to silence the critics. McCaw led them to a successful defence of the crown in 2015 and bowed out of international rugby after the tournament. His tally of 148 caps is an all-time record in international rugby.

BELOW: Two-time Rugby World Cup-winning captain Richie McCaw played a staggering 148 matches for New Zealand between 2001 and 2015.

MOST APPEARANCES: TOP TEN

Pos	Caps	Player (Country, span)
1	148	Richie McCaw (New Zealand, 2001–15)
2	141	Brian O'Driscoll (Lions/Ireland, 1999–2014)
3	139	George Gregan (Australia, 1994-2007)
4	134	Gethin Jenkins (Lions/Wales, 2002–16)
=	134	Sergio Parisse (Italy, 2002–18)
6	132	Keven Mealamu (New Zealand, 2002–15)
7	130	Ronan O'Gara (Lions/Ireland, 2000–13)
8	129	Stephen Moore (Australia, 2005–17)
9	127	Victor Matfield (South Africa, 2001–15)
10	126	Alun-Wyn Jones (Lions/Wales, 2006–18)

MOST APPEARANCES: BY POSITION

Position	Player (Country, Span)	Appearances
Full-back	Mils Muliaina (New Zealand, 2003–11)	84
Winger	Bryan Habana (South Africa, 2004–16)	123
Centre	Brian O'Driscoll (Lions/Ireland, 1999–2014)	141
Fly-half	Ronan O'Gara (Lions/Ireland, 2000–13)	118
Scrum-half	George Gregan (Australia, 1994–2007)	137
No.8	Sergio Parisse (Italy, 2002–18)	127
Flanker	Richie McCaw (New Zealand, 2001–15)	145
Lock	Victor Matfield (South Africa, 2001–15)	127
Prop	Gethin Jenkins (Lions/Wales, 2002–16)	134
Hooker	Keven Mealami (New Zealand, 2002–15)	131

A UNIQUE CASE

Hugh Ferris is a unique case: he played only two matches in international rugby, both of them for different countries – one match for Ireland (against Wales at Swansea on 16 March 1901) and the other for South Africa (against Great Britain at Cape Town on 12 September 1903).

CROSSING THE HOME NATIONS DIVIDE

There is only one instance in history of a player representing two Home Nations countries. As a medical student in Edinburgh, Dr James Marsh played twice for Scotland in 1889. He went on to settle in the Manchester area and played for England against Ireland in 1892.

BELOW: Ireland's Ronan O'Gara played against Italy on 14 occasions between 2000 and 2012 and was on the winning side every time – scoring 180 points in the process.

INTERNATIONAL RUGBY'S YOUNGEST PLAYER

When George Chiriac came on as a replacement for Romania in their match against Belgium in Bucharest on 20 April 1996 (which the home side won 83–5), it marked a moment of rugby history: aged 16 years 141 days, the Bariad-born forward became the youngest player in international rugby history. Not that it was a prelude to greater things: Chiriac had to wait five years before winning his second cap and would go on to make a total of only 19 appearances for his country – the last coming against Namibia at the 2003 Rugby World Cup.

ONE-CAP WONDERS

Of the 18,400 players to have played in international rugby, 4,149 of them only won one cap – a remarkable 22.54 per cent.

JENKINS DRAWS HOME COMFORTS

By the start of the 2015 Rugby World Cup, Gethin Jenkins had overtaken Jason Leonard's long-standing mark (119) as the most-capped prop forward in international rugby history (he now has 134 caps). By 2017, the Welsh stalwart had broken another long-standing record: he has now made 70 appearances at Cardiff's Millennium Stadium – the most appearances at a single ground by any player in international rugby history.

OLDEST DEBUTANT

Although the month of his birth remains uncertain, what is known is that, on 22 January 1923, Frederick Gilbert (born in 1884) made history when he made his debut for England against Wales at Twickenham. At 39 years of age he became, and remains, the oldest-ever debutant in international rugby.

MOST MATCHES AGAINST A SINGLE OPPONENT WITHOUT LOSING

Two players hold the record for playing the most matches against a single opponent without losing – 14. Richie McCaw won all 14 of the matches he played for New Zealand against Ireland between 2001 and 2015, while Ireland's Ronan O'Gara appeared on the winning side in all 14 matches he played against Italy between 2000 and 2012.

ABOVE: The most-capped prop forward in international rugby history, Gethin Jenkins passed Stephen Jones' record for the most appearances at a single ground in 2015 – he has now played 70 times at the Millennium Stadium since 2002.

INTERNATIONAL RUGBY'S OLDEST PLAYER

Kevin Wirachowski made his international debut as a replacement during Canada's 26–13 defeat to England at Wembley on 17 October 1992 and, although he failed to become a regular in the Canucks' line-up, he remained in and around the national squad for the next decade, bowing out of international rugby in record-breaking fashion. When the prop forward from British Columbia came on as a replacement to win his 17th and final cap during Canada's 16–11 defeat to the United States in Vancouver on 18 June 2003, he became, aged 40 years 198 days, the oldest player ever to have made an appearance in an international rugby match.

MOST CONTESTED FIXTURE

There has been no more contested fixture in international rugby history than matches between Australia and New Zealand. The two southern hemisphere giants faced off for the first time in 1903 (New Zealand won the match 22–3) and they have since played a further 162 matches. The two countries compete for the Bledisloe Cup on an annual basis (as part of the Rugby Championship schedule). For the record, New Zealand lead the way with 111 wins to Australia's 43, with seven matches drawn.

YELLOW CARD BITS AND PIECES

A total of 1,870 yellow cards have been issued in international rugby history: the first was shown to Australia's James Holbeck during the Wallabies' clash with South Africa at Pretoria on 23 August 1997, a match the visitors went on to lose 61–22.

A DAMAGING EFFECT

Statistics prove that a team's chances of winning an international rugby match are significantly reduced if one of its players is dismissed: 168 red cards have been issued in international rugby history and on only 56 occasions has a team with a player sent off gone on to win the match – a lowly 33.33 per cent.

ABOVE: Australian centre James Holbeck (with ball) achieved the unfortunate distinction of becoming the first player in international rugby history to receive a yellow card.

MOST RED CARDS (COUNTRY): TOP TEN

Pos	Yellow	Team
1	13	Uruguay
2	12	Fiji
3	11	France
=	11	Italy
=	11	Tonga
6	9	South Africa
7	8	Samoa
=	8	Canada
=	8	Georgia
=	8	United States

MOST YELLOW CARDS IN A MATCH

The record for the most yellow cards issued in a single match is seven, during Uruguay's encounter with Georgia at Montevideo on 30 October 2004: Federico Capo Ortega, Nicolas Brignoni and Ignacio Lussich all spent ten minutes in the sin bin for Uruguay, while Irakli Ninidze, David Zirakashvili, Mamuka Gorgodze and Giorgi Jghenti all received yellow cards for Georgia. Uruguay went on to win the fractious match 17–7.

LEFT: Australia celebrate a rare victory 26–14 victory over New Zealand in Hong Kong on 30 October 2010.

MOST YELLOW CARDS AND GONE ON TO WIN THE MATCH

The record for the most yellow cards received by a team that has gone on to win the match is three, achieved by: Canada against Italy at Rovigo on 11 November 2000 (Canada won 22–17); Uruguay against Georgia at Montevideo on 30 October 2004 (Uruguay won 17–7); Romania against Portugal at Lisbon on 20 March 2010 (Romania won 20–9); Germany against Netherlands at Hanover on 12 November 2011 (Germany won 23–7); Germany against Czech Republic at Prague on 10 March 2012 (Germany won 20–17); Tonga against Scotland at Aberdeen on 24 March 2012 (Tonga won 21–15); Russia against Portugal at Coimbra on 9 March 2013 (Russia won 31–23); Fiji against Japan at Toronto on 29 July 2015 (Fiji won 27–22); Georgia against Uruguay at Tblisi on 13 June 2015 (Georgia won 19–10); USA against Canada at Vancouver on 3 August 2015 (USA won 15–13); and Russia against Germany at Sochi on 13 February 2016 (Russia won 46–20).

ALL BLACK BROWNLIE THE FIRST TO SEE RED

England's match with New Zealand at Twickenham on 3 January 1925 promised to be a titanic struggle. The home side came into the match off back-to-back grand slams, while the visitors were unbeaten since 1921 and were reaching the end of a 32-fixture tour during which they had swept all before them – but nobody expected the fiery clash that ensued. It was a battle from the first whistle, so much so that, after only eight minutes, referee Albert E. French brought the forwards together for the third time and issued a final warning. To little effect: moments later, New Zealand loose-forward Cyril Brownlie stamped on a prostrate England player and was duly ordered from the field, thus becoming the first player in history to be sent off in an international match.

RED CARDS GALORE IN PORT ELIZABETH

It was perhaps the only black mark for South Africa during what was otherwise a glorious march to the Rugby World Cup crown in 1995. Ten minutes from time during the Springboks' final pool match, against Canada at Port Elizabeth on 3 June, what had already been a bruising encounter degenerated into a mass brawl. As a result, South Africa's John Dalton and Canada's Gareth Rees and Rod Snow all received their marching orders. It is the only time in international rugby history that three players have been expelled from the field of play during a single match.

OTHER RED CARD BITS AND PIECES

Although 168 players have been sent off in international rugby over the years, interestingly, none has been sent off more than once in his international career. Uruguay hold the record for having had the most players sent off in international matches, with 13.

BATTLE RAGES AT CARDIFF ARMS PARK

For over 100 years, no player had ever been sent off in a Home Nations Championship match, but that all changed on 15 January 1977 when Wales played Ireland at Cardiff Arms Park. Thirty-eight minutes had passed in an unexpectedly tight contest (the score was locked at 6–6) and Ireland were getting the better of the forward confrontations. And then it all kicked off: when another Welsh line-out was disrupted, Wales prop Geoff Wheel vented his frustration on Ireland's Stuart McKinney; Ireland's Willie Duggan reacted by taking a swing at Welsh lock Alan Martin and a mêlée ensued. When the dust settled, Scottish referee Norman Sanson showed red cards to both Wheel and Duggan – it was the first time in history that two players had been sent off in a single international.

ABOVE: Cyril Brownlie (third row, fourth player from left) was the first player ever to be sent off. The All Black stamped on an England forward and referee Albert E. French – having warned both sets of players three times in the first ten minutes of the match – issued the ultimate sanction on the All Blacks loose-forward.

INSPIRATIONAL McCAW

In years to come, when people look back at the early years of the 21st century, there is little doubt they will regard Richie McCaw as one of the standout players of his generation – if not the standout player. For not only has the legendary All Black helped transform the role of breakaway forward – as the general of the breakdown (winning the ball and slowing down an opponent) – he has also proved an inspirational leader for his country. He captained the All Blacks for the first time during a 26–25 victory over Wales at the Millennium Stadium on 20 November 2004 (in the absence of regular captain Reuben Thorne). The full-time captaincy came his way in 2006 and he ended his first season at the helm hoisting the Tri-Nations trophy. But it was the 2007 Rugby World Cup, the greatest prize in the game (and one which had, mysteriously, eluded the All Blacks since 1987), that McCaw and his team-mates really had their eyes on. They lost 20–18 to an inspired France in the quarter-finals. It was the All Blacks worst-ever showing in the tournament to date. But still the All Blacks, with McCaw still very much in charge, remained the team to beat: they enjoyed further Tri-Nations success in 2008 and 2010 and entered the 2011 Rugby World Cup, this time on home soil, as firm favourites. This time they did not disappoint, beating France 8–7 in the final to confirm their status as the world's best. The good times have not stopped there: they won the renamed Rugby Championship in 2012, 2013 and 2014 and 2015 and defended their Rugby World Cup crown in 2015, after which McCaw retired having led the All Blacks to a record 97 wins in 110 matches.

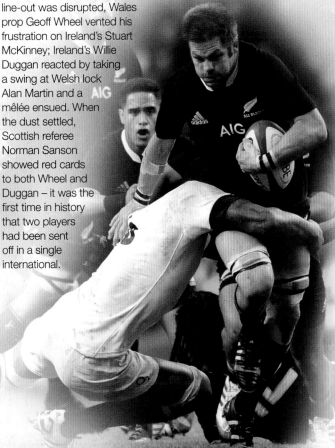

LEFT: The stand-out player of his generation, Richie McCaw has captained New Zealand in 110 matches, winnning 97 of them.

SIX NATIONS CHAMPIONSHIP

The oldest competition in world rugby, it all started in 1893 when the four Home Union countries (England, Ireland, Scotland and Wales) contested the first of what would become the annual Home Nations Championship. It became the Five Nations Championship in 1910 with the inclusion of France and, bar a period of 15 years when France were excluded from the competition (amid rumours of professionalism in the French game), remained that way until 2000, when Italy joined the party and the competition was renamed the Six Nations Championship.

BELOW: Ireland celebrate their Six Nations grand slam triumph in 2018.

TEAM RECORDS

ENGLAND WIN INAUGURAL CHAMPIONSHIP

The first-ever Home Nations Championship – contested between December 1882 and March 1883 – was played under the game's old points system, with matches decided by goals: a goal was awarded for a successful conversion after a try, from a drop goal or from a goal from mark. If the scores were level at the end of play, any unconverted tries were counted to produce a winner; if the scores were still level at that point, the match was declared a draw. The 1882–83 championship came down to a final-match, winner-takes-all showdown between Scotland (who had beaten Wales 3–1 and Ireland 1–0) and England (2–0 winners against Wales and 1–0 conquerors of Ireland) in Edinburgh on 3 March 1883. After the match ended in a 0–0 draw, England won on count-back by two tries to one to become the competition's first winners.

RIGHT: England celebrate a grand-slam-winning 2003 Six Nations Championship campaign. Eight months later they would go on to lift the Rugby World Cup.

OVERALL RECORD

Country (Span)	Home Nations		Five Nations		Six Nations	Overall		Grand Slam	Triple Crowns
Wales (1883–)	7	(4)	15	(8)	4	26	(12)	11	20
England (1883–)	5	(5)	17	(6)	6	28	(11)	13	25
France (1910–31, 1947–)	–		12	(8)	5	17	(8)	9	–
Scotland (1883–)	9	(2)	5	(6)	0	14	(8)	3	10
Ireland (1883–)	4	(3)	6	(5)	4	13	(8)	3	11
Italy (2000–)	–		–		0	0	(0)	0	–

Note: outright wins (shared wins)

FIVE NATIONS CHAMPIONSHIP (1910–31, 1947–99)

The expanded Five Nations Championship (following the inclusion of France) was contested 71 times between 1910 and 1999, with England and Wales leading the way with 23 tournament victories (England with 17 outright wins and six shared titles; Wales with 15 outright wins and eight shared), followed by France (with 20 wins, 12 outright and eight shared) and Ireland and Scotland (11 wins each – Ireland with six outright and five shared titles, and Scotland with five outright wins and six shared titles).

RIGHT: Captain Brian O'Driscoll lifts the 2009 Six Nations Championship trophy after Ireland recorded their first grand slam for 61 years.

HOME NATIONS CHAMPIONSHIP (1883–1909, 1932–39)

The Home Nations Championship was contested 22 times between 1883 and 1909 – with five competitions left uncompleted (in 1885, 1888, 1889, 1897 and 1898). Scotland led the way with eight victories (six outright and two shared), followed by Wales (seven wins – six outright, one shared), England (five wins – three outright, two shared) and Ireland (four wins – three outright, one shared). The competition reverted to the Home Nations Championship between 1932 and 1939, after France were excluded. In this era England won four Home Nations titles (two outright, two shared), Ireland and Wales three each (both one outright, two shared) and Scotland two (both outright).

SIX NATIONS WINNERS

2000	England
2001	England
2002	France (grand slam)
2003	England (grand slam)
2004	France (grand slam)
2005	Wales (grand slam)
2006	France
2007	France
2008	Wales (grand slam)
2009	Ireland (grand slam)
2010	France (grand slam)
2011	England
2012	Wales (grand slam)
2013	Wales
2014	Ireland
2015	Ireland
2016	England (grand slam)
2017	England
2018	Ireland (grand slam)

CHAMPIONS 2003 The Royal Bank of Scotland

RBS

6 NATIONS

CHAMPION The Roy l of Scotla d

CONSECUTIVE GRAND SLAMS AND TRIPLE CROWNS

The record for the most consecutive grand slams is two, held by England (who have achieved the feat three times, in seasons 1913–14, 1923–24 and 1991–92) and France (in 1997–98). Diehard Wales fans also lay claim to the feat, stating that back-to-back triple crowns in the 1908 and 1909 Home Nations Championship, coupled with a pair of victories over France in the same years, equate to a grand slam. France, however, did not join the championship until 1910, so the Welsh claim is merely unofficial. Two teams have won four consecutive triple crowns: Wales (between 1976 and 1979) and England (between 1995 and 1998).

HEAD-TO-HEADS: WINS/DEFEATS/DRAWS

	England	France	Ireland	Italy	Scotland	Wales
England	x	48/34/7	66/49/7	19/0/0	69/39/13	56/54/12
France	34/48/7	x	51/31/7	17/2/0	50/36/2	39/47/3
Ireland	49/66/7	31/51/7	x	18/1/0	59/60/5	48/64/7
Italy	0/19/0	2/17/0	1/18/0	x	7/12/0	2/16/1
Scotland	39/69/13	36/50/2	60/59/5	12/7/0	x	49/70/3
Wales	54/56/12	47/39/3	64/48/7	16/2/1	70/49/3	x

1973: A UNIQUE CHAMPIONSHIP

Shared championships were a common feature of the Home Nations and Five Nations tournaments – there were 19 of them – until 1994, when points difference was used for the first time to break ties between teams, but on only one occasion did all five teams share the spoils. In 1973, England, France, Ireland, Scotland and Wales all finished with a record of won two, lost two to finish locked on four points apiece.

TEMPORARY FIVE NATIONS *AU REVOIR* FOR LES BLEUS

Sporadic wins over Ireland and Scotland apart, it took time for France to find their stride in the Five Nations after they had been admitted to the fold in 1910: they had to wait until 1927 to record their first victory over England and until the following year before they did the same to Wales. But just when it seemed as though French rugby was on the up, rumours of professionalism in the French domestic game started to emerge and, as a result, in 1932 France were banished from the competition – the only team ever to suffer such a fate. Les Bleus were reinstated to the fold in 1947 and have been part of the championship ever since. They won their first title outright in 1959.

THE AZZURRI ENTER THE FRAY

By the mid-1990s, Italy had developed a squad of players that swept all before them in European rugby's second tier and were starting to string together some impressive performances against the world's elite rugby-playing nations, including home-and-away victories over Ireland in 1995 and 1997. It was only right, therefore, that the Azzurri should be given the chance to test their mettle on a regular basis against Europe's elite and, in 2000, they were invited to join an expanded Six Nations Championship. They have found life much tougher on the bigger stage, winning only 12 of 85 matches. Italy have won two matches in a season twice (2007 and 2013) and their best finish was fourth (also in 2013).

ABOVE: Wales did not lose to England, Scotland or Ireland between 1976 and 1979, and they beat England 27–3 in this 1979 encounter at Cardiff Arms Park.

BELOW: Diego Dominguez was one of Italy's brightest stars in their early years in the Six Nations Championship.

GRAND SLAMS AND TRIPLE CROWNS

Team	Grand slams	Triple crowns
England	13	25
Wales	11	20
France	9	n/a
Scotland	3	10
Ireland	3	11
Italy	0	n/a

AZZURRI STILL FINDING THEIR FEET

Italy may have rejoiced when they were finally accepted into the northern hemisphere's premier competition for 2000, but they have found the going hard. The Azzurri have won only 12 of 95 matches (with only two of those victories achieved away from home) and hold unwanted all-time tournament records for: the lowest winning percentage (13.15 – including a 15–15 draw away to Wales in 2006); the worst points difference (-1,815); and conceding the most points in a single tournament (228 in their debut season).

HOME COMFORTS AND AWAY-DAY JOY

England and Wales hold the distinction of having secured the most Six Nations Championship victories at a home venue: England have notched up 153 home wins in 235 matches, whereas as Wales have 153 home wins in 232 matches. England also hold the all-time tournament record for most victories at an opponent's ground, with 105 wins in 237 matches.

SERIAL RECORD-BREAKERS

England have been the championship's (in all its guises) most dominant team over the years. They have collected the most grand slams (13) and triple crowns (25) and hold the all-time tournament records for: the most wins (258); most draws (39); highest winning percentage (58.66); best winning percentage at home (70.00); most matches won away (105); best winning percentage away (44.3 in 237 matches); most points scored (6,675); best points difference (+1,668); most tries scored (927); most penalties (661) and most conversions kicked (501); and most conversions in a single match (nine – from ten attempts – against Italy at Twickenham on 7 February 2001), which they won 80–23 (it was the biggest margin of victory in Five/Six Nations Championship history).

BELOW: Will Greenwood crosses the line for England during their convincing 44–15 victory over Wales in 2001. England ended as Six Nations Championship winners and scored a tournament-record 229 points.

ABOVE: Bill Beaumont led England to grand slam glory in the 1980 Five Nations Championship – one of a record 13 grand slams won by England in the history of the Five/Six Nations Championship.

PLENTY OF LOWS FOR SCOTLAND

Scotland have enjoyed plenty of good times in the Six Nations Championship over the years, with 22 tournament victories (14 outright and eight shared), three grand slams (most recently in 1990) and ten triple crowns, but there have been plenty of low points along the way too: the Scots have won the wooden spoon on 33 occasions and hold the unwanted all-time tournament record for having suffered the most defeats: 255 in 474 matches.

A DARK CLOUD WITH A RECORD-BREAKING LINING FOR ENGLAND

Although England bowed out of the extended 2001 Six Nations Championship in disappointing fashion – losing 14–20 to Ireland in Dublin in the final round of matches (delayed by five months because of an outbreak of foot-and-mouth disease) to miss out on a grand slam (if not the tournament) for a second consecutive year – their performances up until that point, including victories over Wales (44–15), Italy (80–23), Scotland (43–3) and France (48–19), had been nothing short of scintillating. During the course of that championship, England set all-time records for: the most points scored in a single tournament (229), the most tries scored in a single tournament (29) and the most conversions scored in a single tournament (24).

BIGGEST MARGINS OF VICTORY: TOP TEN

Pos	Margin	Winner	Score	Opponent	Venue	Date
1	57	England	80–23	Italy	Twickenham	17 Feb 2001
2	53	Wales	67–14	Italy	Millennium Stadium	19 Mar 2016
=	53	Ireland	63–10	Italy	Rome	11 Feb 2017
4	51	France	51–0	Wales	Wembley	5 Apr 1998
5	48	Wales	51–3	Scotland	Millennium Stadium	15 Mar 2014
6	47	Ireland	60–13	Italy	Lansdowne Road	4 Mar 2000
=	47	England	59–12	Italy	Rome	18 Mar 2000
8	46	England	59–13	Italy	Twickenham	12 Feb 2011
9	44	Ireland	54–10	Wales	Lansdowne Road	3 Feb 2002
10	43	France	56–13	Italy	Rome	19 Mar 2005
=	43	Ireland	58–15	Italy	Lansdowne Road	12 Mar 2016

THE SCOREBOARD TELLS ONLY HALF THE STORY

The history books record that Scotland beat Wales by four goals to nil in the two sides' Home Nations Championship match at Raeburn Place in Edinburgh on 26 February 1887, but few of them describe the devastating manner of their victory. Scotland scored a tournament record 12 tries in the match (five of them by George Lindsay, another all-time tournament record), of which only four were converted. In modern scoring terms, the Scots would have run out 68–0 winners.

ABOVE: Iain Balshaw scored two of England's ten tries during their record-breaking 80–23 win over Italy at Twickenham in February 2001.

LEFT: Dan Parks nails one of Scotland's record-equalling five drop goals during the 2010 Six Nations Championship. This one came against Wales during the Scots' 31–24 defeat at the Millennium Stadium, Cardiff.

SIX NATIONS DROP GOAL BITS & PIECES

France are the Five/Six Nations drop goal kings, having nailed 111 attempts in 374 matches since 1910. In 1967, *Les Bleus* also became the first team to drop five goals in one tournament, a record since equalled by Italy in 2000, Wales in 2001, England in 2003 and Scotland in 2010. The Six Nations record for the most drop goals in a match is three, a feat achieved on six occasions.

SINGLE TOURNAMENT PENALTY JOY

The record for the most penalty kicks scored by a team in a single tournament is 21, set by England in 2013 and equalled by Ireland in 2015. The record for the most successful penalty attempts in a match is seven, a feat achieved on nine occasions, most recently in 2016, when Maxime Machenaud of France made seven (out of seven attempts) against England at the Stade de France in Paris.

THE MOST POROUS DEFENCE

No side in the competition's history has conceded more points than Scotland. The Scots have leaked 6,215 points in 474 matches since the inaugural Home Nations Championship in 1882–83.

TRY-SCORING RECORDS

THE FLYING SCOTSMAN STEAMS INTO THE RECORD BOOKS

Born in Australia and raised in New Zealand, Ian Smith was educated in England (at Winchester College and Oxford University, where he first played rugby) and eventually played for Scotland (he qualified through relatives in the Scottish Borders). Scotland were delighted to secure his services. Nicknamed the 'Flying Scotsman', he made his debut in 1924, helped Scotland to their first grand slam in 1925 (during which he equalled Cyril Rowe's record of most tries in one tournament – 8) and was a mainstay of the Scotland side until 1933. He stands second on the all-time tournament try-scoring list with 24 (behind Ireland's Brian O'Driscoll) and shares the record (with O'Driscoll) for most tries scored in home matches (15).

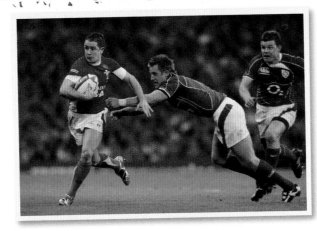

LEFT: Shane Williams scored 14 tries in 22 Six Nations Championship appearances for Wales at Cardiff's Millennium Stadium – a record for one player at single ground.

A SPECIAL DAY FOR THE HEWITTS

Ireland's Home Nations Championship match against Wales at Cardiff on 8 March 1924 was one of the most memorable in the tournament's history – and particularly for the Hewitt family. That day, two brothers, 18-year-old Tom Hewitt (on the wing) and his younger brother Frank (at fly-half), both made their international debuts and both scored a try as Ireland edged to a slender 13–10 victory. During the match, Frank, at 17 years 156 days, had become not only the youngest-ever player to appear in the tournament but also the youngest-ever player to score a Six Nations try.

BELOW: Ireland's Brian O'Driscoll hunts down the tryline en route to becoming the Six Nations' all-time leading try-scorer.

DREAM DEBUT FOR LLEWELLYN

A winger with the unfashionable second-tier Welsh club Llwynpia, Willie Llewellyn launched what would become one of the great careers of Wales's greatest era in spectacular style. On 7 January 1899, against England at Swansea, he scored four tries – a record for a player making their Six Nations debut – as Wales cruised to a convincing 26–3 victory. Llewellyn went on to make a further 19 appearances for Wales and ended his international career in 1905 having scored 16 tries for his country – to stand 13th on Wales's all-time try-scoring list.

THERE'S NO PLACE LIKE HOME FOR SHANE WILLIAMS

Shane Williams made his international debut when he came on as a replacement for Wales during their opening 2000 Six Nations match against France at the Millennium Stadium on 5 February 2000 (the first Six Nations match ever played at the venue) and ended up on the losing side, as France romped to a 36–3 victory. But disappointments at the new home of Welsh rugby have been few and far between for the wing wizard: he went on to score 14 tries in 22 matches there – a Six Nations record for a player at a single ground – before bowing out after the 2011 tournament.

NO AWAY-DAY BLUES FOR HICKIE AND O'DRISCOLL

Two players hold the record for the most tries scored in away matches in the Six Nations Championship as Ireland's Denis Hickie and countryman Brian O'Driscoll have both scored 11 tries in away matches. Hickie achieved the feat in 18 matches; O'Driscoll in 31.

MOST TRIES: TOP TEN

Pos	Tries	Player (Country, Span)
1	26	Brian O'Driscoll (Ireland, 2000–14)
2	24	Ian Smith (Scotland, 1924–33)
3	22	Shane Williams (Wales, 2000–11)
4	18	Gareth Edwards (Wales, 1967–78)
=	18	Cyril Lowe (England, 1913–23)
=	18	Rory Underwood (England, 1984–96)
7	17	George North (Wales, 2011–18)
8	16	Ben Cohen (England, 2000–06)
=	16	Gerald Davies (Wales, 1967–78)
=	16	Ken Jones (Wales, 1947–57)
=	16	Willie Llewellyn (Wales, 1899–1905)

EASTER ROLLS BACK THE YEARS

When Nick Easter left the pitch following England's 19-12 quarter-final defeat to France at the 2011 Rugby World Cup, he might well have done so thinking that, after 47 matches and at the age of 32, his international career was over. And, despite a string of impressive performances for his club side Harlequins, so it seemed. But when England's regular No.8 Ben Morgan broke his leg prior to the 2015 Six Nations, coach Stuart Lancaster turned to Easter to fill the void. Easter did not disappoint: he made four appearances from the bench and scored England's sixth try in their 47-17 victory over Italy at Twickenham. In doing so, he became, aged 36 years 183 days, the oldest try-scorer in the tournament's history.

RIGHT: Nick Easter became the Six Nations' oldest-ever try scorer (36 years 183 days) when he scored England's sixth try in their 47–17 victory over Italy at Twickenham on 14 February 2015.

O'DRISCOLL IS TOP TRY-SCORING CAPTAIN

The leading Ireland player of his generation (and arguably the best of all time), Brian O'Driscoll has captained Ireland a record 41 times in Six Nations Championship matches between 2003 and 2011, and to great effect, too: his 15 tries as captain – out of a total of 26 (to stand top of the tournament's all-time try-scoring list) – are the most by a captain in the competition's history.

HOME/FIVE/SIX NATIONS CHAMPIONSHIP ALL-TIME LEADING TRY-SCORERS: BY POSITION

Position	Player (Country, Span)	Tries
Full-back	Serge Blanco (France, 1983–91)	11
	Stuart Hogg (Scotland, 2012–18)	11
Winger	Ian Smith (Scotland, 1924–33)	24
Centre	Brian O'Driscoll (Ireland, 2000–14)	26
Fly-half	Ronan O'Gara (Ireland, 2000–13)	9
Scrum-half	Gareth Edwards (Wales, 1967–78)	18
No.8	Jamie Heaslip (Ireland, 2008–17)	9
Flanker	Jim McCarthy (Ireland, 1948–55)	8
	Cherry Pillman (England, 1910–14)	8
Lock	Jack Whitfield (Wales, 1920–24)	5
Prop	Martin Castrogiovanni (Italy, 2004–16)	5
Hooker	Eric Evans (England, 1950–58)	5
	Keith Wood (Ireland, 1995–2002)	5

MOST TRIES IN A LOSING CAUSE

The record for the most tries by a player whose team has gone on to lose the match is three, achieved by three players: Robert Montgomery (Ireland) against Wales at Birkenhead on 12 March 1887; Howard Marshall (England) against Wales at Cardiff on 7 January 1893; and Emile Ntamack (France) against Wales at the Stade de France, Paris, on 6 March 1999.

THE LONGEST TRYLESS STREAK

Fast on the road to becoming the most capped Scotland player of all time, Ross Ford made his international debut as a 20-year-old against Australia at Murrayfield on 6 November 2004, and has been the cornerstone of the Scotland pack ever since. The hooker has appeared at three Rugby World Cups (in 2007, 2011 and 2015), made an appearance for the British Lions in 2009 (against South Africa) and holds an unwanted Six Nations Championship record: he has made the most appearances in the competition without ever scoring a try (55).

MOST TRIES SCORED AGAINST A SINGLE OPPONENT

Two players share the record for the most tries scored against a single opponent in Five/Six Nations matches – nine. Ian Smith (Scotland) scored nine tries in eight matches against England between 1924 and 1933; whereas as Shane Williams (Wales) scored nine tries in nine matches against Italy between 2000 and 2011, and the same number of tries in eight matches against Scotland between 2000 and 2011.

BELOW: Scotland's Ross Ford has played 55 Six Nations matches without ever scoring a try.

PREVIOUS PAGES: Gary Ringrose scored the opening try during Ireland's Grand Slam-securing 24–15 victory over England at Twickenham on 17 March 2018.

POINTS-SCORING RECORDS

THE TOURNAMENT'S FIRST POINTS-SCORER

It may not have been the most convincing kicking display in the championship's illustrious history, but when England's Welsh-born three-quarter Arthur Evanson, making his international debut, slotted two conversions in six attempts during England's 2–0 victory over Wales at Swansea on 16 December 1882 (the competition's inaugural match), he became the tournament's first-ever points-scorer.

MOST POINTS IN A LOSING CAUSE

Scotland may have generated all the headlines when they beat Italy 29–27 at the Stadio Olimpico on 17 March 2018 to snatch victory from what seemed to be a certain defeat, but Italy's Tomasso Allen also produced a performance that earned him a place in the record books. The Italian fly-half scored tries, three conversions and two penalties in the match, and his haul of 22 points is an all-time record in the Six Nations for a player who has ended up on the losing side.

MOST POINTS: TOP TEN

Pos	Points	Player (Country, Span)
1	557	Ronan O'Gara (Ireland, 2000–13)
2	546	Jonny Wilkinson (England, 1998–2011)
3	467	Stephen Jones (Wales, 2000–11)
4	406	Neil Jenkins (Wales, 1991–2001)
5	403	Chris Paterson (Scotland, 2000–11)
6	388	Leigh Halfpenny (Wales, 2009–18)
7	357	Jonny Sexton (Ireland, 2010–18)
8	343	Owen Farrell (England, 2012–18)
9	288	Gavin Hastings (Scotland, 1986–95)
10	270	David Humphreys (Ireland, 1996–2005)

SERIAL RECORD-BREAKER

Jonny Wilkinson embarked on what would become one of the most stellar careers in international rugby history when, on 4 April 1998, aged 18 years 314 days, he came on as a replacement for England during their Five Nations Championship victory over Ireland (35–17) at Twickenham. And, despite missing three seasons (2004–06) through injury, the mercurial fly-half went on to break numerous championship records. He leads the way for: the most points in a tournament (89 in 2001); the most points in a single match (35, against Italy at Twickenham on 17 February 2001); the most conversions in a match (9, against Italy at Twickenham on 17 February 2001); the most points at a single ground (329 in 22 matches at Twickenham); the most conversions (89); and the most drop goals (11); and stands second (behind Ronan O'Gara on the tournament's all-time points-scoring list (with 546 points compared to O'Gara's 557).

LEFT: Jonny Wilkinson was pivotal to England's success for more than a decade and he holds numerous all-time Six Nations Championship records.

CAPTAIN KICKS HIS WAY INTO THE RECORD BOOKS

A flawless kicking display from Scotland captain Chris Paterson in the Scots' 2007 Six Nations match against Wales at Murrayfield secured his side a surprise 21–9 victory and him a place in the record books. The long-serving winger's 21 points in the match (thanks to seven successful penalty kicks) is an all-time record for a captain in a Six Nations fixture.

MOST POINTS SCORED BY A FORWARD

A legend in French rugby circles, back-row forward Jean Prat made his debut for France against a British Army XV in Paris on 1 January 1945 – while World War Two was still raging. His finest moments came almost a decade later, in 1954: first, when he scored a barn-storming solo try to secure a 3–0 victory over New Zealand at Colombes, Paris; and, second, later in the year, when he captained France to their first-ever Five Nations Championship title. He bowed out of international rugby the following year, but still holds the distinction of having scored more points (87) than any other forward in the tournament's long history.

LEFT: Ireland's Ronan O'Gara tops the Five/Six Nations Championship's all-time points-scoring list with 557 in 63 matches.

O'GARA: SIX NATIONS POINT-SCORING KING

No player has scored more points in Six Nations Championship matches than Ronan O'Gara. The Ireland fly-half, who also holds the all-time tournament record for kicking the most penalties (109) has amassed 557 points in 63 Six Nations Championship matches between 2000 and 2013. O'Gara has 10 tries, 81 conversions and six drop goals to his name.

MOST DROP GOALS IN A MATCH

The record for the most drop goals in a Six Nations match is three, a feat achieved by four players: Pierre Albaladejo (France) against Ireland at Colombes, Paris, on 9 April 1960; Jean-Patrick Lescarboura (France) against England at Twickenham on 2 February 1985; Diego Dominguez (Italy) against Scotland at Rome on 5 February 2000; and Neil Jenkins (Wales) against Scotland at Murrayfield on 17 February 2001.

JARRETT'S DAY IN THE CARDIFF SUN

Brought into the Welsh line-up for the final match (against England at Cardiff) of what had been a disastrous 1967 Five Nations campaign for Wales – they had lost their first three matches – Keith Jarrett enjoyed a day to remember. The Newport full-back scored 19 points (one try, five conversions and two penalties) – the most by a debutant in the tournament's history – to help Wales to a morale-boosting 34–21 victory. Jarrett went on to win a further nine caps for his country before switching to rugby league (with Barrow) in 1969.

MOST PENALTIES IN A MATCH

The record for the most penalties in a Six Nations match is seven, a feat achieved by eight players: Simon Hodgkinson (England) against Wales at Cardiff on 19 January 1991; Rob Andrew (England) against Scotland at Twickenham on 18 March 1995; Jonny Wilkinson (England) against France at Twickenham on 20 March 1999; Neil Jenkins (Wales) against Italy at the Millennium Stadium, Cardiff, on 19 February 2000; Gerald Merceron (France) against Italy at the Stade de France, Paris, on 2 February 2002; Chris Paterson (Scotland) against Wales at Murrayfield on 10 February 2007; Leigh Halfpenny (Wales) against Scotland at Murrayfield on 9 March 2013; and Maxine Machenaud (France) against England at Stade de France, Paris, on 19 March 2016.

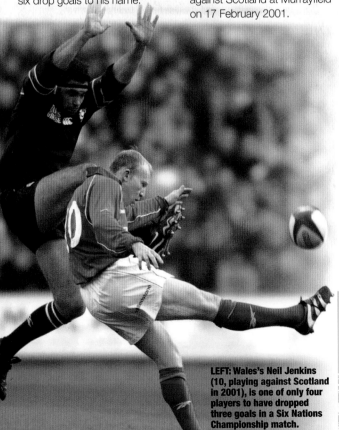

LEFT: Wales's Neil Jenkins (10, playing against Scotland in 2001), is one of only four players to have dropped three goals in a Six Nations Championship match.

ABOVE: Chris Paterson kicked seven penalties against Wales at Murrayfield in 2010.

MOST POINTS AGAINST A SINGLE OPPONENT

Opponent	Points	Player (Country, Span)
England	92	Ronan O'Gara (Ireland, 2000–13)
France	108	Ronan O'Gara (Ireland, 2000–12)
Ireland	107	Stephen Jones (Wales, 2000–11)
Italy	146	Ronan O'Gara (Ireland, 2000–12)
Scotland	116	Ronan O'Gara (Ireland, 2000–13)
Wales	129	Jonny Wilkinson (England, 1999–2011)

APPEARANCE RECORDS

ONE OF IRELAND'S ALL-TIME GREATS

Born and raised in Belfast and educated at Cambridge University, Mike Gibson is many critics' choice as the finest Irish player of all time (until Brian O'Driscoll came along). A player of great versatility – he won caps in four different positions – he made his debut (at fly-half) during a 18–5 Five Nations defeat of England at Twickenham on 8 February 1964. With a professional approach to the game years before the concept appeared on world rugby's radar, his quick hands, ability to break an opponent's backline and tearaway defensive tactics soon marked him out as a special talent. Over a 15-year career that included five British Lions tours, he represented Ireland on 69 occasions – a record that lasted until February 1995. His record for most appearances in the Five/Six Nations Championship, 56 between 1964 and 1979, has since been surpassed by compatriots Ronan O'Gara, Brian O'Driscoll and Rory Best, and Italy's Sergio Parisse.

THAT RECORD-BREAKING LOSING FEELING

A veteran of 65 matches in the Six Nations Championship (who has played in 15 competitions between 2004 and 2018), Italian No.8 Sergio Parisse has the unfortunate distinction of having appeared on the losing side more than any other player in the Six Nations – 55 times.

BELOW: In his 15-season career, Brian O'Driscoll, Ireland's most-capped player, experienced more Home/Five/ Six Nations Championship victories (45) than any other player in the history of the competition.

MOST APPEARANCES: TOP TEN

Pos	Caps	Player (Country, Span)
1	65	Brian O'Driscoll (Ireland, 2000–14)
=	65	Sergio Parisse (Italy, 2004–18)
3	63	Ronan O'Gara (Ireland, 2000–13)
4	60	Martin Castrogiovanni (Italy, 2003–16)
=	60	Rory Best (Ireland, 2006–18)
6	56	Colin Gibson (Ireland, 1964–79)
=	56	Gethin Jenkins (Wales, 2003–16)
8	55	Ross Ford (Scotland, 2006–17)
9	54	John Hayes (Ireland, 2000–10)
=	54	Jason Leonard (England, 1991–2004)

VICTORY A COMMON EXPERIENCE FOR IRELAND'S O'DRISCOLL

No player has enjoyed the sweet taste of Six Nations success on more occasions than Ireland's most capped player, Brian O'Driscoll. The long-serving centre found himself on the winning side 45 times in 63 Six Nations matches between 2000 and 2014.

MOST APPEARANCES AGAINST A SINGLE OPPONENT

Colin Gibson holds the all-time Six Nations record for having played the most matches against a single opponent. The legendary Ireland centre played against England on 15 occasions between 1964 and 1978. He ended up on the winning side eight times and suffered defeat five times, with two matches drawn.

BELOW: A legendary figure in Irish rugby history, and considered among the finest players his country has ever produced, Mike Gibson made 56 appearances in the Five Nations championship, 15 of them against Wales.

MOST APPEARANCES: BY POSITION

Position	Player (Country, Span)	Appearances
Full-back	Tom Kiernan (Ireland, 1960–73)	44
	J.P.R. Williams (Wales, 1969–81)	44
Winger	Rory Underwood (England, 1984–96)	50
Centre	Brian O'Driscoll (Ireland, 2000–14)	65
Fly-half	Ronan O'Gara (Ireland, 2000–13)	59
Scrum-half	Peter Stringer (Ireland, 2000–11)	47
No.8	Sergio Parisse (Italy, 2004–18)	63
Flanker	Martyn Williams (Wales, 1998–2010)	51
Lock	Willie-John McBride (Ireland, 1962–75)	53
Prop	Martin Castrogiovanni (Italy, 2003–16)	60
Hooker	Rory Best (Ireland, 2006–18)	60

THERE'S NO PLACE LIKE HOME FOR WALES' JENKINS

A powerful scrummager and surprisingly swift of foot in the loose, Gethin Jenkins has been a pivotal member of three Welsh Grand Slam-winning squads (2005, 2008 and 2012) and has won more caps for his country (125) than any other player. He already holds one all-time record: he has played the most matches at a single ground – 31 matches at the Millennium Stadium between 2003 and 2016.

YOUNGEST PLAYER

Ireland's Frank Hewitt holds the distinction of being the tournament's youngest-ever player. The Belfast-born fly-half was 17 years 157 days old when he made his debut during Ireland's 13–10 victory over Wales in Cardiff, a match in which he scored a try. He went on to make a further eight appearances for his country.

BELOW: Jason Leonard played in more Six Nations matches (54) than any other player for England.

RIGHT: Philippe Sella (white shirt) holds the France record for most Five/Six Nations Championship appearances with 50.

MOST APPEARANCES: BY COUNTRY

Country	Player (Span)	Appearances
England	Jason Leonard (1991–2004)	54
France	Philippe Sella (1983–95)	50
Ireland	Brian O'Driscoll (2000–14)	65
Italy	Sergio Parisse (2004–18)	65
Scotland	Ross Ford (2006–17)	55
Wales	Gethin Jenkins (2003–16)	56

THE TOURNAMENT'S OLDEST DEBUTANT

His exact date of birth may remain unknown (it was in 1894), but when Frederick Gilbert made his debut for England in their Five Nations Championship match against Wales at Twickenham on 20 January 1923, he became the first, and to date only, 39-year-old to play in the competition (England won the match 7–3). The full-back made only one further appearance for England, against Ireland later that season.

ONE-MATCH WONDERS

Of the 5,008 players to have appeared in the Six Nations Championship in 132 years of competition, 958 of them – a surprising 19.13 per cent – only ever appeared in one match.

THE RED MIST RISES IN PARIS

England's Five Nations Championship match against France at the Parc des Princes in Paris on 15 February 1992 always promised to be a fractious affair. Barely four months had passed since England had out-muscled and out-fought the French to win a tense Rugby World Cup quarter-final at the same venue, and France were out to avenge the defeat. They failed in their mission and, as the clock ticked down, their frustration grew, they imploded, with both Gregoire Lascube and Vincent Moscato being shown red cards. It remains the only instance in the tournament's history in which a team has had two players sent off in a match. For the record, England went on to win 31–13 to secure their second grand slam in two years.

TOURNAMENT RED CARDS

Player	Team	Opponent	Venue	Date
Willie Duggan	Ireland	Wales	Cardiff	15 Jan 1977
Geoff Wheel	Wales	Ireland	Cardiff	15 Jan 1977
Paul Ringer	Wales	England	Twickenham	16 Feb 1980
Jean-Pierre Garuet-Lempirou	France	Ireland	Parc des Princes	21 Jan 1984
Kevin Moseley	Wales	France	Cardiff	20 Jan 1990
Alain Carminati	France	Scotland	Murrayfield	17 Feb 1990
Gregoire Lascube	France	England	Parc des Princes	15 Feb 1992
Vincent Moscato	France	England	Parc des Princes	15 Feb 1992
John Davies	Wales	England	Cardiff	18 Feb 1995
Walter Cristofoletto	Italy	France	Stade de France	1 Apr 2000
Alessandro Troncon	Italy	Ireland	Rome	3 Feb 2001
Scott Murray	Scotland	Wales	Millennium Stadium	12 Feb 2006
Michele Rizzo	Italy	France	Stade de France	9 Feb 2014
Rabah Stimani	France	Italy	Stade de France	9 Feb 2014
Stuart Hogg	Scotland	Wales	Millennium Stadium	15 Mar 2014

CAPTAIN FANTASTIC

Italy's Sergio Parisse has been a constant shining light in an otherwise struggling Italy side from the moment he made his debut for the Azzurri in the tournament against England in Rome on 15 February 2004. And although he holds a number of unwanted tournament records – such as experiencing the most defeats (55) – he is also the holder of one notable record: he has captained his country in more Six Nations matches (47) than any other player.

BELOW: Irish referee Stephen Hilditch made Six Nations history when he sent off France's Gregoire Lascube and Vincent Moscato during Les Bleus' 1992 clash against England at the Parc des Princes, Paris.

ABOVE: One of the Six Nations Championship's stand-out players for more than a decade, Sergio Parisse has led Italy a record 47 times in the tournament.

FAMILIAR FOES

The Six Nations Championship's most contested fixture is that between Ireland and Scotland. The two countries met for the first time in Belfast on 19 February 1883 (a match Scotland won by one goal to nil) and have gone on to contest the fixture on 124 occasions, with Scotland recording 60 wins to Ireland's 59, with five draws.

REDUCING THE CHANCE OF VICTORY

Beware the yellow card! It has been shown to players on 192 occasions in the Six Nations Championship since its introduction in 2000 and statistics reveal that, of teams with a player yellow-carded, only 32.3 per cent have gone on to record a victory – a success rate of roughly one in three.

THE TOURNAMENT'S FIRST RED CARDS

In nearly 100 years of Six Nations Championship matches (in all its guises) there had been tussles, scuffles, full-blown fights and limitless bad behaviour that raised many an eyebrow, but no player had ever been shown a red card. That all changed on 15 January 1977 at Cardiff Arms Park when, after the match had descended into a mass brawl, Scottish referee Norman Sansom dismissed Wales's Geoff Wheel and Willie Duggan (Ireland) for fighting. For the record Wales went on to win the fractious 14-a-side encounter 25–9.

BAD BOY FRENCH

France have enjoyed plenty of good times in the Six Nations in all of its incarnations over the years: winning the tournament on 17 occasions with nine grand slams. But there have been plenty of darker moments along the way: they were banished from the competition between 1932 and 1946; they are the only side to have had two of its players sent off in the same match (against England at Parc des Princes, Paris, on 15 February 1992; and hold the unwanted all-time tournament record for having had more players sent off than any other team: five.

ABOVE: Hard-nosed hooker Vincent Moscate is one of four Frenchman to have seen red in a Six Nations Championship match – an unwanted all-time tournament record Les Bleus share with Wales.

MOST YELLOW CARDS

Pos	Yellow	Country
1	48	Italy
2	42	Scotland
3	36	Wales
4	28	England
5	24	Ireland
6	13	France

BELOW: England's James Haskell has seen yellow on more occasions (five) than any other player in Six Nations history.

HISTORY-MAKING MOMENT ON A DAY TO FORGET FOR SORRY WALES

The first-ever Six Nations Championship match to be played at the new Millennium Stadium in Cardiff – Wales against France on 5 February 2000 – ended in disaster for the home side. Wales opened the scoring through a Neil Jenkins penalty, but things went rapidly downhill for the home side from there. France rallied to lead 9–3 at half-time and were at their rampaging best in the second half. As Welsh indiscipline grew under the mounting pressure, Scott Quinnell was shown a yellow card by referee Chris White – becoming the first player in history to suffer the penalty – and France went on to record a resounding 36–3 victory.

YELLOW CARD FEVER

England's James Haskell is the only player in Six Nations Championship history to have been shown a yellow card on five occasions. The firebrand flanker has seen yellow: v Italy on 7 February 2009; v Ireland on 10 February 2013; v France on 21 March 2015; v Ireland on 27 February 2016; and v Wales on 12 March 2016.

YELLOW CARDS GALORE, BUT STILL EMERGING ON THE WINNING SIDE

The most yellow cards given to a team that has then gone on to win the match is two, a feat that has been achieved by three teams on six occasions. By France: who lost Jean Daude and Emile Ntamack for ten-minute spells but still beat Scotland 28–16 at Murrayfield on 4 March 2000. By Wales, on three occasions: first on 8 March 2008, when they lost Mike Phillips and Martyn Williams but went on to beat Ireland 16–12 at Croke Park, Dublin; then in the 2011 Championship, when they lost Lee Byrne and Bradley Davies against Scotland at Murrayfield, but still recorded a comfortable 24–6 victory; and finally against Italy at the Millennium Stadium in the 2018 tournament, when both Gareth Davies and Liam Williams received yellow cards, but Wales still won the match 38–14. And England: who saw Shane Geraghty and James Haskell sent to the sin bin but still went on to register a 36–11 victory over Italy at Twickenham on 7 February 2009); and lost Dan Cole and James Haskell (again) against Wales at Twickenham on 12 March 2016, but still went on to win 25–21.

THE RUGBY CHAMPIONSHIP

Considered the toughest competition in world rugby, the Rugby Championship – formerly known as the Tri Nations and contested between the three giants of southern hemisphere rugby, Australia, New Zealand and South Africa – was staged for the first time in 1996. Argentina joined the rebranded competition in 2012. New Zealand have been the tournament's dominant team, winning the championship on 15 occasions, with Australia winning four times and South Africa three times.

BELOW: Victory in the 2017 Rugby Championship was New Zealand's sixth tournament success in eight years.

TEAM RECORDS

OVERALL RECORD (1996–2017)

Team	P	W	L	D	%	For	Aga	Diff	Tries	Conv	Pens	Drop
Argentina (2012–2017)	37	3	29	1	10.60	576	1096	520	50	40	79	3
Australia (1996–2017)	109	44	57	4	43.80	2279	2562	-283	229	159	263	9
New Zealand (1996–2017)	111	80	24	1	76.66	3072	1935	+1137	329	232	312	9
South Africa (1996–2017)	111	42	59	4	41.90	2271	2605	-334	214	157	273	22

LEFT: New Zealand celebrate victory in the inaugural Tri-Nations Championship in 1996. the All Blacks have gone on to collect 12 futher titles and have set a whole host of records along the way.

ALL BLACKS SET HOST OF RECORDS

New Zealand have been the dominant team since the Tri-Nations/Rugby Championship's inception in 1996. They won the tournament's first-ever match (thumping Australia 43–6 in Wellington on 6 July 1996) and went on to win their remaining three matches to claim the inaugural title with a 100 per cent record. It set the tone for things to come. New Zealand have claimed 15 titles, registered a record 80 wins (with a winning percentage of 76.66) and also hold the all-time competition records for: the most tries (329), the most points scored (3,072), the best points difference (+1,137), kicking the most conversions (232) and penalties (312).

FIRST TRI-NATIONS TITLE FOR THE SPRINGBOKS

Having endured miserable campaigns in the 1996 and 1997 Tri-Nations championships (winning only two of their eight matches), reigning world champions South Africa finally hit their stride in the tournament in 1998. They opened their account with a hard-fought victory over Australia in Perth (14–3), beat New Zealand in Wellington (13–3, to hand a first-ever defeat to the All Blacks in the competition) and battled to their first-ever Tri-Nations title with home wins over New Zealand (24–23 at Durban) and Australia (29–15 at Johannesburg).

RIGHT: South Africa, the reigning world champions at the time, collected the first of their three Tri-Nations titles in 1998.

TOURNAMENT STALEMATES A RARITY

Twenty-two years of Tri-Nations/Rugby Championship competition have seen 144 matches played with New Zealand notching up 80 wins, Australia 44 wins, South Africa 42 wins and Argentina (who entered the fray in 2012) with three victories to their name. Strangely, only five of those matches have ended in a draw: Australia v South Africa in 2001(14–14); Argentina v South Africa in 2012 (16–16); Australia v New Zealand in 2014 (12–12); and Australia v South Africa, twice in 2017 (23–23 and 27–27).

TOURNAMENT CHAMPIONS

1996	New Zealand
1997	New Zealand
1998	South Africa
1999	New Zealand
2000	Australia
2001	Australia
2002	New Zealand
2003	New Zealand
2004	South Africa
2005	New Zealand
2006	New Zealand
2007	New Zealand
2008	New Zealand
2009	South Africa
2010	New Zealand
2011	Australia
2012	New Zealand
2013	New Zealand
2014	New Zealand
2015	Australia
2016	New Zealand
2017	New Zealand

	Argentina	Australia	New Zealand	South Africa
Argentina	x	1/10/0	0/11/0	2/8/1
Australia	10/1/0	x	12/33/1	22/22/3
New Zealand	11/0/0	34/12/1	x	35/12/0
South Africa	8/2/1	22/22/3	12/35/0	x

A GOLDEN AGE FOR THE WALLABIES

Australia did not enjoy the best of starts to life in the Tri-Nations, finishing bottom in 1996 and 1997, but they recorded two wins for the first time in 1998, repeated the feat in 1999 (including a morale-boosting 28–7 victory in their final match against champions New Zealand) and used their improved performances as a platform from which to launch the most successful period in their history. They won the Rugby World Cup (for the second time) later that year and carried that form into the 2000 Tri-Nations, winning three and losing one of their matches to claim the title for the first time. They defended their crown the following year thanks to a pulsating 29–26 final-match win against New Zealand in Sydney. They would have to endure a ten-year wait before collecting a third title. A fourth title arrived in 2015.

MOST POINTS IN A SINGLE TOURNAMENT

New Zealand used the 2016 Rugby Championship to dispel any thoughts anyone might have had that their performances might falter after several long-standing players, such as Richie McCaw and Dan Carter, retired after the 2015 Rugby World Cup. The All Blacks were at their peerless best, winning all six of their matches (three of them by more than 30 points) and scored a tournament record 262 points in the process.

ABOVE: Back-to-back tournament wins in 2000 and 2001 marked a zenith in Australia's Tri-Nations form; and then came a ten-year wait for a third crown.

AUSTRALIA RETURN TO WINNING WAYS

If back-to-back crowns in 2000 and 2001 signified a Tri-Nations golden era for Australia, then the nine tournaments that followed were the Wallabies' dark ages: 14 wins from 41 matches meant they could only watch on with envy as New Zealand and South Africa took the spoils. But that all changed in 2011: an impressive 39–20 opening win against South Africa may have been followed by a 30–14 defeat to New Zealand, but the Wallabies rallied to win their final two matches.

MOST POROUS DEFENCE

South Africa hold the unwelcome distinction of having conceded more points than any other team in the competition's history (2,605 in 111 matches – an average of 24.47 per match), compared to Australia's 2,562 and New Zealand's 1,935. Argentina hold the record for having conceded the most points in a single tournament (235 in six matches in 2017 – an average of 39.17 per match).

RIGHT: South Africa's Joe van Niekerk dives over Australia's line to score the Springboks' second try in their title-clinching 23–19 win in 2004.

A CAMPAIGN TO FORGET FOR SORRY SOUTH AFRICA

South Africa embarked on the defence of their Tri-Nations title in 1999 with a disappointing 28–0 defeat to New Zealand in Christchurch and, a week later, crashed 32–6 to Australia in Brisbane. Things barely improved for the Springboks at home when New Zealand beat them 34–18 in Pretoria, but at least they recorded a face-saving victory in their final match of the campaign against Australia in Cape Town (10–9). However, the victory did not prevent them from finishing bottom of the table and, to compound their misery, their tournament haul of 34 points is the lowest in Tri-Nations history.

SPRINGBOKS RALLY TO CLAIM THRILLING TRI-NATIONS CROWN

The ninth edition of the Tri-Nations (in 2004) turned out to be a cliffhanger. New Zealand opened up with two straight home wins (16–7 against Australia in Wellington and 23–21 against South Africa in Christchurch) to head the table. Then Australia won both of their home matches (23–18 against New Zealand at Sydney and 30–26 against South Africa in Perth). The state of play was simple: victory for either Australia or New Zealand in their final match (away to South Africa) would virtually guarantee them the title; the Springboks, on the other hand, had to win both of their remaining home matches to stand any chance of lifting the crown. They started well, beating New Zealand in Johannesburg (40–26), and then pipped Australia in a pulsating winner-takes-all showdown at Kings Park, Durban (23–19), to win the tightest Tri-Nations in history.

BELOW: Bryan Habana scores one of South Africa's nine tries during the Springboks' 73–13 rout of Argentina at Johannesburg on 17 August 2013.

THE BOKS BATTER THE PUMAS

Anyone looking to further their argument that Argentina were out of their depth during their first years in the Rugby Championship need not look beyond their performance against South Africa at Johannesburg on 17 August 2013. The Pumas (still looking for their first win in the competition) found themselves on the wrong end of a hammering. South Africa ran in nine tries (seven of them in the second half, to run out comprehensive 73–13 winners. It is the largest victory ever recorded in the competition.

BIGGEST MARGINS OF VICTORY: TOP TEN

Pos	Winner	Score	Opponent	Venue	Date
1	South Africa	73–16	Argentina	Johannesburg	17 Aug 2013
2	New Zealand	57–0	South Africa	North Shore City	18 Sep 2017
3	Australia	49–0	South Africa	Brisbane	15 Jul 2006
4	South Africa	53–8	Australia	Johannesburg	30 Aug 2008
5	New Zealand	57–15	South Africa	Durban	8 Oct 2016
6	South Africa	61–22	Australia	Pretoria	23 Aug 1997
=	New Zealand	54–15	Argentina	La Plata	29 Sep 2012
8	New Zealand	43–6	Australia	Wellington	6 Jul 1996
9	Australia	54–17	Argentina	Rosario	5 Oct 2013
10	New Zealand	52–16	South Africa	Pretoria	19 Jul 2003

ALL BLACKS' EDEN PARK FORTRESS

Teams rightfully fear the prospect of playing New Zealand at Eden Park, Auckland (the scene of the All Blacks' two Rugby World Cup triumphs in 1987 and 2011), as the stadium has been nothing short of a fortress for them in Tri-Nations/Rugby Championship matches. The All Blacks have won all 14 of the games they have played there – the most by any team at a single ground in the competition's history. New Zealand have also recorded a 100 per cent record at two other grounds: at Loftus Versfeld Stadium in Pretoria (where they beat South Africa in three matches: 34–18 in 1999; 52–16 in 2003 and 45–26 in 2006) and at the National Stadium in Johannesburg, when they beat South Africa in two matches there (29–22 in 2010 and 32–16 in 2012). Unsurprisingly, given their success in the competition, New Zealand also hold the record for most home wins (46) and most away wins (34).

SOUTH AFRICA EDGE A CLASSIC

South Africa's clash against New Zealand at Johannesburg on 19 August 2000 has entered rugby folklore as one of the greatest matches in the game's history. South Africa raced into a 33–13 lead before New Zealand mounted a thrilling comeback to lead 37–36. Braam van Straaten edged the Springboks ahead and an Andrew Mehrtens penalty restored the All Blacks' lead before a Werner Swanepoel try secured South Africa's victory (46–40). New Zealand's of 40 points in the match are the most scored by a losing team in Rugby Championship history.

ZERO POINTS SCORED IN A GAME

Team	Score	Opponent	Venue	Date
South Africa	0–28	New Zealand	Dunedin	10 Jul 1999
South Africa	0–49	Australia	Brisbane	15 Jul 2006
New Zealand	0–19	South Africa	Cape Town	16 Aug 2008
Australia	0–22	New Zealand	Auckland	25 Aug 2012
South Africa	0–57	New Zealand	North Shore City	18 Sep 2017

ABOVE: Thinus Delport races clear of the All Black to score the first of South Africa's six tries in their epic 46–40 victory over New Zealand in Johannesburg in 2000. New Zealand's tally of 40 points is a record for a losing team in the competition.

RIGHT: New Zealand No.8 Kieran Reid drives forward the All Blacks' 23–22 victory over Australia at Sydney in the 2010 Tri-Nations Championship. The All Blacks' one-point victory is one of only ten in the tournament's history.

TRY-SCORING HIGHS AND LOWS

New Zealand's impressive march to the 2016 Rugby Championship crown, during which they won all six of their matches, saw them cross the try-line on 38 occasions to set an all-time tournament record. South Africa hold the unwanted record for the fewest tries scored in a single Tri-Nations campaign: in 2001, admittedly a low try-scoring year, they crossed the line just twice in four matches and, not surprisingly, finished the tournament bottom of the table.

LOWEST TOURNAMENT TRY COUNT

Although the 2001 Tri-Nations championship – won by Australia following their pulsating final-match victory over New Zealand in Sydney (29–16) – may have been one of the most exciting campaigns of recent times, it will not be remembered for the participants' try-scoring exploits: the three teams scored only 13 tries in the tournament's six matches – the fewest in Tri-Nations history.

ONE-POINT WINNING MARGIN

Team	Score	Opponent	Venue	Date
South Africa	14–13	Australia	Perth	18 Jul 1998
South Africa	24–23	New Zealand	Durban	15 Aug 1998
South Africa	10–9	Australia	Cape Town	14 Aug 1999
Australia	24–23	New Zealand	Wellington	5 Aug 2000
Australia	19–18	South Africa	Durban	26 Aug 2000
South Africa	21–20	New Zealand	Rustenberg	2 Sep 2006
New Zealand	19–18	Australia	Sydney	22 Aug 2009
New Zealand	23–22	Australia	Sydney	11 Sep 2010
Australia	14–13	Argentina	Perth	14 Sep 2013
Australia	24–23	South Africa	Perth	6 Sep 2014
New Zealand	25–24	South Africa	Cape Town	7 Oct 2017

MOST DROP GOALS

Overall:	22	South Africa
Match:	2	South Africa v New Zealand, Johannesburg, 19 July 1997
		South Africa v Australia, Pretoria, 30 July 2005
		South Africa v Australia, Cape Town, 16 June 2007
		South Africa v Australia, Pretoria, 1 October 2016
Tournament:	4	South Africa in 2005

MOST PENALTIES

Overall:	312	New Zealand
Match:	9	New Zealand v Australia, Auckland, 24 July 1999
Tournament:	29	South Africa in 2009

MOST CONVERSIONS

Overall:	232	New Zealand
Match:	8	South Africa v Argentina, Johannesburg, 17 August 2013
Tournament:	28	New Zealand in 2017

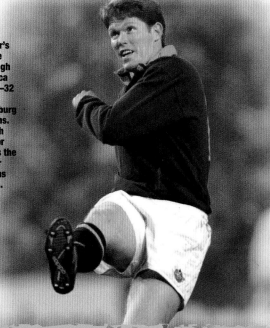

RIGHT: Jannie de Beer's two drop-goals in the match were not enough to prevent South Africa from slipping to a 35–32 defeat against New Zealand in Johannesburg in the 1997 Tri-Nations. Surprisingly, although repeated on two other occasions, it remains the most drop-goals ever scored in a Tri-Nations Championship match.

TOP TRY-SCORER HABANA

So fast he was once raced against a cheetah (the cheetah won), Bryan Habana has been a breath of fresh air since he made his debut for South Africa in 2005 and has gone on to become one of international rugby's biggest stars. He scored 12 tries in his first 12 games for the Springboks and soon made his mark in the Rugby Championship: scoring twice against Australia at Perth in only his third game in the competition. The tries have continued to flow: he scored seven tries in the 2012 Rugby Championship and by the end of the 2016 tournament had scored an all-time competition record 21 tries.

THERE'S NO PLACE LIKE HOME

Born and raised in Auckland, Doug Howlett enjoyed a lengthy and highly successful 62-Test career with the All Blacks and ended his international stint as his country's all-time leading try-scorer, with 49. He enjoyed considerable success in Tri-Nations fixtures at Eden Park, once scoring three tries in a match there (against Australia in 2005) and five overall in four matches at Auckland's main stadium.

TRY ON DEBUT

Nine players have scored tries on their debuts in Tri-Nations/Rugby Championship matches – Warren Brosnihan (South Africa, 1997), Lloyd Johannson (Australia, 2005), Chris Feauai-Sautia (Australia, 2013), Bernard Foley (Australia, 2013), Codie Taylor (New Zealand, 2015) and Jesse Kriel (South Africa, 2015); Nehe Milner-Skudder (two tries, 2015 – he is the only player to score twice on debut); Curtis Rona (Australia, 2017); and David Havili (New Zealand, 2017).

DRAWING A BLANK

A cornerstone of a powerful South African pack, Tendai Mtawarira has made 39 appearances in the Rugby Championship, since his debut during the Springboks' 16–9 defeat to Australia at Perth on 19 July 2008, and has not scored a single try. No player has endured a lengthier try-less run in the competition's history.

NO AWAY-DAY BLUES FOR SMITH

A versatile back whose searing pace means he can play as a wing, outside-centre, or full-back, Ben Smith has been a vital component of New Zealand's dominance in recent years – and is arguably one of the most under-rated players in world rugby. He has enjoyed particular success on the road in Rugby Championship matches, scoring an all-time tournament record 12 tries in 11 away matches. Compatriot Joe Rokocoko and South Africa's Bryan Habana stand second on the list with 11.

TOURNAMENT'S FIRST-EVER TRY

New Zealand's Zinzan Brooke holds the distinction of having scored the first-ever try in a Tri-Nations/Rugby Championship match. The No.8 achieved the feat during the All Blacks' 43–6 victory over Australia at Wellington on 6 July 1997 in the competition's first-ever match.

BELOW: New Zealand's Ben Smith has scored more tries in away games (12) than any other player in the tournament's history.

BELOW: Bryan Habana tops the all-time Rugby Championship try-scoring list with 21.

MOST TRIES: TOP TEN

Pos	Tries	Player (Country, Span)
1	21	Bryan Habana (South Africa, 2005–16)
2	18	Ben Smith (New Zealand, 2012–17)
3	17	Richie McCaw (New Zealand, 2002–15)
4	16	Christian Cullen (New Zealand, 1996–2002)
5	15	Joe Rokocoko (New Zealand, 2003–10)
6	13	Adam Ashley-Cooper (Australia, 2005–16)
=	13	Doug Howlett (New Zealand, 2001–07)
=	13	Julian Savea (New Zealand, 2012–16)
9	12	Israel Dagg (New Zealand, 2010–17)
10	11	Jean de Villiers (South Africa, 2004–15)
=	11	Ma'a Nonu (New Zealand, 2008–15)

NOKWE MAKES HIS MARK FOR THE BOKS

They may have finished bottom of the pile in the 2008 Tri-Nations, but South Africa rounded off what had otherwise been a disappointing campaign in style. The star of their comprehensive 53–8 victory over Australia in Johannesburg on 30 August was Jongi Nokwe. Making only his third appearance for the Boks, the winger scored four tries in the match before leaving the field through injury in the 51st minute. It remains the most tries by a player in a Rugby Championship match.

YOUNG GUN O'CONNOR SETS NEW RECORD

Currently one of the most exciting prospects in world rugby, James O'Connor became Australia's second youngest Test player when he made his debut against Italy at Padova on 8 November 2008. Despite his tender years, he is already being compared to Aussie great Tim Horan, and he made history on 5 September 2009 when he scored Australia's second try in their 21–6 victory over South Africa at Brisbane to become, aged 19 years 62 days, the youngest-ever try-scorer in a Tri-Nations match.

ABOVE: Jongi Nokwe's third match for South Africa was a very special one. Despite having to be taken off with an injury after only 51 minutes, the flying winger had already scored a Tri-Nations Championship record four tries in the Springboks 53–8 rout of Australia at Johannesburg in August 2007.

UNLIKELY RECORD FOR RONCERO

Rodrigo Roncero established a reputation as one of the world's most destructive scrummagers during his 14-year, 55-match career with the Pumas, but it is his try-scoring exploits that earned him a place in the record books. When he crossed the line in the 12th minute of Argentina's match against New Zealand at Wellington on 8 September 2012, to give his side a 5–3 lead, he became, aged 35 years 204 days, the oldest try-scorer in the competition's history (beating Frank Bunce's record that had stood for more than 15 years). His joy was brief, however, as New Zealand recovered and went on to win the match 21–5.

RIGHT: Rodrigo Roncero's sixth international try was a record-breaking one: it saw him become the oldest ever try-scorer in the Tri-Nations/Rugby Championship.

ALL-TIME LEADING TRY-SCORERS: BY POSITION

Position	Player (Country, Span)	Tries
Full-back	Christian Cullen* (New Zealand, 1996–2002)	13
Winger	Bryan Habana (South Africa, 2005–16)	21
Centre	Ma'a Nonu (New Zealand, 2008–15)	11
Fly-half	Beauden Barrett (New Zealand, 2012–17)	8
Scrum-half	Justin Marshall (New Zealand, 1996–2004)	9
	Will Genia (Australia, 2009–17)	9
No.8	Kieran Read (New Zealand, 2009–17)	9
Flanker	Richie McCaw (New Zealand, 2002–15)	17
Lock	Mark Andrews (South Africa, 1996–2001)	3
	Victor Matfield (South Africa, 2001–15)	3
Prop	Tony Woodcock (New Zealand, 2005–15)	7
Hooker	Keven Mealamu (New Zealand, 2003–15)	5

MAGICAL McCAW

New Zealand's Richie McCaw is the only of only two players in history (Dan Carter is the other) to win the IRB's International Player of the Year award on three occasions, in 2006, 2009 and 2010). The flanker has been a shining light for New Zealand ever since he made his debut for the All Blacks against Ireland in November 2001. And McCaw has enjoyed much success in the Rugby Championship, too, scoring 17 tries in 58 matches – the most by any forward in the tournament's history.

MOST OVERALL TRIES AGAINST ONE OPPONENT

Opponent	Tries	Player (Country)	Matches
Argentina	9	Julian Savea (New Zealand, 2012–15)	8
Australia	10	Richie McCaw (New Zealand, 2002–15)	28
New Zealand	8	Bryan Habana (South Africa, 2005–16)	24
South Africa	9	Christian Cullen (New Zealand, 1996–2002)	11

POINTS-SCORING RECORDS

CARTER LEADS THE WAY

Dan Carter's tournament debut came as a try-scoring replacement during New Zealand's 50–21 defeat of Australia at Sydney on 26 July 2003, but he had to wait almost a year for his second appearance. Since 2004, however, the man who stands at the top of international rugby's all-time leading points-scoring table has been the creative, driving force behind a dominant All Blacks team that has collected seven titles in nine years. He has also set many tournament records: most points (554 in 41 matches); most points in one tournament (99 in 2006); most points at one stadium (105 in seven matches at Auckland's Eden Park); most penalties (120); and most conversions (76).

MOST POINTS ON DEBUT

Great things were expected of Tom Taylor when he made his debut for New Zealand against Australia at Wellington on 24 August 2013. He was the son of Warwick Taylor, who had played for the All Blacks between 1983 and 1988 and the nephew of Murray Taylor, who had won seven caps for New Zealand. And he did not disappoint, scoring 14 points (one conversion and four penalties) in the match – the most by any player on debut in the Rugby Championship. He went on to make two further appearances.

ABOVE: South Africa's Morne Steyn enjoyed a stellar debut season in the 2009 Tri-Nations Championship and broke a host of records as the Springboks went on to claim the title.

THE HIGHEST POINTS-SCORING CAPTAIN

If two Rugby World Cup-winning triumphs, in 2011 and 2015, confirmed Richie McCaw's standing as one of the game's all-time greats, then a string of standout performances in the Rugby Championship over the years put him on the path to greatness. McCaw played in a record 58 matches in the competition between 2002 and 2015 and also holds the record for the most points scored in Rugby Championship matches by a captain (70 – thanks to 14 tries).

LEFT: New Zealand's kicking machine Dan Carter is the only player in the history of the Tri-Nations/Rugby Championship to have scored more than 554 points.

SENSATIONAL STEYN MAKES HIS TRI-NATIONS MARK

Bulls fly-half Morne Steyn burst on to the international rugby scene when he nailed a last-gasp penalty for South Africa against the British and Irish Lions at his home ground, Pretoria, on 27 June 2009 to secure a 28–25 win and an unassailable 2–0 series lead. He carried this form into the 2009 Tri-Nations championship, scoring all of his side's points in their 31–19 victory over New Zealand at Durban (to break Andrew Mehrtens' record for the most points scored by a player in a single Tri-Nations match), and ended South Africa's title-winning campaign having set the new tournament mark for the most penalties in a single tournament (23) and for the most drop goals in a single tournament (3). In 2010, he scored 24 points in South Africa's 39–41 defeat to Australia in Bloemfontein to break yet another Tri-Nations record: it is the most points scored by a player who has finished on the losing side.

MOST POINTS IN A TOURNAMENT: TOP FIVE

Pos	Points	Player (Country)	Year
1	99	Dan Carter (New Zealand)	2006
2	95	Morne Steyn (South Africa)	2009
3	88	Morne Steyn (South Africa)	2013
4	84	Carlos Spencer (New Zealand)	1997
5	82	Dan Carter (New Zealand)	2008

PRETORIUS' CLAIM TO FAME

Supremely gifted in attack – he has fast feet, good hands and an eye for a gap – Andre Pretorius' perceived weakness in defence curtailed what many thought would be a glittering international career. The diminutive fly-half made his debut for South Africa aged 23 against Wales at Bloemfontein on 8 June 2002, scoring three penalties in a 34–19 victory. And when he scored 24 points against Argentina in his third match, the future looked bright. But injuries – and that perceived defensive weakness – started to take their toll. Pretorius was in and out of the Boks' starting XV until 2007, after which he disappeared from the international scene. He does have one claim to fame, however. He is the only player in Tri-Nations/Rugby Championship history to have scored a try, a conversion, a penalty and a drop-goal in a single match. He achieved the feat during the Boks' 23–30 defeat to New Zealand at Durban on 10 August 2002.

MOST POINTS AGAINST A SINGLE OPPONENT

Opponent	Points	Player (Country, Span)
Argentina	100	Bernard Foley (Australia, 2013–17)
Australia	273	Dan Carter (New Zealand, 2003–15)
New Zealand	155	Matt Burke (Australia, 1996–2004)
South Africa	245	Dan Carter (New Zealand, 2004–13)

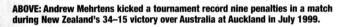

ABOVE: Andrew Mehrtens kicked a tournament record nine penalties in a match during New Zealand's 34–15 victory over Australia at Auckland in July 1999.

ABOVE: South Africa's Andre Pretorius is the only player in Tri-Nations/Rugby Championship history to score a try, a conversion, a penalty and a drop-goal in a single match.

UNUSUAL RECORD FOR EALES

John Eales holds many records in international rugby history: in 1999, he was captain of Australia when they became the first team to win the Rugby World Cup twice and he was also the first Australia captain to lead his side to back-to-back Tri-Nations tournament victories. But he also another unusual record: he is the only forward in the tournament's history to score points via the boot – he kicked four penalties.

KICKING MASTERCLASS PROPELS MEHRTENS INTO RECORD BOOKS

New Zealand fly-half Andrew Mehrtens was the main architect behind his side's comfortable 34–15 victory over Australia at Auckland on 24 July 1999. The South African-born Canterbury fly-half scored 29 points in the match (a record since broken by Morne Steyn), including nine penalties (a tournament record that stands to this day) and a conversion.

MOST POINTS: TOP TEN

Pos	Points	Player (Country, Span)
1	554	Dan Carter (New Zealand, 2003–15)
2	390	Morne Steyn (South Africa, 2009–16)
3	328	Andrew Mehrtens (New Zealand, 1996–2004)
4	271	Matt Burke (Australia, 1996–2004)
5	266	Matt Giteau (Australia, 2003–15)
6	210	Percy Montgomery (South Africa, 1997–2008)
7	207	Beauden Barrett (New Zealand, 2012–17)
8	203	Nicolas Sanchez (Argentina, 2012–17)
9	199	Bernard Foley (Australia, 2013–17)
10	198	Stirling Mortlock (Australia, 2000–09)

INTERNATIONAL RUGBY'S MARATHON MAN

When George Gregan retired from the game in 2007, he did so as the most capped player in international rugby history (with 139 appearances for Australia since his debut in 1994). Most of his records have since been beaten (most notably when Brian O'Driscoll surpassed his all-time Test appearance tally in 2014), but he still holds one Tri-Nations/ Rugby Championship record. He has made more appearances against South Africa in the tournament than any other player (25).

BELOW: Once international rugby's most-capped player, George Gregan made a record 25 appearances against South Africa in the Tri-Nations/Rugby Championship.

MOST APPEARANCES: TOP TEN

Pos	Caps	Player (Country, span)
1	58	Richie McCaw (New Zealand, 2002–15)
2	54	Keven Mealamu (New Zealand, 2003–15)
=	54	Bryan Habana (South Africa, 2005–16)
4	51	Jean de Villiers (South Africa, 2004–15)
5	49	Victor Matfield (South Africa, 2001–15)
6	48	George Gregan (Australia, 1996–2007)
7	47	Nathan Sharpe (Australia, 2002–12)
=	47	Tony Woodcock (New Zealand, 2005–15)
=	47	Adam Ashley-Cooper (Australia, 2005–16)
=	47	Kieran Read (New Zealand, 2009–17)

ONE-CAP WONDERS

Of the 649 players to appear in Rugby Championship matches, 72 of them have only ever made one appearance in the competition – 11.09 per cent.

CAPTAIN FANTASTIC

In 2001, New Zealand sought to reinvigorate their line-up with fresh talent. One of the players they turned to was Richie McCaw, an openside flanker who had impressed at both Under-19 and Under-21 levels. It proved an inspired selection as New Zealand won the Tri-Nations in 2002 and 2003 and rugby aficionados immediately knew that, in McCaw, the All Blacks had unearthed a special talent. A standout performer for New Zealand against the British Lions in 2005, he was appointed captain of the All Blacks on a full-time basis the following year. Since then, under his command, New Zealand have enjoyed some of the best moments in their history winning seven Tri-Nations/ Rugby Championship titles in ten years and the Rugby World Cup in 2011 and 2015. Not surprisingly, McCaw holds the competition record for the most matches won by a player (47) and also for the most matches played in the tournament by a single player (58).

TRY-SCORING ONE-CAP WONDERS

Two players have played only one match in the tournament but marked that appearance with a try: Lloyd Johannsson (Australia) against New Zealand at Auckland on 3 September 2005 (New Zealand won the match 34–24); and Chris Feauai-Smith (Australia) v South Africa at Cape Town on 28 September 2013 (South Africa won the match 28–8).

A LONG WAIT FOR DALE SANTON

After a long domestic career with Boland and then Western Cape-based franchise Eagles (during which he established a reputation as a fiery hooker), as well as a few outings with the Emerging Springboks (whom he captained against the British and Irish Lions as long ago as 1997), Dale Santon was finally handed his senior debut for South Africa in their Tri-Nations clash with Australia at Cape Town on 12 July 2003. He thus became, at 33 years 328 days, the oldest debutant in the tournament's 15-year history.

LEFT: All Blacks captain Richie McCaw has won more Rugby Championship matches than any other player: 47 victories in 58 games.

THE TRI-NATIONS' YOUNGEST PLAYER

One of the most exciting young talents in world rugby, James O'Connor became the second youngest Australian debutant in history when, aged 18 years 126 days, he came on as a replacement against Italy at Padova on 8 November 2008. He made his first full start for his country, also against Italy, at Canberra on 13 July 2009 (and scored three tries in the match), but he was named as a replacement for the Wallabies' 2009 Tri-Nations opener against New Zealand in Auckland on 18 July. However, when he came on as a 61st-minute replacement for Berrick Barnes, he became, aged 19 years and 13 days, the youngest player in Tri-Nations history. Not that his first experience in the tournament was a winning one: the All Blacks won the match 22–16.

LUCKY CHARM

Flanker Ardie Savea had a lot to live up to when he made his debut for the All Blacks against Wales at Auckland on 11 June 2016. He is the younger brother of Julian Savea, New Zealand's try-scoring machine who seems destined to break all of his country's try-scoring records. But the younger Savea has proved to be some player in his own right, as he vies with Sam Kane for possession of New Zealand's No.7 jersey. When he has played, he has proved to be something of a lucky charm for the All Blacks, particularly in Rugby Championship matches: he has played 11 times in the tournament and has been on the winning side on every occasion.

RIGHT: New Zealand's Ardie Savea has been on the winning side in all 11 of the games he has played in the Rugby Championship between 2016 and 2017.

UNFORTUNATE RECORD FOR PUMAS LEGEND

Juan Martin Fernandez Lobbe will go down in history as one of Argentina's greatest-ever players. A versatile back-row forward who can occupy either the openside flanker or No.8 berth, he made his debut for the Pumas in 2004 and was one of his country's standout performers at the 2007 Rugby World Cup – a tournament in which Argentina shocked the rugby world by finishing third.

The Pumas' performances at that tournament would ultimately lead to their inclusion in the Rugby Championship and a chance to test their mettle against Australia, New Zealand and South Africa. And no Argentine player has suffered more than Fernandez Lobbe: he has played in 17 matches in the tournament and has never tasted victory (a record), suffering 16 defeats and one draw (against South Africa, 16–16, at Mendoza on 25 August 2012) along the way.

MOST APPEARANCES: BY POSITION

Position	Player (Country, Span)	Appearances
Full-back	Mils Muliaina (New Zealand, 2003–11)	37
Winger	Bryan Habana (South Africa, 2007–16)	54
Centre	Jean de Villiers (South Africa, 2005–15)	44
Fly-half	Dan Carter (New Zealand, 2003–15)	38
Scrum-half	George Gregan (Australia, 1996–2007)	48
No.8	Kieran Read (New Zealand, 2009–17)	46
Flanker	Richie McCaw (New Zealand, 2002–15)	58
Lock	Victor Matfield (South Africa, 2001–15)	49
Prop	Tony Woodcock (New Zealand, 2005–15)	47
Hooker	Keven Mealamu (New Zealand, 2003–15)	54

LEFT: Australia's James O'Connor is the youngest player to appear in the Rugby Championship and also the competition's youngest-ever try-scorer.

MORE MCCAW RECORDS

A Rugby World Cup-winning captain in 2011 (thus ending New Zealand's much-chronicled 24-year wait for the game's biggest prize) and 2015 and one of only two men in history to win the IRB Player of the Year Award on three occasions (in 2006, 2009 and 2010), Richie McCaw's status among the game's all-time greats is already secure. And he's enjoyed plenty of success in the Tri-Nations/Rugby Championship too, leading New Zealand to seven titles in ten years since he was appointed full-time captain in 2006, posting a record of 47 wins in 58 matches. Both the number of wins recorded and matches played are all-time tournament records for a captain.

TOURNAMENT RED CARDS

Player	Team	Opponent	Venue	Date
Andre Venter	South Africa	New Zealand	Auckland	9 Aug 1997
Marius Joubert	South Africa	Australia	Johannesburg	17 Aug 2002
Drew Mitchell	Australia	New Zealand	Melbourne	31 July 2010
Bismarck du Plessis	South Africa	New Zealand	Auckland	14 Sep 2013
Tomas Lavanini	Argentina	South Africa	Salta	26 Aug 2017
Damian de Allende	South Africa	New Zealand	Cape Town	7 Oct 2017

TRI-NATIONS JOY FOR KIWI HENRY

Graham Henry will always be celebrated in New Zealand as the man who ended the country's 24-year wait for Rugby World Cup glory. But his record in the Tri-Nations was also exemplary. The All Blacks took the title five times during Henry's reign as coach (between 2004 and 2011), comfortably making him the most successful coach in the tournament's history.

MOST AND FEWEST YELLOW CARDS IN A TOURNAMENT

The yellow card has become a regular feature in Tri-Nations/Rugby Championship matches since the first one was shown in 1997. In all, 110 have been shown, on average more than one every other game. The most shown yellow cards shown by referees in a single tournament was 16 in 2013. Surprisingly, however, three tournaments have been completed without a single yellow card being shown: in 1998, 1999 and 2011 (when each tournament comprised just six matches).

ABOVE: Five Tri-Nations titles in seven years bears testimony to Graham Henry's substantial impact on New Zealand rugby, but he will always be remembered as the coach who helped the All Blacks win the Rugby World Cup on home soil in 2011.

MOST YELLOW CARDS IN A MATCH

The record for the most yellow cards shown in a match is four, on two occasions: during South Africa's 28–8 victory over Australia at Cape Town on 28 September 2013 (two for South Africa and two for Australia); and during New Zealand's 36–10 victory against Argentina in Buenos Aires on 30 September 2017 (two for New Zealand and two for Argentina).

MATCHES WON WITH A YELLOW CARD

Statistics show that only 41 times (in 77 matches) has a team gone on to win a Tri-Nations/Rugby Championship tie after one of their players has received a yellow card – 53.25 per cent.

SPRINGBOKS SUFFER A RED CARD BUT STILL SEE OFF THE WALLABIES

South Africa are the only side in Tri-Nations Championship history of to have won a match despite having had a player sent off. The Springboks' Marius Joubert was red-carded in their match against Australia at Ellis Park, Johannesburg, on 17 August 2002, but still held on to win 33–31. In both other cases, the team with a player sent off has gone on to lose.

LEFT: With 47 wins in 58 Tri-Nations/Rugby Championship matches, Richie McCaw is the most successful captain in the tournament's history.

MOST YELLOW CARDS (COUNTRY)

Pos	Number	Country
1	32	Australia
=	32	South Africa
3	25	New Zealand
4	11	Argentina

SOUTH AFRICA'S VENTER THE FIRST TO SEE RED

New Zealand's clash with South Africa at Eden Park, Auckland, on 9 August 1997 was fraught with tension from the moment the Springboks refused to face the All Blacks' traditional pre-match haka, and the match was on a knife-edge when the second half kicked off with the home side holding a slender 23–21 lead. And then came a history-making moment that changed the course of the match: South Africa's Andre Venter became the first-ever player in the Tri-Nations to be sent off (for stamping). The floodgates duly opened and New Zealand romped to a 55–35 victory.

SURVIVING THE YELLOW-CARD ODDS

The Tri-Nations record for the most yellow cards received by a team that has gone on to win the match is two, a feat achieved on 13 occasions: by Australia against South Africa at Brisbane on 27 July 2002 – won 38–27; by South Africa against Australia at Durban on 21 August 2004 – won 23–19; by South Africa against New Zealand at Durban on 1 August 2009 – won 31–19; by New Zealand against South Africa at Johannesburg on 6 October 2012 – won 32–16; by New Zealand against South Africa at Auckland on 14 September 2013 – won 29–15; by South Africa against Australia at Cape Town on 28 September 2013 – won 28–8; by New Zealand against South Africa at Johannesburg on 5 October 2013 – won 38–27; by Australia against Argentina at Rosario on 5 October 2013 – won 54–17; by New Zealand against Australia at Auckland on 23 August 2014 – won 51–20; by Australia against New Zealand at Sydney on 8 August 2015 – won 27–19; by Australia against Argentina at Perth on 17 Sep 2016 – won 36–20; by New Zealand against Argentina at Buenos Aires on 1 Oct 2016 – won 36–17; by Australia against Argentina at Twickenham on 8 Oct 2016 – won 33–21; and by New Zealand against Argentina at Buenos Aires on 30 September 2017 – won 36–10.

YELLOW PERIL FOR HOOPER

After starring for Australia at the 2011 IRB Junior World Championships (in which the Wallabies finished third), and following that up with a standout 2012 season for the Brumbies, Michael Hooper finally made his senior international debut for Australia (as a replacement) during the 9-6 defeat to Scotland at Newcastle on 5 June 2012. The openside flanker made his first full appearance against New Zealand later that year and has been an ever-present in the Wallabies pack ever since. He has set an unwanted record along the way, however. He is the only player in the Rugby Championship's history to have been shown a yellow card on four occasions: against South Africa at Brisbane on 7 September 2013; against South Africa at Cape Town on 28 September 2013; against Argentina at Mendoza on 4 October 2014; and against Argentina at Twickenham on 8 October 2016.

THE FIRST TRI-NATIONS YELLOW CARD

The first player in Tri-Nations history to be shown a yellow card was Australia's James Holbeck in the Wallabies' final match of the 1997 campaign, against South Africa at Pretoria on 23 August. The Springboks went on to record a comfortable 61–22 victory, condemning the Wallabies to a bottom-place finish.

WORLD RUGBY RANKINGS AND AWARDS

The World Rugby Rankings, introduced on 9 September 2003, is a system used to rank the world's international teams based on their results, with all teams given a rating between 0 and 100. The rankings are based on a points-exchange system in which sides take or gain points off each other depending on the result of a match. The points gained or lost in a match depend on the relative strengths of each team and the margin of defeat or victory, with an allowance made for teams who have home advantage. Due to the singular importance of the event, points-exchanges are doubled for Rugby World Cup matches. When the system was introduced, England, as a result of their 2003 Rugby World Cup victory, were installed at no.1, but New Zealand, thanks largely to their dominance in the Tri-Nations championship, have been the most consistently ranked no.1 team, holding the top spot for approximately 75 per cent of the time between 2003 and 2011. First presented in 2001, the World Rugby Awards are bestowed annually by the game's world governing body to honour significant achievements in the sport, with the Player of the Year award considered the most prestigious accolade.

BELOW: Beauden Barrett showed New Zealand there was life after Dan Carter, and was named World Rugby Player of the Year in 2016 and 2017.

Pos	Member Union	Rating Point	Pos	Member Union	Rating Point
1	New Zealand	93.99	26	Brazil	56.81
2	Ireland	89.11	27	Netherlands	56.52
3	England	86.23	28	Germany	54.42
4	Australia	85.49	29	Korea	54.39
5	Scotland	83.83	30	Kenya	54.24
6	South Africa	83.81	31	Chile	54.04
7	Wales	83.41	32	Czech Republic	53.30
8	France	79.10	33	Switzerland	53.25
9	Argentina	78.22	34	Uganda	50.69
10	Fiji	77.93	35	Lithuania	50.69
11	Japan	75.66	36	Poland	50.46
12	Georgia	73.96	37	Malta	49.67
13	Tonga	71.87	38	Ukraine	49.64
14	Italy	71.10	39	Morocco	48.97
15	USA	69.23	40	Paraguay	48.54
16	Samoa	69.03	41	Colombia	48.36
17	Romania	68.25	42	Sri Lanka	48.27
18	Uruguay	65.37	43	Tunisia	47.76
19	Russia	63.27	44	Zimbabwe	47.59
20	Spain	63.09	45	Moldova	47.12
21	Canada	61.98	46	Madagascar	46.76
22	Hong Kong	59.66	47	Guyana	46.56
23	Portugal	59.51	48	Malaysia	46.26
24	Namibia	58.93	49	Senegal	45.85
25	Belgium	58.09	50	Cote d'Ivoire	45.56

BELOW: It's been another exceptional year for the All Blacks: six out of six wins in the Rugby Championship; a nail-biting 1–1 series draw with the British Lions; and still the No.1 ranked team in world rugby.

51	Trinidad & Tobago	45.51	79	India	35.75
52	Cayman Islands	45.20	80	Peru	35.70
53	Mexico	45.12	81	St Vincent &	
54	Cook Islands	45.11		The Grenadines	34.91
55	Croatia	44.46	82	Denmark	34.89
56	Singapore	44.26	83	Barbados	34.88
57	Latvia	44.06	84	Serbia	34.87
58	Philippines	43.44	85	Tahiti	33.79
59	Israel	42.86	86	Bahamas	33.76
60	Sweden	42.84	87	China	33.58
61	Kazakhstan	42.14	88	Swaziland	32.04
62	Venezuela	41.87	89	Uzbekistan	31.29
63	Luxembourg	41.20	90	Mauritius	31.27
64	Jamaica	40.37	91	Rwanda	30.98
65	Chinese Taipei	39.35	92	Pakistan	30.74
66	Papua New Guinea	39.27	93	Costa Rica	30.00
67	Botswana	39.22	=	Ghana	30.00
68	Hungary	38.75	95	Bulgaria	29.94
69	Andorra	38.44	96	Norway	29.52
70	Bosnia & Herzegovina	38.39	97	Indonesia	28.73
71	United Arab Emirates	37.93	98	Finland	28.53
72	Guam	37.85	99	Niue Island	28.45
73	Nigeria	37.71	100	Cameroon	26.33
74	Thailand	37.68	101	Solomon Islands	24.40
75	Austria	37.40	102	Monaco	23.17
76	Bermuda	37.39	103	Greece	22.55
77	Slovenia	37.21	104	Vanuatu	21.45
78	Zambia	36.72	105	American Samoa	19.53

ABOVE: Dylan Hartley's England suffered a disappointing defence of their Six Nations crown in 2017, but still stand third in the world rankings.

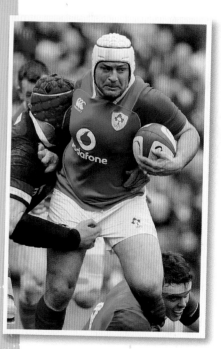

ABOVE: Rory Best became only the third Irishman to lead his side to a Grand Slam. Ireland are now at an all-time high No.2 in the rankings.

WORLD RUGBY AWARDS

2001

IRB International Player of the Year: **Keith Wood (Ireland)**
IRB International Team of the Year: **Australia**
IRB International Coach of the Year: **Rod Macqueen (Australia)**
IRB International Young Player of the Year: **Gavin Henson (Wales)**
IRB International Women's Player of the Year: **Shelley Rae (England)**
IRB Referee Award for Distinguished Service: **Ed Morrison (England)**
IRB Spirit of Rugby Award: **Tim Grandadge (India)**
IRB Distinguished Service Award: **Tom Kiernan (Ireland)**
IRB Development Award: **Jorge Brasceras (Uruguay)**
IRB Chairman's Awards: **Kath McLean, Sir Terry McLean, Albert Ferrasse, John Eales**

2002

IRB International Player of the Year: **Fabien Galthié (France)**
IRB International Team of the Year: **France**
IRB International Coach of the Year: **Bernard Laporte (France)**
IRB International U19 Player of the Year: **Luke McAlister (New Zealand)**
IRB International U21 Player of the Year: **Pat Barnard (South Africa)**
IRB International Sevens Team of the Year: **New Zealand**
IRB International Women's Player of the Year: **Monique Hirovanaa (New Zealand)**
IRB Referee Award for Distinguished Service: **Colin Hawke (New Zealand)**
IRB Distinguished Services Award: **Allan Hosie (Scotland)**
IRB Spirit of Rugby Award: **Old Christians Club (Uruguay)**
IRB Development Award: **John Broadfoot (England)**
IRB Chairman's Awards: **Bill McLaren, George Pippos (posthumously)**

2003

IRB International Player of the Year: **Jonny Wilkinson (England)**
IRB International Team of the Year: **England**
IRB International Coach of the Year: **Sir Clive Woodward (England)**
IRB International U19 Player of the Year: **Jean Baptiste Payras (France)**
IRB International U21 Player of the Year: **Ben Atiga (New Zealand)**
IRB International Sevens Team of the Year: **New Zealand**
IRB Spirit of Rugby Award: **Michael and Linda Collinson (Swaziland)**
IRB Award for Distinguished Service: **Bob Stuart (Australia)**
IRB Referee Distinguished Service Award: **Derek Bevan (Wales)**
IRB International Women's Personality of the Year: **Kathy Flores (United States)**
IRB Development Award: **Tan Theany and Philippe Monnin**
IRB Chairman's Awards: **Vernon Pugh (Wales)**

2004

IRB International Player of the Year: **Schalk Burger (South Africa)**
IRB International Team of the Year: **South Africa**
IRB International Coach of the Year: **Jake White (South Africa)**
IRB International U19 Player of the Year: **Jeremy Thrush (New Zealand)**
IRB International U21 Player of the Year: **Jerome Kaino (New Zealand)**
IRB International Sevens Team of the Year: **New Zealand**
IRB International Sevens Player of the Year: **Simon Amor (England)**
IRB Spirit of Rugby Award: **Jarrod Cunningham (New Zealand)**
Vernon Pugh Award for Distinguished Service: **Ronnie Dawson (Ireland)**
IRB Referee Award for Distinguished Service: **Jim Fleming (Scotland)**

IRB International Women's Personality of the Year: **Donna Kennedy (Scotland)**
IRB Development Award: **Guedel Ndiaye (Senegal)**
IRB Chairman's Award: **Marcel Martin (France)**

2005

IRB International Player of the Year: **Dan Carter (New Zealand)**
IRB International Team of the Year: **New Zealand**
IRB International Coach of the Year: **Graham Henry (New Zealand)**
IRB International U19 Player of the Year: **Isaia Toeava (New Zealand)**
IRB International U21 Player of the Year: **Tatafu Polota-Nau (Australia)**
IRB International Sevens Team of the Year: **Fiji**
IRB International Sevens Player of the Year: **Orene Ai'i (New Zealand)**
IRB Spirit of Rugby Award: **Jean Pierre Rives (France)**
Vernon Pugh Award for Distinguished Service: **Peter Crittle (Australia)**
IRB Referee Award for Distinguished Service: **Paddy O'Brien (New Zealand)**
IRB International Women's Personality of the Year: **Farah Palmer (New Zealand)**
IRB Development Award: **Robert Antonin (France)**
IRB Chairman's Award: **Sir Tasker Watkins (Wales)**

2006

IRB International Player of the Year: **Richie McCaw (New Zealand)**
IRB International Team of the Year: **New Zealand**
IRB International Coach of the Year: **Graham Henry (New Zealand)**
IRB International U19 Player of the Year: **Josh Holmes (Australia)**
IRB International U21 Player of the Year: **Lionel Beauxis (France)**
IRB International Sevens Team of the Year: **Fiji**

IRB International Sevens Player of the Year:
Uale Mai (Samoa)
IRB Spirit of Rugby Award: **Polly Miller**
Vernon Pugh Award for Distinguished Service: **Brian Lochore (New Zealand)**
IRB Referee Award for Distinguished Service: **Peter Marshall (Australia)**
IRB International Women's Personality of the Year: **Margaret Alphonsi (England)**
IRB Development Award: **Mike Luke (Canada)**

2007

IRB International Player of the Year: **Bryan Habana (South Africa)**
IRB International Team of the Year: **South Africa**
IRB International Coach of the Year: **Jake White (South Africa)**
IRB Under-19 Player of the Year: **Robert Fruean (New Zealand)**
IRB Sevens Player of the Year: **Afeleke Pelenise (New Zealand)**
IRB Sevens Team of the Year: **New Zealand**
IRB Women's Personality of the Year: **Sarah Corrigan, referee (Australia)**
IRB Referee Award for Distinguished Service: **Dick Byres, retired (Australia)**
Vernon Pugh Award for Distinguished Service: **José María Epalza (Spain)**
Spirit of Rugby Award: **Nicolas Pueta (Argentina)**
IRPA Try of the Year: **Takudzwa Ngwenya (United States)**
IRPA Special Merit Award: **Fabien Pelous (France)**
IRB Development Award: **Jacob Thompson (Jamaica)**

2008

IRB International Player of the Year: **Shane Williams (Wales)**
IRB International Team of the Year: **New Zealand**
IRB International Coach of the Year: **Graham Henry (New Zealand)**

IRB Junior Player of the Year:
Luke Braid (New Zealand)
IRB International Sevens Player
of the Year:
D.J. Forbes (New Zealand)
IRB Spirit of Rugby Award:
**Roelien Muller and Patrick
Cotter**
IRB Referee Award for
Distinguished Service:
**Andre Watson (South
Africa)**
IRB International Women's
Personality of the Year:
Carol Isherwood (England)
IRPA Special Merit Award:
Agustin Pichot (Argentina)
IRB Development Award: **TAG
Rugby Development Trust
and Martin Hansford (South
Africa)**
IRPA Try of the Year:
Brian O'Driscoll (Ireland)

2009

IRB International Player of the
Year: **Richie McCaw
(New Zealand)**
IRB International Team of the
Year: **South Africa**
IRB International Coach of the
Year: **Declan Kidney (Ireland)**
IRB Junior Player of the
Year: **Aaron Cruden (New
Zealand)**
IRB International Sevens Player
of the Year:
Ollie Phillips (England)
IRB Spirit of Rugby Award:
L'Aquila Rugby (Italy)
IRB International Women's
Personality of the Year: **Debby
Hodgkinson (Australia)**
IRPA Special Merit Award:
Kevin Mac Clancy
IRPA Try of the Year: **Jaque
Fourie (South Africa)**

2010

IRB International Player of the
Year: **Richie McCaw
(New Zealand)**
IRB International Team of the
Year: **New Zealand**
IRB International Coach of the
Year: **Graham Henry
(New Zealand)**
IRB Junior Player of the Year:
Julian Savea (New Zealand)
IRB International Sevens Player
of the Year:
Mikaele Pesamino (Samoa)
IRB Spirit of Rugby Award:
Virreyes RC (Argentina)
IRB International Women's
Personality of the Year: **Carla
Hohepa (New Zealand)**
IRB Development Award: **Brian
O'Shea (Ireland)**

IRB Referee Award for
Distinguished Service:
Colin High

2011

IRB International Player of the Year:
Thierry Dusautoir (France)
IRB International Team of the
Year: **New Zealand**
IRB International Coach of the
Year: **Graham Henry
(New Zealand)**
IRB Junior Player of the Year:
George Ford (England)
IRB International Sevens Player
of the Year:
Cecil Afrika (South Africa)
IRB Spirit of Rugby Award:
Wooden Spoon
IRB International Women's
Personality of the Year:
Ruth Mitchell (England)
IRB Development Award:
Rookie Rugby
IRB Referee Award for
Distinguished Service: **Keith
Lawrence (New Zealand)**
IRB Try of the Year
**Radike Samo (Australia v
New Zealand)**
IRPA Special Merit Award:
George Smith (Australia)
Vernon Pugh Award for
Distinguished Service:
Jock Hobbs

2012

IRB International Player of the
Year: **Dan Carter
(New Zealand)**
IRB International Team of the
Year: **New Zealand**
IRB International Coach of the
Year: **Steve Hansen
(New Zealand)**
IRB Junior Player of the Year:
**Jan Serfontaine
(South Africa)**
IRB International Sevens Player
of the Year: **Tomasi Cama
(New Zealand)**
IRB Spirit of Rugby Award:
Lindsay Hilton (Canada)
IRB Development Award:
South Africa Rugby Union
IRB Referee Award for
Distinguished Service:
Paul Dobson (South Africa)
IRB Try of the Year
**Bryan Habana (South Africa
v New Zealand**
Vernon Pugh Award for
Distinguished Service:
Viorel Morariu (Romania)

2013

IRB International Player of the
Year: **Kieran Read
(New Zealand)**

IRB International Team of the
Year: **New Zealand**
IRB International Coach of the
Year: **Steve Hansen
(New Zealand)**
IRB Junior Player of the Year:
Sam Davies (Wales)
IRB International Sevens Player
of the Year:
**Tim Mikkelson (New
Zealand)**
IRB Women's Sevens Player of
the Year:
**Kayla McAlister (New
Zealand)**
IRB Spirit of Rugby Award:
**Yoshiharu Yamaguchi
(Japan)**
IRB Development Award:
**Ange Guimera (Brazil/Ivory
Coast)**
IRB Referee Award for
Distinguished Service:
Michel Lamoulie (France)
IRB Try of the Year: **Beauden
Barrett (New Zealand v
France)**
Vernon Pugh Award for
Distinguished Service:
Ian McIntosh (South Africa)
IRB Special Award:
Robin Timmins

2014

World Rugby Player of the Year:
**Brodie Retallick
(New Zealand)**
World Rugby Team of the Year:
New Zealand
World Rugby Coach of the Year:
**Steve Hansen
(New Zealand)**
World Rugby Try of the Year:
**Francois Hougaard
(South Africa v New
Zealand)**
IRB Sevens Player of the Year:
Samisono Viriviri (Fiji)
IRB Women's Player of
the Year:
Magali Harvey (Canada)
IRB Women's Sevens Player of
the Year:
Emilee Cherry (Australia)
IRB Referee Award for
Distinguished Service:
Bob Francis (New Zealand)
IRB Spirit of Rugby Award: **Vor
Vivendo o Rugby Project
(Brazil)**
IRB Development Award:
Bidzina Ivanishvili (Georgia)
Vernon Pugh Award for
Distinguished Service:
Ray Williams (Wales)

2015

World Rugby Player of the Year:
Dan Carter (New Zealand)

World Rugby Team of the Year:
New Zealand
World Rugby Coach of the Year:
Michael Cheika (Australia)
World Rugby Breakthrough
Player of the Year: **Nehe
Milner-Skudder (New
Zealand)**
IPRA Try of the Year:
Julian Savea (New Zealand)
World Rugby Sevens Player of
the Year:
Werner Kok (South Africa)
World Rugby Women's Player of
the Year:
**Kendra Cocksedge
(New Zealand)**
World Rugby Women's Sevens
Player of the Year: **Portia
Woodman
(New Zealand)**
World Rugby Referee Award:
Nigel Owens (Wales)
2015 Rugby World Cup Best
Moment:
Japan beating South Africa
IRPA Special Merit Award:
**Brian O'Driscoll (Ireland),
Nathan Sharpe (Australia)**
Award for Character:
Pakistan Rugby Union
Vernon Pugh Award for
Distinguished Service:
Nigel Starmer-Smith

2016

World Rugby Player of the Year:
**Beauden Barrett
(New Zealand)**
World Rugby Team of the Year:
New Zealand
World Rugby Coach of the Year:
**Steve Hansen
(New Zealand)**
World Rugby Breakthrough
Player of the Year:
Maro Itoje (England)
IPRA Try of the Year:
Jamie Heaslip (Ireland)
World Rugby Sevens Player of
the Year:
**Saebelo Senatia (South
Africa)**
World Rugby Women's Player of
the Year:
Sarah Hunter (England)
World Rugby Referee Award:
**Alhambra Nievas (Spain)/
Rasta Rasivhenge (South
Africa)**
IRPA Special Merit Award: **Jean
de Villiers (South Africa)**
Award for Character:
**Rugby Opens Borders
(Austrian Rugby Union)**
Vernon Pugh Award for
Distinguished Service:
Syd Millar

2017 WORLD RUGBY AWARD WINNERS

WORLD RUGBY PLAYER OF THE YEAR:
BEAUDEN BARRETT (NEW ZEALAND)

Any fears New Zealand's rugby fans had that Dan Carter's post-2015 Rugby World Cup retirement would create an unfillable void in the All Black line-up have been eased by the performances of Beauden Barrett. After picking up the World Rugby Player of the Year Award in 2016, he became only the second player to win the game's most prestigious individual award two years in a row (after compatriot Richie McCaw in 2009 and 2010). He received the award ahead of four other nominees in All Blacks team-mate Rieko Ioane, England and British Lions duo Owen Farrell and Maro Itoje and Australia full-back Israel Folau. Barrett said: "I'm very proud and surprised. I wanted to be better than last year and I still think I have plenty more to go. The Lions series put us under the most pressure I have probably felt in a black jersey… We learnt a lot from that series, particularly taking that into the World Cup."

WORLD RUGBY TEAM OF THE YEAR:
NEW ZEALAND WOMEN

New Zealand won a fifth Women's Rugby World Cup title in August after beating defending champions England 41-32 in a thrilling finale in Belfast. The Black Ferns were the top point and try scorers in the tournament. This success came after New Zealand hosted the International Women's Rugby Series in June with the hosts beating Australia and Canada before losing to England. New Zealand are the first women's team to receive the accolade.

WORLD RUGBY COACH OF THE YEAR:
EDDIE JONES (ENGLAND)

Now in his second year, Eddie Jones led England to nine victories in 2017 with the only loss coming against Ireland in the Six Nations finale. A second Six Nations title was followed by a two-test series win in Argentina in June and victories over Argentina, Australia and Samoa to take his record to 22 wins in his 23 tests in charge.

ABOVE: New Zealand's Rieko Ioane had a spectacular breakthrough season in 2017.

WORLD RUGBY BREAKTHROUGH PLAYER OF THE YEAR:
RIEKO IOANE (NEW ZEALAND)

The winger marked his All Blacks debut with a try against Italy, but it is in 2017 that Rieko Ioane truly made his mark on the international stage with 10 tries in 11 starts. The 20-year-old scored twice in his first start against the British and Irish Lions at Eden Park and claimed another double in his first Bledisloe Cup match in August.

IRPA TRY OF THE YEAR:
JOAQUIN TUCULET (ARGENTINA)

Voted for by rugby fans on Twitter, Joaquín Tuculet's score for Argentina in the first test against England in June was named the IRPA (International Rugby Players' Association) Try of the Year 2017. A breakout that began deep in his team's own 22 after Juan Manuel Leguizamon fielded an England kick and the ball found its way to Matias Orlando, the centre slicing through the visitor's defence with ease. He found Emiliano Boffelli in support, the test debutant straightening the attack before releasing Tuculet to sprint away from the defence to finish off the free-flowing move.

WORLD RUGBY SEVENS PLAYER OF THE YEAR: PERRY BAKER (UNITED STATES)

The oldest of the nominees at 31, Perry Baker enjoyed a season to remember in 2016-17, topping the charts for tries and points scored on the HSBC World Rugby Sevens Series with 57 and 285 respectively. The USA Eagles flyer has electric pace and can make something out of nothing, but has now developed the all-round game to go with his natural speed.

LEFT: The USA's Perry Baker was the standout performer on the Sevens circuit in 2016–17.

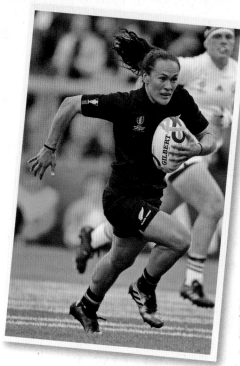

LEFT: Portia Woodman helped New Zealand to the Women's World Cup crown in 2017.

IRPA SPECIAL MERIT AWARD: RICHIE MCCAW (NEW ZEALAND); RACHAEL BURFORD (ENGLAND)

Two-time Rugby World Cup winning captain Richie McCaw is the world's most capped player with 148 tests for the All Blacks, 110 of them as captain. A three-time World Rugby Men's Player of the Year, the 36-year-old was an outstanding leader on the field but also off it. He is Patron of the New Zealand Rugby Foundation and the Catwalk Trust, supporting players and their families following serious injuries and funding research aiming to overcome paralysis after spinal court injuries.

Rachael Burford is a Rugby World Cup winner, having won the title with England in 2014. She has contributed extensively to player welfare and the game in general by sitting on a number of panels, including the World Rugby Laws Review Group, Rugby Committee and Women's Advisory Committee. She became the first female Board Member of the Rugby Players' Association in 2014.

WORLD RUGBY WOMEN'S PLAYER OF THE YEAR: PORTIA WOODMAN (NEW ZEALAND)

New Zealand winger Portia Woodman was named the World Rugby Women's Player of the Year 2017 after helping the Black Ferns win a fifth Women's Rugby World Cup title in Ireland in August. She received the award ahead of four other nominees in Black Ferns team-mate Kelly Brazier, England winger Lydia Thompson and France back-row duo Romane Menager and Safi N'Diaye Woodman said: "Obviously just winning the Team of the Year award shows just how good our team is, and they make me look good. They do all the work and I am out there on the sideline just waiting for the ball."

WORLD RUGBY REFEREE AWARD: JOY NEVILLE (IRELAND)

A veteran of 70 caps for Ireland, Joy Neville is now creating history in the world of refereeing in a year that has seen her take charge of the Women's Rugby World Cup 2017 final in August and referee her first men's international in Rugby Europe's Conference 2 North in October. This month she is acting as assistant referee for three men's matches, having recently signed a professional contract with the IRFU.

WORLD RUGBY WOMEN'S SEVENS PLAYER OF THE YEAR: MICHAELA BLYDE (NEW ZEALAND)

Michaela Blyde enjoyed a breakthrough season in 2016-17. Her potential had always been clear to see, but Portia Woodman's move into the forwards gave her the chance to make a starting spot her own. Blyde's performances saw her finish as top try-scorer with 40, take her place in the HSBC World Rugby Women's Sevens Series Dream Team.

AWARD FOR CHARACTER: EDUARDO ODERIGO (ARGENTINA)

A criminal lawyer, Eduardo "Coco" Oderigo spent 15 years working in the courts of Buenos Aires before a visit to Unit 48 at San Martin prison gave him the idea of teaching rugby and its core values to the inmates. Fundación Espartanos was born out of his desire to help prisoners reintegrate into society and weekly training sessions began in 2009. Eight years on, more than 500 prisoners are involved in the programme which has spread throughout Argentina, supported by local clubs and coaches.

VERNON PUGH AWARD FOR DISTINGUISHED SERVICE: MARCEL MARTIN (FRANCE)

Regarded as a pioneer and visionary figure, Marcel Martin spent more than 50 years involved in the development of rugby in France and was one of the main architects of the major political and sporting changes in rugby. A long-time Board member of the Fédération Française de Rugby Board and Ligue Nationale de Rugby. He passed away in May, aged 83.World Rugby Hall of Fame in 2009.

RIGHT: Beauden Barrett was the 2017 World Rugby Player of the Year.

PICTURE CREDITS

The publishers would like to thank the following sources for their kind permission to reproduce the pictures in this book.

Action Images: /Reuters: 41TL, 68TR

Alamy: /EFE News Agency: 40

Colorsport: 28BR, 55T, 137TL, 175BR; /Colin Elsey: 31L, 54C, 72T, 73BL; /Paul Seiser: 152TR

Getty Images: 51B, 99TR, 102C, 139T, 165BR; /Allsport: 100TL, 101BL, 106BL; /Odd Andersen/AFP: 17C, 24B, 92, 120TL, 165BL; /Pierre Andrieu/AFP: 23T; /Anthony Au-Yeung: 176R, 190T; /Steve Bardens: 91R; /Al Bello: 43TR; /Daniel Berehulak: 35B, 57BR; /Torsten Blackwood/AFP: 61BL; /Hamish Blair: 31B; /Lionel Bonaventure/AFP: 26BL, 113B; /Shaun Botterill: 25BL, 30TL, 44TL, 52TL, 101TR, 127R, 153B; /Gabriel Bouys/AFP: 76TR, 142T, 150BR, 157BR; /Bob Bradford/CameraSport: 5CL; /Simon Bruty: 20TL, 72BL, 122BR; /Martin Bureau/AFP: 23BL, 113L, 128R, 132; /Glenn Campbell/AFP: 63L; /David Cannon: 36B, 79BL, 167BR, 169TR; /Jean Catuffe: 4C, 21B; /Central Press: 102BL; /Central Press/Hulton Archive: 107L; /Russell Cheyne: 17BL, 21TR, 56BR; /Mike Clarke/AFP: 138BL; /Phil Cole: 58BL, 93TR, 122BL; /David Cooper/Toronto Star: 89TL; /Michael Cooper: 33T, 137R, 151BL; /Gareth Copley: 168R; /Mark Dadswell: 133L; /Carl de Souza/AFP: 61T; /Delmas/AFP: 21L; /Adrian Dennis/AFP: 29BR; /Paul Ellis/AFP: 77BL; /Darren England: 55R; /FPG: 90; /Paul Faith/AFP: 187BR; /Dante Fernandez/LatinContent: 94R; /Franck Fife/AFP: 48-49, 63TR, 87C, 134T, 142B; /Julian Finney: 22R, 75BL; /Stu Forster: 24R, 34BR, 65BL, 103BR, 110-111, 121TR, 126TR, 151TR, 163BR, 165TL; /Gallo Images: 116-117; /John Gichigi: 162BL; /Paul Gilham: 28C, 34C, 163C; /Georges Gobet/AFP: 118; /Laurence Griffiths: 45L, 187T; /Steve Haag/Action Plus: 4R; /Richard Heathcote: 33B, 66BR, 112TR; /Mike Hewitt: 7, 8-9, 17TR, 26TR, 35TL, 129BR; /Hagen Hopkins: 4CR, 96-97; /Kent Horner: 94B; /Ben Hoskins: 73TR, 166B; /Hulton Archive: 25T; /Roger Jackson/Central Press: 166BR; /Daniel Jayo: 170-171; /Tom Jenkins: 114-115; /Alexander Joe/AFP: 109B; /Hannah Johnston: 135B, 175TR; /David Jones: 67TR; /Ed Jones/AFP: 152BL; /Keystone/Hulton Archive: 98B; /Saeed Khan/AFP: 140-141; /Glyn Kirk/AFP: 42B, 148BR, 154-155; /Toshifumi Kitamura/AFP: 56BL, 131T, 146TR; /Mark Kolbe: 91BL; /Patrick Kovarik/AFP: 124BL; /Jean-Philippe Ksiazek/AFP: 23BR; /Nick Laham: 52BR, 128BL; /Ross Land: 32T, 86R, 106TR, 109TL, 124C, 138TR, 182TR, 183TL; /Bertrand Langlois/AFP: 88; /Pascal Le Segretain: 81L; /Mark Leech/Offside: 15B; /Matt Lewis: 66BL; /Warren Little: 5L, 121BR; /Philip Littlejohn/AFP: 75T; /Alex Livesey: 39R, 67B, 93C, 126BL; /Silvia Lore/NurPhoto: 4L; /Juan Mabromata/AFP: 82-83, 87BR, 133TR, 177BR; /Nigel Marple: 179BL; /Stephen McCarthy/Sportsfile: 98T; /John McCombe: 108BR; /Jamie McDonald: 36C, 38BL, 164; /Chris McGrath: 50B, 53BL; /Charles McQuillan/World Rugby: 191TL; /Marty Melville: 77TR; /Marty Melville/AFP: 122C; /Craig Mercer/CameraSport: 160-161; /Damien Meyer/AFP: 22BL, 87T; /Brendan Moran/Sportsfile: 12-13, 39BL; /Sandra Mu: 130BL; /Peter Muhly/AFP: 27BR; /Jean-Pierre Muller/AFP: 133BR; /Adrian Murrell: 107T, 109TR, 143BR; /Kazuhiro Nogi/AFP: 57TL, 181BL; /Mark Nolan: 81TR, 181; /Brendon O'Hagan/AFP: 60B, 144BL; /Alejandro Pagni/AFP: 59TL; /Park Ji-Hwan/AFP: 69TL; /Peter Parks/AFP: 54B; /Gerry Penny/AFP: 14, 158B; /Hannah Peters: 144TR, 191B; /Tertius Pickard/Gallo Images: 70-71, 123BR; /Ryan Pierse: 86BL; /Popperfoto: 45BR, 103TL, 159TR; /Steve Powell: 158TR; /Power Sport Images: 69BR, 190B; /Adam Pretty: 15R, 47, 57BL, 100BL, 123C, 127TR; /Vaughn Ridley: 89BR; /Matt Roberts: 176BL; /David Rogers: 2, 4CL, 10-11, 16BL, 20BR, 27R, 29T, 37TL, 37BR, 38TR, 38BR, 42C, 44BR, 53TR, 53BR, 59R, 61C, 64, 76BL, 78, 79TR, 79BR, 80, 95L, 95BR, 104R, 107BR, 108L, 108BC, 120BR, 123TL, 125C, 125TR, 127BL, 130T, 134B, 135TR, 139B, 143TL, 146B, 147TL, 148T, 156R, 156B, 162T, 169BL, 172BR, 173BR, 174BR, 177TL, 178TR, 178BL, 180BL, 182BL; /Miguel Rojo/AFP: 136R; /Will Russell: 183BR; /Tom Shaw: 159BL; /Vano Shlamov/AFP: 137BL; /Christophe Simon/AFP: 129C; /Cameron Spencer: 5R, 99BL, 173TL, 180C; /Ben Stansall/AFP: 112B; /Billy Stickland: 101BR; /Mike Stobe: 46; /Mrs Dulce R Stuart: 27TL; /Rob Taggart/Central Press/Hulton Archive: 43B; /Bob Thomas: 15TL, 16TR, 19T, 19B, 74B, 85, 119, 167TR; /Bob Thomas/Popperfoto: 153T; /Touchline: 74R, 145BL; /Harry Trump: 55BL; /Yoshikazu Tsuno/AFP: 50C; /Claudio Villa: 30BR; /Phil Walter: 18, 58R, 60T, 113TR, 131BC, 131BR, 147BR, 149TL, 184-185, 186; /Anton Want: 105TR; /Lee Warren/Gallo Images: 174TL; /William West/AFP: 32B, 84, 105BL, 130BR; /Graham Wilson/Action Plus: 150TL; /Nick Wilson: 51T, 91T, 179TR; /Dave Winter/Icon Sport: 5CR; /Andrew Wong: 65TR; /Greg Wood/AFP: 62R, 104BL; /Jonathan Wood: 62BL

Offside Sports Photography: /Mark Leech: 128C; /Marca Media: 41R; /Photosport: 172TL

PA Images: 157T; /Paul Barker: 136C; /Empics Sport: 102T; /Tom Honan: 68BL; /Jurgen Kessler/DPA: 41B; /Ross Kinnaird: 168BL; /Dianne Manson/AAP: 35C; /Tony Marshall: 125BL; /Neal Simpson: 145TR, 149BR

Every effort has been made to acknowledge correctly and contact the source and/or copyright holder of each picture and Carlton Books Limited apologises for any unintentional errors or omissions that will be corrected in future editions of this book.